Listening Publics

For Adam, Madeleine and Lance

Listening Publics

The Politics and Experience of Listening in the Media Age

KATE LACEY

polity

The right of Kate Lacey to be identified as Author of this Work has been asserted in accordance with the UK Copyright, Designs and Patents Act 1988.

First published in 2013 by Polity Press

Polity Press
65 Bridge Street
Cambridge CB2 1UR, UK

Polity Press
350 Main Street
Malden, MA 02148, USA

ISBN-13: 978-0-7456-6024-0
ISBN-13: 978-0-7456-6025-7(pb)

A catalogue record for this book is available from the British Library.

Typeset in 11 on 13 pt AGaramond Pro
by Toppan Best-set Premedia Limited
Printed and bound in Great Britain by the MPG Printgroup, UK

The publisher has used its best endeavours to ensure that the URLs for external websites referred to in this book are correct and active at the time of going to press. However, the publisher has no responsibility for the websites and can make no guarantee that a site will remain live or that the content is or will remain appropriate.

For further information on Polity, visit our website: www.politybooks.com

Contents

Acknowledgements

This research has been supported by the Arts and Humanities Research Council and by the University of Sussex. I am also grateful to the archivists at the Bundesarchiv at Berlin-Lichterfelde (BArch) and the BBC Written Archives at Caversham (WAC) for their help and expertise, and to the European Institute for Community and Culture for permission to reprint material first published in *Javnost: The Public* 18(4), 5–20, in an article entitled, 'Listening overlooked: an audit of listening as a category in the public sphere'. I am also grateful to Andrea Drugan, Lauren Mulholland, Ian Tuttle and Neil de Court at Polity for all their support and expertise in bringing this book to publication.

I should also thank all those colleagues who have listened to various parts of this work at conferences and symposia over the years, and have made comments that have helped me think through these ideas and persevere with them. In particular, the international network of radio scholars has been a wonderfully supportive and friendly forum, even when I have railed against the very idea of 'radio studies'. I have also been enormously privileged and pleased to be invited to participate in the AHRC-funded transatlantic Early Broadcasting History Network and in the Australian Research Council-funded 'Listening Project' based in Sydney. The Southern Broadcasting History Group has provided endless stimulation and support closer to home, where I also have the very good fortune to work with some brilliant colleagues at the University of Sussex. These, then, are the people from those networks and beyond to whom I owe particular thanks for their advice, engagement and encouragement: Caroline Bassett, Jonathan Bignell, Michael Bull, Hugh Chignell, Andrew Crisell, Julie Doyle, Tanya Dreher, John Ellis, David Hendy, Ben Highmore, Michele Hilmes, Pat Holland, Cathy Johnson, Irmi Karl, Gholam Khiabany, Peter Lewis, Justine Lloyd, Jason Loviglio, Andy Medhurst, Jamie Medhurst, Monika Metykova, Sharif Mowlabocus, Sally Munt, Siân Nicholas, Penny O'Donnell, Kate O'Riordan, Derek Paget, John Durham Peters, Corey Ross, Polly Ruiz, Paddy Scannell, Kristin Skoog, Cate Thill, Sue Thornham, Rob Turnock and Janice Winship.

I am fortunate to be able to count many of these colleagues as friends, but there are other friends and family I ought to thank for helping me, against the odds, to try to keep the work-life balance in check: Jackie

Alexander, Anita Barnard, Peter Copley, Thomas Gardner, Liz James, Sarah and Andrew Leyshon, Vicky Lloyd, Caroline and Paolo Oprandi, Angela Pater, Karen Reader, Jo Stein, Sarah Thorne, Ann Downie, Peter Lacey, Phil Wilkes, Alison Fisher, Rachel, Jacob and Lottie Lacey. More than anything, I want to acknowledge the endless love, support and sound advice from my amazing parents, Pat and Malcolm Lacey.

This book has been a long time in the writing. My wonderful partner, Lance Downie, has had to live with it taking away my attention for far too long, and I am fortunate and grateful that he has been so understanding. It might have been written sooner had our children, Madeleine and Adam, not come along in the middle of it, but I want to thank them anyway, for putting it all in perspective, but mostly for just making every day more delightful.

Preface

This book is about listening in the modern mediated public sphere. It traces how listening changes in relation to successive media forms and how the act of listening figures in modern public life. In so doing, it deals with an aspect of modern life that is ubiquitous and significant – but that has been strangely overlooked. Ever since the late nineteenth century, the recording, manipulation and transmission of sound has opened up the possibility of new industries, new prospects for the commodification of sound, new artistic practices, new cultures of listening, new subjectivities and, not least, new publics. And yet *listening* has been a curiously absent category in most treatments of media history and in most theorizations of the public sphere. It is a curious absence because listening is actually right at the heart of questions of communication and public life. Listening is essential to the engagement with most of our media, albeit that the act of listening which is embedded in the word 'audience' is rarely acknowledged. It is a no less curious absence in theories of the public sphere, where the objective of political agency is often characterized as being to find a voice – which surely implies finding a public that will listen, and that has a will to listen.

The starting point for this book is the idea that the arrival of sound media gradually 're-sounded' the modern public sphere that had been 'de-auralized' in the age of print, and that this has had profound consequences for the conduct and experience of public life, not least in the way in which the cultures and practices of *listening* have come to take on a renewed public significance alongside those of reading and looking. The central argument is that thinking about listening as an activity in public life opens up profound questions for the understanding of mediated experience, public participation and civic engagement. In short, *Listening Publics* aims to reveal listening as a critical category that can enhance our understanding of modern media, politics and experience.

Kate Lacey, Brighton, June 2012

Listening Overlooked

1　Listening In and Listening Out

Listening has long been overlooked in studies of the media as well as in conceptualizations of the public sphere. It is a curious oversight, given the centrality of listening to communicative, experiential and public life. The aim of these first two chapters is to offer an overview of just how critical is the role of listening in mediated public life.

The curious neglect of listening in relation to media and the public sphere has a long and complex history, but is crucially bound up with a cultural hierarchy of the senses that privileges the visual over the auditory (witness the trio of visual metaphors in the paragraph above!), and a logocentric frame in which listening is encoded as passive in opposition to the *acts* of writing, reading and speech. This widespread association of listening with passivity has rightly been called 'one of the worst ideas ever to infest cultural criticism' (Peters 2006: 124), and this book will present ample historical and theoretical evidence to challenge that association. In so doing, it will also engage with the way in which the active/passive distinction is one of those critical and complex binaries that tends to be mapped all too easily onto other powerful (and often gendered) binaries, not least the public/private distinction. Indeed, it is the association of listening with passivity and with the private sphere that has surely hindered it being properly attended to either as a critical public disposition or as a political action.

Defining Terms

These central binary oppositions – active/passive, public/private – are conceptually problematic, often paradoxical, but remarkably persistent and powerful. Clearly there is little chance of arriving at a single definition of 'public' or 'private' to encompass all the contradictory uses; yet neither can the distinction simply be ignored, since it is clearly *meaningful*, for all its inconsistencies. They are not simply adjectives to describe the social world but rather 'tools for arguments about and in that world' (Gal 2002: 79). Such arguments include ideological and normative debates about the 'proper' separation of the spheres, with all the concomitant fears from either end of the political spectrum about the 'colonization' or 'contamination' of one sphere by the attributes and practices of the other. Though the terms

3

persist, their meaning is neither stable nor absolute, their referential content shifting according to context and perspective. Linguistic anthropologist Susan Gal (2002) has usefully suggested that the public/private divide – and, by extension, I would argue, the active/passive distinction – should be thought of less as a simple binary opposition than as a series of *fractal* distinctions, a recursive division that can be projected onto different social objects and in broader or narrower contexts, with often contradictory outcomes. For example, the dictionary definition recognizes listening as active in relation to hearing, yet listening at the same time is insistently described as passive in relation to other communicative actions. Similarly, the individual reception of impersonal public speech via public media in private spaces begins to illustrate the kind of complex and contradictory ways in which the terms are invoked against the backdrop of an ever-changing media landscape. The proliferation and variety of ways in which the terms have been invoked in different times and places have to be taken seriously while at the same time not mistaken for a single overarching distinction.

Of course the 'activity' of audiences has long since been acknowledged in terms of how people engage with the media and the variety of 'readings' they bring to bear on the texts they encounter. Audiences are understood to be 'at work' in accessing, decoding and mobilizing mediated communication. But contemporary reception studies have been fascinated by the television viewer, the film spectator, the reader of magazines, romances and newspapers and the user of web pages. There are astonishingly few studies of contemporary audiences as *listeners*, except perhaps as listeners to music – despite the fact that modern audience research began with the study of listeners to radio. So, while the notion of the active audience in principle extends to the listening audience, the absence of particular accounts of active listeners has served to perpetuate the commonsense understanding of listening as a passive mode of reception. And even if listening is recognized as an audience activity, the recognition has rarely been extended to thinking about the potential forms and consequences of that activity as a political phenomenon in the public sphere.

But if this project was initially born of a frustration with the neglect of listening in relation to the media and the public sphere, during the intervening years between conception and completion, it has been nurtured by a resurgent interest in the auditory – a veritable 'sonic turn' in cultural studies (Drobnik 2004: 10) – that is not unconnected to the increasingly prevalent place that the auditory plays in contemporary culture, in terms of wider access to the production, manipulation and consumption of sound in all its forms. Certainly this book is not unique in arguing that an acoustic dimension be restored to the standard visualist histories of technological and social changes that have characterized the modern mediated public sphere. This book draws on and supplements some of those histories, but the focus is not on sound itself, nor sound technologies per se, but rather the way in which the new possibilities for recorded and transmitted sound shaped – and were shaped by – the idea of listening as a public act, and the consequences that had for what it means to be a member of the public. It is, then, the qualities, practices, experiences and interpretations of listening as a communicative activity in the public sphere that is the central concern.

Although the notion of the public sphere is no longer exclusively associated with the model that Habermas (1962/1991) set out, it is, nevertheless thanks to a creative translation of his term '*Öffentlichkeit*' (literally, 'openness' or 'publicness') that the spatial metaphor of the 'sphere' is introduced into Anglophone discussions of politics and civil society (Peters 1993: 542–3). This accident of translation is perhaps particularly fortuitous for an analysis of listening as a public activity. Sound surrounds, and can be approached from any and every direction, whereas the visual field is fixed and has to be presented face-on. These different qualities of sound and vision are as much cultural constructs as they are descriptions of physical or physiological reality, but as such they have been enormously powerful as metaphors mobilized in competing models of subjectivity, communication and public life. The spherical character of acoustic space was particularly significant in the work of Marshall McLuhan who, since his early collaborations with the 'communications group' in Toronto, had contrasted it to the linearity of visual space in terms that will echo through the discussions that follow (Carpenter and McLuhan 1960; Schafer 2007: 83–4; Cavell 2010: 142–5). In *Law of Media*, written with his son Eric, he offered the following summary of what was at stake in the contrasting conceptualizations of space:

> Visual space, created by intensifying and separating that sense from interplay with the others, is an infinite container, linear and continuous, homogenous and uniform. Acoustic space, always penetrated by tactility and other senses, is spherical, discontinuous, non-homogenous, resonant, and dynamic. Visual space is structured as static, abstract figure minus a ground; acoustic space is a flux in which figure and ground rub against and transform each other (McLuhan and McLuhan 1988: 33).

For McLuhan, visual space is an intellectual construct, a technological effect of alphabetic perception. Acoustic space, by contrast, is grounded in experience. Visual space is conceived as a unified field of perception; acoustic space as a discontinuous field of relations. Visual space breaks up into categories and groups; acoustic space is a 'resonant sphere' with no centre and no margins. The relativity and dynamism of space was increasingly recognized in a series of profound revolutions in art, science and technology in the late nineteenth and early twentieth centuries (examples would include Picasso's cubism, Schoenberg's atonality, Le Corbusier's architecture, Einstein's theories of relativity, and the development of quantum physics) that for McLuhan are set against the 'ground' of electric technology and represent a technologically determined return to the 'common sense' of acoustic space (McLuhan 2004: 69).

If the visual space of print culture was associated with rationality, objectivity, abstraction, linearity, individualism and nationalism, then, McLuhan argued, electronic culture reverses those attributes to favour partiality, involvement, experience, simultaneity, collectivity and globalism. From this perspective, acoustic space sits somewhere between the physical and the virtual, just as the public sits somewhere between the real and the imaginary. By extension, listening becomes the defining mode of experience under these new conditions, not only metaphorically, but also literally, by virtue of the new media technologies of recording and transmission.

It is not coincidental, as Stephen Connor (1997: 208–9) has argued, that this destabilization and reconfiguration of the soundscape coincided with reconceptualizations of the modern self as unstable, malleable and fragmented. In fact, the qualities of the auditory resonate in a variety of ways with modernist, feminist and postmodern conceptualizations of subjectivity, not least because privileging an acoustic subjectivity throws into disarray conventional distinctions between interior and exterior worlds, public and private, active and passive, even subject and object (Bhaba 1992; Salvaggio 1999; Ihde 2007). The new sound media of the phonograph, the telephone and the radio radicalized these attributes of auditory experience, for the first time in history ripping sound away from its secure and organic location in time and space, and shattering the once stable connection between sound and vision, between sound and body.

So my intention in this book is to examine the listening relation in modern public life rather than focus on what was listened to. Of course, the distinction is only an analytical one and has its limitations – the sounds people listened to will still resonate through the pages that follow – but the distinction is a necessary step in moving beyond the conventional histories of media, or sound technologies or specific media audiences in order to connect the material history of listening to the idea of listening as a public act.

The distinction has its roots in the fact that 'to listen' is both an intransitive and a transitive verb. In other words, it is possible to listen without necessarily listening *to* anything. Listening can therefore be understood as being in a state of anticipation, of listening *out* for something. The listening public in this sense is an always latent public, attentive but undetermined. Any intervention in the public sphere is undertaken in the hope, faith or expectation that there is a public out there, ready to listen and to engage. One of the features of public discourse that distinguishes it from other forms of collective address is precisely that it is addressed to an indeterminate set of people defined only insofar as they participate in or find themselves interpellated in the discourse that addresses them.

This 'listening out' is in a sense the mirror image, or perhaps the necessary corollary, of the indiscriminacy of the public address. There is a faith in the moment of address that there is a public out there, and there is a faith in the act of listening that there will be some resonance with the address. We are familiar with the idea of the reading public, an idea that suggests a potential, the sum of people with the critical skill of literacy, rather than the readers of any one particular publication. Yet the idea of the listening public that emerged with the infant sound media at the turn of the last century – and that has dominated ideas of the audience ever since – has tended to be associated with particular texts or media, with no connotations of latent critical practice. Early radio, for example, was attended by the usual mix of utopian idealism and cultural pessimism that habitually surrounds the emergence of new media. For both sides it rapidly came to stand as the paradigmatic mass medium. With its rapid adoption by whole populations, the simultaneity of its centralized and monologic address to a vast atomized and domesticated audience together with its 'immediate' sensory appeal, it seemed to offer either the possibility of a newly inclusive democratic forum fit for the modern age, or a pernicious threat to a participatory democracy and an effective public sphere. When 'screen radio', as television was once called, arrived, it only intensified the debates. This is familiar territory. What is rarely considered, however, is the role that listening played in this history and in these debates. For some, the return to the spoken word breathed new life into public communication and opened it up to all, reinvigorating public participation. For others, the identification of the public as an audience of listeners as opposed to readers was the quintessential proof of the passification of the public, rendered mute and helpless in its position as listener in a culture that celebrates and privileges the freedom of *expression*. The relegation of listening (standing in for media consumption as a whole) as a public activity remains clearly evident in contemporary celebrations of 'interactivity' and 'produsing' and so on, where the 'progress' is more often identified in the proliferation of voices and opportunities for expression than in the proliferation or quality of opportunities to listen.

In other words, most treatments of listening within media and cultural studies tend to privilege the action of listening *in* to something, to use the telling phrase adopted in the early years of radio. 'Listening' in such formulations tends to be relatively unproblematized, presented simply as the natural receptive mode of consuming media messages in sound. Even when listening is taken to be a sense *formation*, the apperception of sound tends to be examined at the level of intimate, individual experience. Despite the growth in 'sound studies', academic treatments of listening rarely attend to the connections between the act of 'listening in' to specific media texts, the sensory experience of listening and a political philosophy of listening. This book challenges such a restricted understanding of the listening public by identifying listening as a category that bridges *both* the realm of sensory, embodied experience *and* the political realm of debate and deliberation. Moreover, it will make the case that, unlike a reading public constituted of individuals in isolation, a listening public is made up of listeners inhabiting a condition of plurality and intersubjectivity. Its ambition is to think these different aspects of listening together, to address the public aspect of listening, an aspect which has at least as much to do with listening out, as listening in – listening as a form of radical openness, literally, *Öffentlichkeit* – the German term commonly translated as 'the public sphere'.

Listening In/As a Public

The analytical separation of 'listening out' (an attentive and anticipatory communicative disposition) from 'listening in' (a receptive and mediatized communicative action) opens up a space to consider listening as an activity with political resonance. Indeed, it becomes possible to think of listening as a political action in its own right. Where political theory has concentrated on the rights and responsibilities of speech and expression, the intention here is to examine the rights and responsibilities of those listening *in the act of listening* (that is to say, the object of enquiry is not on the activities that follow on as a consequence of having listened, for example the production of more speech or other forms of political action). This apparently simple switch of focus opens up surprisingly far-reaching speculations about the guarantee of plurality in modern political society (the role of 'auditing' political discourse), and proposes listening as a powerful conceptual corrective to nostalgic political models based on idealized notions of the face-to-face dialogic encounter.

This image of the 'face-to-face' indicates how our dominant communicative models tend to be conceptualized in terms of a visual logic and a dyadic exchange, rather than in terms of an embodied and pluralistic encounter. It is a construct that implicitly privileges interpersonal, private conversation over impersonal, public communication. 'Face-to-face' also implies a 'live' and 'immediate' exchange, but in the age of electronic mediation, liveness, of course, can also happen at a distance – a radical sensory reorganization of communicative experience that was first registered as a listening experience via the sound media of the telegraph, the telephone and the radio. If 'face-to-face' is coupled with 'live' as some sort of ideal of communicative exchange, then the communications media are always to be found wanting.

This is just one example of how beginning from a perspective that takes listening seriously can usefully recast some of the most fundamental tenets of communication theory. This has nowhere more profound consequences than in balancing the normative ideal of free speech with a normative freedom of listening that encompasses both a responsibility and a right to listen. In chapter 8, the concept of 'freedom of listening' will be proposed as a necessary corollary to the 'freedom of speech', and that listeners be understood not just as an 'audience' for public discourse, but as 'auditors' of public exchanges, performances and plurality. Where the freedom of speech is a right ascribed to the individual, I will argue there is a 'freedom of listening' that, by contrast, inheres in the space *between* individuals, and is concerned precisely with guaranteeing the context within which freedom of expression can operate not as speech, but as *communication*.

However, it is sensible to point out in these introductory remarks that while the central argument of *Listening Publics* is for listening to be considered as an activity in the public sphere, it will be taken as read that this listening is necessarily just one activity among others. Listening is neither autonomous nor primary either as a sensory or a communicative activity. The neglect of listening as a public action has, however, been so pervasive and so profound, that the case has to be put as strongly as possible, even if doing so runs the danger of appearing to make overblown claims for listening as the principal or most profound dimension of communicative activity in the public sphere. True, the acknowledgement of listening as public action can open up new ways of thinking about old questions, and is a necessary corrective, but it would be absurd to claim listening as a self-sufficient activity, let alone a sufficient political activity. On the other hand, the starting point of this book is that to have ignored listening as an activity in the public sphere for so long is equally absurd.

Listening in the Literature

Counter to this general trend of neglect, there are two aspects of the cultural work of listening that have been the subject of much attention, although they will play only a tangential role in this book. The first is the 'skill' of listening in therapeutic, interpersonal or pedagogic situations; the second is the 'art' of listening to music and other sonic forms. The former tends to concentrate on the psychology of the individual listener, and is rarely applied to public or mediated situations. For example, the International Listening Association was founded in 1979 to 'identify, and institutionalize "listening" as a legitimate area of scholarly enquiry' (Wolvin et al. 1999: 111). It subsequently launched a journal that in 1995 became *The International Journal of Listening*, where the focus is, with a few notable exceptions, very much on interpersonal communication from the perspective of cognitive psychology and is very often concerned with a kind of 'strategic' listening in business, education and the professions (Gehrke 2009: 2; Beard 2009: 15; Wolvin 2010). Where media are considered within this framework, it tends to be the interpersonal forms like telephony. Another related body of work considers the skill of listening as a research method in interview-based disciplines like journalism, anthropology and sociology (Wiley 1998; Merritt and McCombs 2004: 105; O'Donnell 2009; Erlmann 2004; Angel-Ajani 2006; Burghart 2008; Forsey 2010; Back 2007, 2009).

Meanwhile, the specialist musicological discourses on listening tend to treat music (and sonic arts generally) as an aesthetic more than a sociological or political phenomenon, and so these, too, lie broadly beyond the remit of this book.[1] Yet the importance of music in the development and expansion of the listening public, and indeed the political role of music more broadly, cannot be denied. It is clear that the rapid and ubiquitous adoption of sound technologies in modern public life have been significantly driven by the desire for more music to be more accessible to more people in more and more different situations. Certainly music has brought people together in 'listening publics', and of course music can have its own political force, directly or indirectly. Moreover, musical and other aesthetic and cultural experiences are inescapably social, of course, however much they seem also to be individual, affective experiences (Bourdieu 1986). To this extent, music will feature in the story, albeit rather *sotto voce*, if only for the pragmatic reason of keeping the project within manageable limits, and in recognizing that listening to music in modern public life has already been the subject of many studies, from histories of recording technologies to genealogies of musical genres, from stories of fans and analyses of youth cultures to textual analyses of protest songs and biographies of musicians with a political edge. Still, in many considerations of music in public life, the idea of the listening public tends to be conflated with the notion of particular taste publics and identity politics, and the wider public dimension folds in again around the individual and around listening as a practice of individual consumption.

'Sound' and the excavation of 'soundscapes' tend to fare better than 'listening' per se. In 2005, Michele Hilmes commented sardonically that sound studies have been 'hailed as an "emerging field" for the last hundred years' and that it might well remain that way, 'always emerging, never emerged' (Hilmes 2005: 249), although the growing number of degree courses, research centres and anthologies in the field suggest that it is becoming more established (Bull and Back 2003; Morat 2011; Pinch and Bjisterveld 2011; Sterne 2012). Whatever its status, it has certainly been a dynamic one in recent years, albeit widely distributed across different disciplines that do not always speak (or listen) to each other, and where the production of sound tends to receive more critical attention than its reception. Much of the most important work in historical sound studies has concentrated on attempts to reconstruct historical soundscapes, for example the contested sounds of Shakespearean or Victorian England, nineteenth-century rural France, colonial America or the American Civil War (Corbin 1998; Smith 1999, 2001; Picker 2003; Cullen Rath 2003). Not coincidentally perhaps, most studies of this sort seem to deal with periods that pre-date the era of recordable sound, almost as if we could turn to a more direct 'record' of more recent soundscapes. The ambition of this book is not to reconstruct the modern media soundscape (which would be to try to recreate a sense of *what* was heard in particular times and places), but to try to think through how innovations in media technologies might have impacted on *ways of listening* in a reconfigured soundscape in which sounds were no longer in the same way bound to a specific time and place and to ask the question what impact that might have had on public life and listening as a political activity.

Finally, there are plenty of media histories on which this study draws. This book does not claim to offer sustained chronological or institutional histories of the media, for its historical span is too broad and its conceptual ambition lies elsewhere. The notion of the 'listening public' does not arise in relation to a single medium or at any single identifiable historical moment, but is, rather, a latent term that appears in different guises in various contexts throughout the modern media age. Instead, the focus is on moments of transition, be they moments of technological development or political change, inasmuch as they present 'privileged moments of genuine uncertainty and improvisation' (Boddy 2004: 3), that can potentially destabilize preconceived notions of the public consequences of now familiar political and media ecologies. In the spirit of Miriam Hansen's (1991) work on early cinema publics, the book begins with the contention that, in periods of transition with successive sound media, we might well expect to find the activity of listening as an explicitly contested terrain in the public sphere, which in turn raises the possibility of identifying alternative listening publics that lie behind the dominant historical narrative of a *passified* audience.

It is predominantly in these periods of innovation and instability that the debates, discourses and decisions that helped to shape the social application of these various technologies are at their most prolific and urgent. The phonograph and the radio will be taken as the archetypal technologies of this new era of sound, representing the key attributes of all subsequent sound media, recording and transmission. For that reason, the weight of the historical evidence presented in this book lies between the 1870s and the 1930s when there was a veritable 'aural awakening' (Biocca 1990) by virtue of there being *more* sound, (certainly more music), and also a greater variety of sounds being produced by the sound factories of recording studios and radio stations. The simple possibility of playback, of *repeating*, of listening again and again to the self-same sounds, be that for study or amusement, was nothing short of revolutionary. Sound for the first time could be captured, repeated, slowed down, speeded up, reversed, and could be transmitted to far-flung times and places – all literally unheard of possibilities just a few years before. The modern ear, then, was faced with a richer sonic environment to decipher than ever before, new businesses grew up as veritable 'empires of sound' (Millard 1995), and listening to mediated sound became established as a public phenomenon. Moreover, this period also saw the extension of the vote to women and the working class, the upheavals of war and economic depression, and the sharpening ideological divide between right and left. For all these various reasons, the debates about the proper role of the emergent media in a democratic culture were particularly urgent, and the foundations that were laid when these media were in their infancy resonated throughout the twentieth century and into our contemporary digital media culture.

Given the extensive public attention to the new horizons opened up by the auditory technologies of telegraphy, telephony, phonography and radio, there is a surprisingly impoverished vocabulary for writing about mediated listening. There are no easy auditory equivalents to the visual concepts of the 'gaze' or the 'glance', 'surveillance', 'voyeurism' or 'spectatorship'. Despite increasing scholarly attention to the sound of cinema and of television, this somehow has not widely translated into attending to the question of 'listenership'. The very word rings oddly – in fact the OED offers it only as a noun to describe 'the estimated number of listeners to a broadcast programme or to radio (*specifically as opposed to television*)' [my italics], whereas the common definition of 'spectatorship' is 'the state of being a spectator or beholder'. In short, 'listenership' is the quantitative product of a media event, while 'spectatorship' is an existential condition. One of the themes of this book is that the modern technologies of mediation have, in fact, contributed to the production of 'listenership' not only as a collective noun, but as a state of being and a civic disposition.

And yet studies of both media and politics are shot through with auditory terminology though on the whole we remain deaf to the implications of such language. Within political discourse, analyses of political relations are often framed in terms of 'harmony' or 'discord', where judgements can be 'sound', and ideas can 'resonate', where people can act in 'concert' or produce a 'cacophony', and where 'having a voice' is central to all kinds of politics. And of course, democratic theory places great weight on 'the freedom of speech', without quite recognizing that speech is sounded out, and therefore demands a listener. The most significant example of this auditory terminology is obviously the word 'audience', which etymologically clearly privileges the listening relation in the process of communication, and yet has all but lost that particular association. There is potentially much at stake in recovering an understanding of that listening dimension if only because modern citizens habitually spend a significant proportion of their lives as members of audiences in one form or another. For all the attention to 'the spectacle' in modern culture, there are in fact few spectacles that unfold in utter silence. But the shift to an acoustic rather than a visual register in understanding the mediated world also, I will argue, offers productive ways of thinking about even purely visual culture inasmuch as it shifts our attention from the subjectivity of the individual to the intersubjectivity of the public, plural world.

Audiences as Listening Publics

'Audience', according to the OED, refers to the action, state, condition or occasion of hearing, or 'an assembly of listeners'. The modern idea of an audience certainly retains that notion of a collectivity. An 'audience of one' is a phrase that draws attention to the rarity of being a singular member of an audience. 'Audience' is a collective noun for the activity of listening that has been assimilated for other activities, precisely because no parallel nouns existed that gave the same sense of collectivity. 'Readership', for example, still conjures up a vision of individual readers; 'spectatorship' remains primarily an abstraction associated with individual viewers, not the cinema public. And yet the inescapable collectivity suggested by the word 'audience' resides in its relation to sound and listening (Ong 1982: 74).

This sense of 'the audience', in the singular, this image of a unity created out of the diversity of a group of individuals, lies at the heart of much of the mistrust of 'mass' media, since the 'mystery of the collective noun' conjures up the idea of a singular body with 'a collective consciousness that is analogous to a unified individual subject', despite all evidence and experience to the contrary. Addressing this problem in relation to theatrical audiences, Alice Rayner (1993: 3–6) has argued that since 'the audience' is made up of diverse individuals and since the constitution of the audience changes over time (rather like the pronoun 'we'), it makes less sense to talk about the ontology of the audience than to talk about it in terms of 'the listening function that would constitute the action of audience'. Thought of in these terms, the audience 'is an instance of intersubjective relations with specific reference to the act of listening', and since listening involves a fundamental openness towards others,[2] listening and the action of audience is an act that is both political and 'fundamentally ethical'.

It is this sense of openness in relation to others in the act of listening that connects with definitions of the public, although 'public' is another of those apparently ordinary but extraordinarily complex words that defy easy definition. Already in these first few pages, it has appeared as a noun in the singular and in the plural, as an adjective that either stands alone or is conjoined with other nouns, like 'sphere' or 'life'. And always tagging along is its equally difficult other half: 'private' (Weintraub and Kumar 1997). It would be impossible to give a definitive, or even concise definition, of 'public' – even the OED struggles, acknowledging as an opening gambit that, 'the various senses pass into each other by many intermediate shades of meaning'. But for all its nuances, as an adjective it means something to do with being open so that all may see or hear; and as a noun, something that describes a community, nation or people as a whole. Yet 'the public' is not coterminous with these other collective nouns. Michael Warner (2002: 50) points to the essential circularity in the idea of 'a public', which is, at least in principle, simply 'a space of discourse organized by nothing other than discourse itself', a self-creating and self-organizing space that 'exists *by virtue of being addressed*'. However, despite acknowledging that a public is constituted by being addressed, in the very next sentence Warner supposes the only way of being *actively* involved in a public is in 'speaking, writing and thinking'. In short, there is no active part to play in being addressed: 'merely paying attention is enough to make you a member' (Warner 2002: 62).

This innocuous phrase 'merely paying attention' is worth unpacking, for the 'merely' suggests that paying attention comes easily. And yet 'to pay attention' would suggest precisely an intentional effort to engage with the 'speaking, writing and thinking' of others, presumably by listening, reading and more thinking. Since it is hard to conceive of literacy as something that is not a skill, or of reading or thinking without intent, the 'merely paying attention' seems to be a reference to listening (looking would also fit here, but 'appearing' is not granted the status of a public activity in Warner's trio of possibilities). So here, albeit implicitly, is an acknowledgement of the *critical* role of listening in becoming a member of a public – critical, that is, both in the sense of crucial, and in the sense of a rational disposition.

The media are doubly implicated in the modern constitution of things public: first, by virtue of their role in publicizing events, ideas and performances; and second, by virtue of their role in enabling the constitution of the public – or rather, *publics* – as an imagined community with an intersubjective horizon. The media also have various public functions according to liberal political theory: to hold the state to public account, to act as a forum for public information, debate and civic participation, and to channel the voice of the people as public opinion. There is, of course, a vast scholarly literature that engages with the term in very precise ways in a variety of political and sociological traditions,[3] and some of those debates will reveal themselves in the chapters that follow, but the term is left deliberately open here, in order to explore the variety of ways in which listening plays out as a public activity. The idea of a singular, overarching public is a rhetorical fiction, albeit perhaps a necessary or inevitable one, and there are instances where the idea of a single 'listening public' maps on to such a fiction; but on the whole, the theoretical, historical and empirical evidence suggests the presence of multiple publics with distinct characteristics, functions and political capital, overlapping and interrelating in potentially significant ways. By focusing on an activity like listening that is central to so much public engagement and yet has been almost entirely ignored as a critical category in considerations of the public sphere, it is possible not only to delineate some specific incarnations of the public which have escaped attention, but also to indicate some of the ways in which those overlaps and interrelationships have played out.

Certainly there is a tendency and a temptation to set up publics and audiences as opposites, the one made up of (potentially) active citizens, the other made up of more or less passive consumers. The term 'public' commonly has a strong normative dimension, whereas 'audience' is more commonly a descriptive term. This dichotomy has a long history and is evidently ideological, especially in the way in which audiences – as opposed to publics – are ascribed feminine, emotional and racialized characteristics, and are thereby frequently denigrated. Richard Butsch has explored the ways in which 'the audience' has been produced in discourse, by both participants and observers, highlighting how those produced by cultural authorities *about* the audience are more powerful – and accessible to the historian – than those produced *by* members of the audience. Moreover, those dominant discourses have tended to characterize the audience as a problem, as something to be tamed, regulated or exploited for commercial gain. Audiences in this sense share a conceptual lineage with 'the crowd' and 'the mass', the one made up of people sharing the same physical space, the other made up of people dispersed and isolated by virtue of media technologies. Both provoke fears that the individual – together with their individuality, their reason and their independence – is lost and vulnerable under such conditions. The dispersed media audience remains broadly invisible – and inaudible – a fact which has rendered it phantasmatic, at turns less alarming than the sight of an unruly mob and yet in some ways more disturbing for its unknowability.

And yet there is much that 'public' and 'audience' have in common – not least the very people who are being categorized. Both are made up of 'members' drawn from the general population, taking up 'a situated role that people temporarily perform' (Butsch 2008: 3). People in either role constitute a collectivity that is reflexively aware of other members of that grouping, engage in discussion and reflection and shape and share in (national) events. Indeed, efforts to increase civic participation in public affairs often turn to mediated forums to generate interest and discussion, apparently harnessing the vivacity of the audience to resuscitate the ailing public. But even these more positive treatments of the audience have tended to posit membership of an audience as just a staging post in becoming an informed citizen, a necessary, but separate, step towards participating actively in the public sphere. In such formulations, participation in an audience acts as a preparatory stage for the constitution of a public, albeit that not all audience activity is connected to the political in this way (Livingstone 2005). This raises questions about the experiential dimensions of citizenship and the *practices* that link private identity and experience to the public sphere (Couldry et al. 2007a: 28). Citizenship in this sense is understood not simply as a right or an attribute, but in the republican or radical democratic sense of a habitual practice, 'motivated by circumstance and obligation, cultivated through education and experience, consistently performed' (Barney 2007: 39; see also Eley 2002: 230). Listening is a particularly interesting category in relation to these debates about the connections between audiences and publics precisely because it bridges the conventionally political realm of debate and deliberation and the realm of sensory, embodied experience.

'Listening' is distinct from 'hearing', but not separate. Although it can be useful analytically to distinguish between listening and hearing, the distinction is not a straightforward one, nor should it be mapped simply onto the problematic binaries of mind and body, culture and nature, cognition and perception. One definition of listening is the *active* direction of the sense of hearing. Lisbeth Lipari (2010: 349) summarizes the significance of this distinction as follows: 'Etymologically *listening* comes from a root that emphasizes *attention* and *giving* to another, while *hearing* comes from a root that emphasizes *perception* and *sensation* of sound.' But 'listen', like 'lust', also shares a common root in the Old English 'list' – to like, desire or lust to do something. It is a concept that combines agency and desire.[4] So listening is both a public activity and a private experience, and it can be both these things at the same time. This is significant in considering the role of listening in a world of mediation, where the media have served to challenge and redraw once familiar distinctions between public and private. The reintroduction of the spoken word into the 'impersonal' address of public discourse, for example, brought with it a sense of presence and 'the present' associated with listening to the human voice that was absent from the disembodied written word. Politics in the broadest sense does not play out only in institutions and officially sanctioned spaces, but also in the production and reproduction of immediate, everyday life; or rather, it plays out precisely in the *articulation* between formal political space and everyday experience, an articulation that is grounded in a sense-making process. Just as there is a double articulation (Silverstone 1994) to media in their textual and material aspects (technological and environmental), so mediated listening restores a double articulation to the reception of public speech as information and affect.

Habermas' account of the emergence of the public sphere notably rests on a similar formulation in identifying an 'audience-oriented subjectivity' (1962/1991: 49) rooted in the intimate familial sphere as a prerequisite for the circulation of rational critical discourse on political practice. Habermas here acknowledges the way in which print culture – literary as much as political – was meaningful to specific readers at the same time as it was meaningful to unspecified others, a mode of address described as 'a ground condition of intelligibility for public language' (Warner 1992: 378). The reference to the *audience* orientation of the subject is telling here, because

17

it recognizes a moment in the development of a public sensibility in which reading takes on (or returns to) the status of collective listening. These ideas will be developed further in later chapters, but for the moment it is enough to recognize that in properly understanding 'the audience' as a 'listening public', new light is cast on the conventional – and problematic – delineations between 'audiences' and 'publics'.

Polyphonic Cultural History

Listening Publics is not, however, intended as an abstract treatise on listening or publics, though it does draw on and connect with phenomenological and other philosophies of listening and theories of the public sphere. Rather it is intended as a contribution to a cultural and material history of listening in modernity, which is to say it takes listening to be a cultural practice that changes under changing historical and material conditions. Given the immense technological transformations in communicative practice since the late nineteenth century, it seems apposite to consider how listening has been configured in relation to changing techniques and technologies of mediated sound – while recognizing that listening is not necessarily or straightforwardly determined by those technologies. That relation is a dialectical one, where the techniques and technologies of mediated sound are transformed in their turn in relation to the figure of the listener (and in relation to a host of other cultural, social, political, technical and economic factors). As James Lastra (2000: 4) put it in his history of cinema sound:

> Vision was neither the only sense to be transformed nor the only one to act as an agent of transformation. Hearing was just as surely dislocated, 'mobilized,' restructured, and mechanized. The 'annihilations' of space and time affected hearing as much as seeing, and acoustic experience was as thoroughly commodified as its optical counterpart.

This book draws on disparate sources to provide both new historical narratives of the modernization of listening as well as making an argument for the centrality of listening as a category in public life across the long twentieth century. The broad historical sweep – from the late nineteenth century to the early twenty-first – is a self-conscious bid to counter the 'rhetoric of amnesia' around new media, to reveal those patterns or meanings that only emerge over very long periods of time and that might exceed the lifespan or specific national version of any particular media form. It also takes an interdisciplinary and cross-national approach to the problematic of historicizing the act of listening by presenting some of the cultural and political responses in Europe and America to the possibilities thrown up by technological innovations in the mediation of sound. Along the way it offers a mix of medium theory, institutional histories, textual analysis and political philosophy. Examples will be drawn primarily from the US, UK and Germany, in an attempt to draw connections and contrasts between the various nationally inflected histories, although this is not intended as a fully fledged comparative history as such. These three countries have much in common as Western states negotiating the processes of modernization, and there was much direct and indirect communication between them in relation to media trade and policy (Hilmes 2012). But there were also significant differences politically, economically and culturally. Relatively few media histories, particularly perhaps those concerned with broadcasting, go beyond the national context, but a cross-national perspective offers the chance of building on that literature to examine listening strategies within contrasting media systems, be they democratic or authoritarian, elitist or populist, public service or commercial.[5]

The book begins with a broad, though naturally not exhaustive, overview of the 'modernization' of listening in relation to a succession of media technologies, from the written word to current social media trends. The three following chapters explore aspects from this history in more detail, looking in turn at how ideas of realism, noise and liveness figure in the construction of listening publics in the age of spectacle. The focus then shifts to the practices and experiences of listeners encountering mediated sound in private and public spaces. The final section turns to the implications of these new cultures of listening for more abstract and philosophical questions about the politics and ethics of listening in a mediated world, to argue that critical attention to the roles and responsibilities of listening holds up a sounding board to the ethics of media production and policy.

Although media from papyrus to the iPod will appear in these pages, it is the phonograph and the radio which take centre stage, standing in for the paradigmatic innovations of recordability and transmission of sound that have transfigured the entire media landscape. But this is not a medium-specific study. Carolyn Marvin (1988: 4–6) long since cautioned against the biases of 'artefactual histories' that tend to assume audiences are produced and their actions determined by the technological properties of artificially separated media. In tracing the history of any technology, the tributary sources can be almost infinitely extended, although often enough we tell ourselves only partial histories, inflected with the prejudices of hindsight. On the other hand, contemporary media questions can alert us to blindspots in previous iterations of media histories. Today's vocabulary of intermediality, multimedia, immersion and convergence, for example, helps us more clearly to see how distinctions between the various media are historically contingent (Altman 2004: 15; Elsaesser 2006; Wurtzler 2007: 11).

Listening as a political activity is not contained by mediated sound, let alone by any single medium, however defined. For that reason, too, listening cannot be considered only in relation to non-visual media. The questions about mediated listening as a public phenomenon that arise in relation to these particular instances of recorded and broadcast sound are also relevant to the plethora of audiovisual media, analogue and digital, mainstream and alternative, global and local that characterize contemporary culture and everyday life. As will be argued in the next chapter, the first media technology to have 'modernized' listening was the written word; indeed, to the extent that listening is the most fundamental mode of communicative reception, understanding and reflexivity, it makes just as much sense to talk about listening to print as it does to speak of 'reading' a film.[6] Given the qualities of plurality, intersubjectivity and liveness associated with the listening position, this is more than idle wordplay, as it potentially opens up new ways of thinking about the reception of mediated texts in general.

To the extent that different media do allow for different experiences and affordances, there is also a sense in which the media together have increasingly come to 'define a space that is increasingly mutually referential and reinforcive, and increasingly integrated into the fabric of everyday life' and have correspondingly become 'resources for thought, judgement and action, both personal and political' (Silverstone 2006: 5). Roger Silverstone coined the term 'mediapolis' to describe this space, suggesting that, while the public sphere is made up of more than just the media, to all intents and purposes the media have arguably come to constitute the very idea of 'publicness' in the modern world, and they have come to provide a material grounding and context for our sense of commonality, our common sense. This book argues that the act of listening needs to be attended to as one of the central ways of making sense of this mediated space, and not just in relation to specific audio media. The role of listening in public life has changed and become more pronounced with the advent of mediated sound, while the constitution of the listening public under these new mediated conditions has in turn expanded the dimensions and experience of public life.

Despite these explanations, the attempt to engage with listening publics across media, across such a long period of time and across national boundaries is perhaps foolhardy, and certainly some readers might find the rapid switching between fragments from different contexts disconcerting, compared to more conventional media histories. But this way of working has emerged somewhere between a pragmatic response to the lack of sustained engagement with mediated listening and a principled attempt to work within a 'polyphonic paradigm' (Curtis 1978). This involves a multidimensional, analogical approach to cultural enquiry, an 'acoustic' approach that looks for plausible relationships alongside the provable, cause-and-effect relations privileged in logical and visual paradigms. It is the product of collecting fleeting or implicit references to listening in a wide variety of public and academic discourses, drawing together a range of sometimes competing historical voices, piecing together various historical fragments in an attempt to create a fresh analysis. It draws on some original archival sources (though listening is not a well catalogued subject!) and reports in contemporary newspapers, magazines and journals, as well as synthesizing references from an eclectic range of literatures to demonstrate the embeddedness of listening cultures in the public sphere and experience.

In fact, it is worth qualifying the assertion that mediated listening in the public sphere has been ignored. It would be more accurate to say it has not received much *sustained* attention. There is actually no shortage of commentary on listening during the period under review. At one level, this is obvious. It could hardly be the case that such an important aspect of experiential and informational life could have been entirely overlooked in either popular, specialist or technological discourse. Indeed, references to the modernization of listening and the development of the listening public do appear in media histories, but generally in a fragmentary, accidental or oblique way. Meanwhile studies on sound media specifically tend to focus more on the production and textuality of sound and its individuated reception, rather than its public dimensions. There are many aspects of the narrative that follow that deserve greater amplification or that magnify particular moments from more complex stories, but the variety of material presented is required in order to attend to the connections between the sensory experience of listening, the philosophy of listening, and the act of listening in; and to restore the question of listening in public and as a public to a range of media histories.

By exploring the negotiation of listening practices in relation to these moments of media transition, *Listening Publics* hopes to offer an historical perspective from which to reconsider contemporary media technologies and public soundscapes, but also to make an argument for considering listening as a critical activity in public life.

2   The Modernization of Listening

Listening, which can be defined as the active direction of the sense of hearing to discern meaning from sound, is a *cultural* practice. Listening practices are therefore neither natural nor immutable, but can change over time, according to context and material conditions. Nor are listening practices arbitrary, for they are shaped by and feed back into relations of power. Although this insight is hardly new, it is still worth reiterating at the outset of this chapter, as there remains something stubbornly counter-intuitive about the idea that our senses are not simply natural faculties – neither universal, trans-historical nor straightforward.

Historiographical Questions

The question then arises of how listening might change over time and under different conditions. Technology plays its part. Archaeologists and cultural historians have shown how people have long crafted instruments and spaces to manipulate sound and create specialized listening environments, and that a fascination with the disembodied voice runs throughout human history (Peters 1999; Connor 2000; Scarre and Lawson 2006; Hendy 2010). The new sound media, then, for all their radical novelty, are part of a much longer history of changing listening practices and cultures. However, the central premise of this book is that the relatively recent possibility of listening to sounds mediated across time and distance did not just change the experience of listening, but reconfigured the experience of public life. This chapter suveys how listening has changed in relation to changing media technologies, notwithstanding the conceptual and methodological difficulties in approaching such a question.

First of all, the question is not how listening has been changed *by* media technologies. Listening practices cannot be mapped predictably or straightforwardly onto changes in technology, or even changes in the soundscape more generally. Like any other cultural practice, listening is embedded in the complex realities of unequal power relations, cultural specificities and the dynamics of continuity and change. Second, the notion of 'modernization' cannot be conflated with any simple narrative of 'progress'. At any one time there are likely to be multiple 'auditory regimes' that co-exist – more or less prominently, more or less securely established. It is at best a shorthand term for the processes of negotiation and reflexivity in relation to modernity in all their complexity and ambivalence. Nor is the selection of British, German and American examples intended to suggest that these Western histories of listening are either definitive or archetypal, although they have been influential. Indeed, the very mutability of listening practices in Western modernity raises the question – for another time – about how histories of listening have played out in other times and places. Finally, the evidentiary basis for speculating about the modernization of listening is necessarily limited and partial, and can often be traced only through tangential, fragmentary or elusive references, especially in addressing the question of how transition was *experienced* – whether as sudden or gradual change, revolutionary or incremental, universal or differentiated among particular classes or communities.

Despite all these hurdles and caveats, it is nevertheless remarkable how rarely the transfiguring of the auditory has featured in the standard accounts of the transformations of experience wrought by the processes of modernization, which otherwise recognize new modes of organizing vision, new mimetic forms of expression, new forms of self-reflexivity, and new experiences of space, time and everyday life. In fact, the modernization of listening is intimately bound up in all these transformations which were, in turn, part of the broader processes of industrialization and urbanization – the disembedding of social, ethnic and gender relations, increased social and geographic mobility, the rise of mass production and mass consumption, new conceptions of leisure and so on. Furthermore, the new sound media were emerging into an auditory environment that was already undergoing tremendous change. And all of these processes had consequences for the reconfiguration of the public and the private, and provide the broader context in which an analysis of the modernization of listening must be conducted.

Alain Corbin (1995: 182) has argued all aural histories are indebted to the pioneering work of Lucien Febvre who in the 1930s set out to write a history and anthropology of human sensibilities. Febvre suggested that human progress and the triumph of reason represented a kind of 'hearing loss' as vision began to pre-empt the other senses in the experiential ordering of the world. Indeed, he identified the early modern period in European history as a transition from the 'age of the ear' to the 'age of the eye', an argument that was to resurface in the work of Marshall McLuhan, who famously privileged the role of the media in this historical transformation. Significantly, though, McLuhan argued the mediated experience of the electronic age, while still bearing the imprint of the visual, was characterized by the properties of acoustic space. While there are undeniably limitations in these attempts to describe all-embracing shifts from 'the ear to the eye' or 'the visual to the acoustic' (as Febvre himself demonstrated), the 'hegemony of vision' is certainly a powerful trope in studies of modernity, and is reflected in the continuing scholarly attention to all the varieties of 'visual culture' (Levin 1993; Mirzeoff 2002; Casetti 2008; Howells and Negreiros 2012).

It is a truism that the only access historians have to information about any shifts in the modes of perception is shaped by and revealed through prevailing discourses. Certainly the history of listening is hard to filter through the persistent privileging in Western discourses of vision over audition.[1] The distanciation, differentiation and domination associated with the visual mastery of the world was a product of the coupling of artistic perspectivalism with Cartesian ideas of subjective rationality (the eye as the I), bound up with the rise of scientific and technological rationality (Jay 1992, 1993: 68; Crary 1993; Connor 1997: 203–4). This hegemonic visual model of knowledge and subjectivity has, of course, come under sustained philosophical critique for its positing of an ahistorical, disembodied and disembedded subject and for its operation within a more or less explicitly gendered and racialized framework in which the neutral, objective, progressive and penetrating visuality of modern Western culture is contrasted with the primitive, affective and feminized aurality of the ethnic Other (Schmidt 2000: 21). But for all its imperial dominance, Cartesian perspectivalism has not been the *only* way of seeing in modern Western history. Scholars like Jay and Crary have identified the ruptures, discontinuities and multiplicity of viewing positions within and across historical moments and in relation to different techniques and technologies of spectatorship. In this regard, the literature on visual culture provides an important lesson in thinking about listening[2] – the need to be sensitive to the historical specificity and plurality of listening positions, the ways in which listening practices might be implicated in gendered, classed and racialized discourses, and indeed to think about the interplay with vision and the other senses.

Despite the burgeoning scholarship on sound and aurality, there is still a long way to go before histories of auditory culture will match the range and volume of scholarly attention to the modernization of vision, but Jonathan Sterne's magisterial account of the cultural origins of mediated sound, *The Audible Past*, has been hugely influential in putting the modernization of listening onto the agenda. Sterne (2003: 2) shows how during the long nineteenth century there was 'a series of conjunctures among ideas, institutions, and practices [that] rendered the world audible in new ways and valorized new constructs of hearing and listening'. This produced the conditions for the development of reproductive sound technologies – an argument which radically inverts the conventional idea that listening changes because of technological innovations. Sterne argues that a specialist 'audile technique' which had developed in scientific and medical discourses crossed over into mediatized listening with the telegraph, and was eventually brought into the realm of mass media and everyday life (Sterne 2003: 137–8).

Central to the story of *The Audible Past* are the *transducers* – devices that turn sound into something else, such as electricity or digits, and then back again (Sterne 2003: 22). But behind these technological phenomena Sterne identifies a major historical reversal in scientific and technical thinking from the mid eighteenth century onwards – namely a move to focusing on the ear rather than the mouth as the model for sound reproduction – in other words, on the techniques of *reception* rather than production. Helmholtz saw that sound is a nervous reaction, a *sensation*, that happens in the ear. This insight opened up the possibility of synthesizing sound (Sterne 2003: 65) by displacing the focus on the sound object (primarily speech and music) with a concern for vibration and frequency – in other words, with 'sound itself, irrespective of its source' (Sterne 2003: 33). This challenges the common assumption that sound is 'naturally' out there, waiting to be 'captured' and reproduced with as much fidelity as the technology can muster. The ear *already* mediates sound. It filters the sonic environment, selectively distinguishing meaningful from meaningless sound, which is a cultural activity as much as a physiological one. What is more, the cultural norms that determine this process of selection must, by definition, be historically contingent. That means the widespread presence of sound technologies (themselves produced to meet cultural and social imperatives) has changed those cultural norms; has changed, in other words, the 'nature' of sound itself, and certainly our practices of listening.

Modernized listening was characterized by the 'individuation of acoustic space, the stratification of sounds and the separation of hearing from the other senses' (Sterne 2003: 155) and prefigured, Sterne argues, all subsequent incarnations of mediated listening. Listening, just like visual techniques of observation, became 'articulated to notions of science, reason and rationality', becoming a 'technical skill [that could] be developed and used toward instrumental ends'. Listening, then, became 'a site through which modern power relations can be elaborated, managed, and acted out' (Sterne 2003: 93).

This book argues the modernization of listening goes beyond these processes of 'individuation' and has important public and intersubjective dimensions. But Sterne's recognition of listening as a site and practice of power relations is a useful reminder that the auditory realm does not simply offer a positive or benign corrective to the dominance and disciplinary regime of the visual. The senses are all geared to power in different ways and to different effect through history. That power relations can also operate through the act of listening is also a useful reminder that the act of listening is far from being as passive, immutable and unremarkable as so commonly assumed. Listening, it is safe to assume, has always been available as a site of power relations, always alongside and in relation to the other senses, but perhaps never more explicitly contested than in the modern era which, as Sterne (2003: 182) puts it, 'marks a new level of plasticity in the social organization, formation, and movement of sound'. Sterne's interest lies with the conditions that allowed for this plasticity, rather than how this plasticity 'reified' into particular media forms. This book, too, is interested in uncovering some of those moments of 'plasticity', although the emphasis is less on the technical and economic pressures that funnelled media potentials into their eventually familiar moulds, than in exploring the implications of these histories for the formations of new kinds of publics.

It is with this in mind that the following overview of the modernization of listening is offered. It cannot pretend to be exhaustive, and it is perhaps misleadingly mediacentric, but it aims simply to pick out some transformational 'moments' where the possibilities or practices of listening within a mediated public sphere were thrown into particular relief.

Writing, Reading and Listening

Even in terms of a media history, the modernization of listening does not begin with the invention of the modern audio media of telephone, phonograph or radio, because the first media technology to affect the listening experience was the written word. With writing, spoken language began to be disembodied and transplanted from the realm of the auditory into the visual. What had once been ephemeral and intangible became permanent and material. Plato (1956: 69) has Socrates explain to Phaedrus this 'strange quality' of writing that turns speech into a silent image:

> the painter's products stand before us quite as though they were alive; but if you question them, they maintain a solemn silence. So, too, with written words: you might think they spoke as though they made sense, but if you ask them anything about what they are saying, if you wish an explanation, they go on telling you the same thing, over and over forever.

Leaving aside the oft-noted irony of this written appeal against the written word, what is striking here is the recognition of a world of discourse falling silent, being muted. There is nothing left to *listen* to. Listening, in other words, is identified as being at the very heart of the dialogic and dialectical process. For Plato's Socrates, the silencing of language is a threat to recall and understanding; writing is passive, conservative, unresponsive and ultimately deadening. It is in the act of listening that the word is kept alive.

It would be wrong, however, to overplay how writing silenced speech, not only because people went on, naturally, talking and listening to each other, but because writing in a sense *stored* sound, at least once it began to develop an acoustic dimension in the form of phonograms, as it did first in ancient Egypt and Babylon. The phonetic alphabet that emerged around 1500 BC was a major development, but it was the addition of vowel sounds in the Greek alphabet that marked the breakthrough to a written representation of sounded speech. Once sound had been captured in this way, it was freed from its ephemerality and locatedness – the sound of speech could be reproduced by the reader at any time, anywhere. Or perhaps more accurately, the speech could be sounded out, since the abstraction of the vowel system stopped short of reproducing regional dialects, vocal timbres and emotional inflections. Those parts of language remained tied to the body, to the particularities of an individual. The phonic alphabet was a levelling device, in principle accessible to all regardless of context and yet, in its sounding out, adaptable to endless individual modulation. This decontextualization is writing's status as reminder, the displacement of memory that Socrates so decried. But it is also the very thing that has been credited (most famously by writers like Havelock, Innis, McLuhan and Ong) with enabling – or at least stimulating – the development of new levels of abstraction, objectivity and analysis. Havelock (1986) even argued it was the 'acoustic efficiency' of the Greek alphabet that made democracy possible. Where previous scripts had been complex, mysterious and arcane, the Greek alphabet corresponded so nearly to the sounds of speech that it was accessible to all, opening up the once closed and elitist world of letters in principle, if not in practice, to all.[3]

The technology of writing had a gradual but insistent and revolutionary impact on oral societies and culture – which is to say, it transformed the relations and practices of speaking and listening. It is not that there was less to listen to, but that listening became more differentiated. Nor is it simply that some words were read and some listened to, for reading *included* listening – listening to the sounds of the language, either read aloud or with the inner voice. Indeed, so efficient a system was the alphabet that it barely registers to the proficient reader as a series of visible marks, and so, as Havelock put it, 'it ceased to interpose itself as an object of thought between the reader and his recollection of the spoken tongue' (in McLuhan and McLuhan 1988: 15). In other words, despite the involvement of the eye, writing is a recording device for the ear.

Derrick de Kerckhove (1997: 104), one of the foremost proponents of the 'alphabet effect', argued that writing produced two 'modes' of listening, the oral and the literate, the former 'global and comprehensive', the latter 'specialized and selective', the one 'cosmocentric and spatial', the other 'linear, temporal and logocentric'. For de Kerckhove, the triumph of literate over oral listening in the visualized culture of the West has amounted to a kind of societal 'hearing loss'. Yet while the recognition of different *kinds* of listening is instructive, the interpretation seems tinged with unnecessary nostalgia for 'real' communication, communication that is unmediated. It is also marked by the sort of 'denigration of vision', to borrow Jay's term, that often appears in writing that attends to sound, as if the senses were in some sort of internecine battle in which the critic has to take sides. Although the process of inscription itself marked the separation of sight from sound, it was a process that nevertheless came from sound and returned to sound.[4] For example, when Greek orators used scripts, just like contemporary public speakers they fostered techniques to give the impression of spontaneity and improvisation, and were very conscious of adapting tone, volume and gesture to optimize the delivery of the spoken word (Liebersohn 2005: 318). The script was adapted, in other words, to the listening public. Indeed, it is likely Plato wrote in the form of the dialogue to facilitate their being read aloud, believing a written text could be made sense of fully only in the process of *sounding* it out (Yamagata 2005: 120–1). In one dialogue designed to demonstrate the superiority of the spoken word, he shows Socrates improvising and revising speeches in response to his listeners' questions. In so doing, he makes clear the activity of the listeners in contributing to the production of the written text and its understanding.[5]

In this short discussion, it is already possible to discern a number of tropes that recur throughout the history of mediated communication: questions of authenticity, realism and transparency; questions about memory, archiving and the proliferation of information at the expense of knowledge; questions about dissemination and dialogue, propaganda and interactivity; questions of the word, the spirit and the body. And there is already a sense of foreboding about the new technological future and a certain nostalgia for what went before.

Oral and written traditions continued (and continue) to co-exist and the one continued to inform and inflect the other. The two traditions existed side by side in European culture through the Middle Ages (albeit often in different spheres of influence, for example oral custom and written law), but with written culture, broadly speaking, on the advance, and oral culture being *realigned* – increasingly informed and contextualized by written texts (Stock 1990: 19–21). The rise of 'textuality' had immense implications, not least the promotion of rationality, the emergence of a new kind of 'public' and a new relation to 'experience'. Interestingly, because illiteracy was still the norm for vast swathes of the population, the 'textual communities' that emerged during the Middle Ages are as often referred to as 'listeners' as 'readers'. Even into the early print era, reading would have been experienced primarily as 'a listening process, simply set in motion by sight' (Ong 1982: 121).

The rise of *silent* reading is a complicated story bound up with changes in the accessibility and portability of books, a gradual move from a monastic to a scholastic reading culture, and the privatization of reading afforded by both the spread and form of printed materials (Littau 2006: 14–17). Technologically, the origins of silent reading have been traced to an innovation of Irish medieval scribes which began to spread across Europe from the seventh century, namely the separation of individual words by a space (Saenger 1997: 11). Until then, words had run into each other because vowel letters had allowed for the unambiguous transcription of *pronounced* speech. The ancients found no virtue in easy, speedy, or 'reference' reading. Reading aloud (slowly and carefully deciphering meaning from words that ran into each other) fostered comprehension, close reading, dialogue and the important skill of memorizing. Reading in the ancient world was 'public, taxing and loud' (Fischer 2003: 18). Modern silent reading works with 'lexical images' that do not necessarily need to be sounded out but still create voices in the head. It was further facilitated by the improved legibility of the machinic word on the page, and by the mass production of portable texts that allowed private, domesticated reading in place of the collective listening to the reading aloud of a unique manuscript. The bodily traces of an author's hand were eliminated in the anonymity of the publisher's print, and their words more rarely passed through the speech organs and into the ears of their readers (Kittler 1999: 8–9; Lupton 2004: 16–17).

The printed word, freed from the shackles of time, geography and community, took on a disembodied authority and, so the argument goes, helped to produce the modern subject as rational observer. Silent reading was regarded as purified, freed from the intervention of the body and calling upon a higher interiority (Kittler 1995: 84). Reading out loud fell from favour, save for specific ceremonial or pedagogical situations. Speech, and specifically the sonorous properties of speech that act for listeners as markers of difference, particularity and alterity, remained – until the intervention of modern technologies of sound recording and reproduction – firmly bound to time, place and the body.

But the rise of print culture and silent reading did not entirely silence the public sphere. First, it is possible to trace the continuing fascination with aurality through the plentiful acoustic images that figure in the printed works of the Renaissance and Enlightenment (Woolf 2004; Erlmann 2010). Second, the institutionalization of the bourgeois public sphere in *parliaments* (and the formation of a variety of publics in other spaces) continued the tradition of conducting politics through the sound of debate (enabled and enhanced by the gradual dismantling of apparatuses of censorship). Thirdly, the proliferation of texts generated a huge amount of *talk* – not only in the literary salons and coffee houses, but in the warp and weft of everyday life (Rosenfeld 2011: 327–8). Nevertheless, the 'de-auralization' of the world in the age of print and the consequent shift in 'the relation of the spoken word to the visual image' (Carey 1986: 35) has been the starting point for many of the most influential analyses of the modern condition and modern visual culture. The rest of this chapter now turns to the 're-auralization' of the public world.

Revolutions in Sound

The revolutionary media of the nineteenth century were named as writing devices – the photograph that wrote light, the telegraph that wrote across distance, the cinematograph that wrote movement and the phonograph that wrote sound. This naming self-consciously marked these startlingly new technologies as bound up with the most ancient recording technology of all.

The first of the 'graphical' innovations in sound was the telegraph. It was Morse telegraphy that first opened the way to the transmission of information over distance and accelerated the compression of time and space that has become axiomatic for the modern condition. The listening technique associated with this pioneering technology contributed to a notion of a manipulable private acoustic space that was ripe for ideological and commercial exploitation, as Sterne has so eloquently argued. However, telegraphy does not feature very much in this book precisely because the specialist form of its encoding and decoding rendered it a privatized and individualized mode of communication in terms of reception and experience, despite its impact on the public spheres of news and business. It is not insignificant that a new training of the ear was necessitated right at the beginning of this most fundamental transformation of the modern condition, but in many ways this decoding was more like reading than listening (indeed even less like listening than reading the written word). In fact, it was the desire for a more accessible voice telegraphy that inspired the invention of the telephone, and the search for an automated transcription service for the telegraph that inspired the phonograph.

With time, the telephone came to be applied most typically as a system of interpersonal rather than public communication. Indeed, the intimacy of the telephone is striking, bringing voices as close to the ear as in a whisper. And yet, it is an uncanny intimacy – a mediated immediacy, a displaced presence, an estranged familiarity (Ronell 1989). It is a new and thoroughly modern experience of listening. But if the telephone was adopted primarily as a form of interpersonal, or *privatized* communication, its early marketing involved a variety of public demonstrations that pointed to alternative trajectories. Demonstrations would 'broadcast' music or speech to audiences gathered elsewhere in public halls to witness – and covet – the latest technological wonder of the age (Fischer 1992: 60–85). New technological and scientific discoveries were commonly presented at public events, often a mix of education and entertainment, and these events can be instructive in understanding not only the contingency of how new technologies found their social and commercial applications, but also, the liminality of public and private modes of listening. In terms of the telephone, for example, private conversations were displayed as public event, and remind us how even this most intimate form of technologized listening was enabled by the construction of a public communications network.

Telephony represented a radical extension of the ability to listen at a distance. But phonography represented something altogether new. Sound had never before been stored *as sound*. Sound recording represents both a paradigmatic shift in representational practice and 'perhaps the most radical of all sensory reorganizations in modernity' (Peters 1999: 160–1). This deceptively simple device (patented in 1878) that transposed sound waves into physical and *reproducible* form released sound from the bounds of both time and place, and realized eternal dreams of immortalizing the human voice. Edison's 'talking machine' was a sensation – and the possibility of reproducing sound over time and distance eventually helped transform once again the organization and experience of public life.

The phonograph might be best known as a talking machine, but it was also a *listening* machine, for it both recorded and reproduced sound, the machine's great horn functioning first as an ear and only then as a mouth.[6]

Once again, this latest technological wonder was 'introduced to the public' in places of learning and entertainment (Gitelman 2006: 13). Visitors would be invited to listen back to themselves, a profoundly new and uncanny experience (Kahn 2001: 8–9). But the phonograph at first 'stumbled hard against [the] public sphere' which at that time was constituted predominantly as the sphere of the written word (Gitelman 2006: 13). In the contemporary imagination, the phonograph did not only talk and listen, it was also a writing machine. Conceived as an *inscription* device, it resonated in the familiar world of print and found a public at least in part because of the associations with the existing public sphere of readers. This early phonographic 'public' was not constituted *by* the new medium, nor was the medium experienced on what might be called its own terms, but rather, as Gitelman (2006: 13) argues, 'as party to the existing, dynamic (and extrinsic) logics of writing, print media, and public speech'.

Yet the emphasis on the phonograph's graphical rather than sonic qualities, inevitably tells only part of the story. Gitelman (2006: 28) describes how these first phonographic outings 'variously interrogated the normal habits of writing, reading, and speaking', but does not explicitly consider the impact it might have had on *listening*, although the interrogation described here is conducted precisely via a new and public mode of listening. The analogy to writing would suggest reading is the appropriate term; but the inscription is not a sign system to be decoded like an alphabet, but more an interim inscription, the conversion of which back into soundwaves provides for a sense of *immediate* communication. Of course, the practices and expectations of a reading public were not suddenly overturned; and the insight that a new medium emerges into an already existing formation is hugely important, but nevertheless, it is still possible to see in this moment a significant move towards the constitution of a new and modern listening public.

In 1888, Edison had compared his 'perfected phonograph' to early cuneiform writing on baked clay cylinders, though his wax cylinders had the advantage of speaking 'for themselves' and did not have to 'wait dumbly for centuries to be deciphered' (in Gitelman 1999: 281). It is precisely because the deciphering process lies in listening rather than reading, that the analogy with writing begins to strain. While we have become used, analytically and metaphorically, to the idea of 'reading' texts in whatever form they are manifested, it is self-evidently a skill, an accomplishment. It is taught and learned; it is acquired or not. Listening too can be a skill, an accomplishment honed by effort, but it is certainly of a different order to reading, which might be thought of as deciphering an encoded code, not the code itself. Listening is part of language acquisition itself, but also part of simply being in the world, and therefore, broadly speaking, seems to come naturally. In contrast to reading, listening itself *seems* to offer an unmediated connection to the world, and more specifically to the world of language. The phonograph, then, was a writing device that promised *freedom* from reading (and indeed from the chore of putting pen to paper), with all that might mean for democratizing access to public life and letters. In one of his utopian addresses about his new invention Edison (1878: 534) wrote:

> The advantages of [talking] books over those printed are too readily seen to need mention. Such books would be listened to where now none are read. They would preserve more than the mental emanations of the brain of the author; and, as a bequest to future generations, they would be unequaled.

So in transcending the need to read, the phonograph would paradoxically rescue 'the book' from decline and make literature accessible to the (still often illiterate) masses. Listening, then, at the dawn of the modern media age is explicitly posited as a new and more democratic mode of participation in the public sphere. To this extent, the phonograph was just one material incarnation of a more widespread desire during this period to transcend the limitations of print and to make the experience of reading more immediate, primarily by attempts to capture, graphically and stylistically, the characteristics of an individual's speech (Camlot 2003: 148–9), to recognize reading, in other words, as a form of mediated listening.

But for the time being this vision was hindered by technical limitations like the relatively short recording time. It was not until the 1930s that a 'Victorian-length' novel was recorded in its entirety – even then requiring dozens of double-sided discs (Camlot 2003: 151; Rubery 2011). The same limitations applied to music of course, with cultural elites ambivalent about the dissemination of great musical works that had to be listened to piecemeal. The phonograph's destiny seemed entwined with that of the popular song and the comedy turn. But the promise of immortality and entry into a new marketplace encouraged artists to persist with the phonograph, despite its rude interruptions. This 'talking machine' would breathe life into the written word, and preserve an author's living voice, the conduit to their character and their very identity. It could even bring an author back to life, and many men and women in public life were keen at first to have their voices recorded for posterity. And yet, by 1905 the novelty had worn off to such an extent that one commentator could lament, with some irony, that the priorities of the industry were failing to serve not only the present public interest, but the interests of the public yet to come:

> Something of the magnetic personality of Gladstone, the charm of Tennyson, is conveyed to us by the medium of these cylinders. Why then should the airy elusiveness of Mr Balfour, the manly candour of Mr Chamberlain and the shrinking modesty of Mr Winston Churchill be lost to future generations? Why should the eloquence of Lord Rosebery perish, whilst 'Stop Your Tickling Jock' is immortalised?[7]

There will be much more about phonography and its publics in the following chapters, but the term 'listening public' really came into its own when radio technology found its social application as broadcasting; when, in other words, there was a congregation of listeners separated by distance but united in the immediate reception of sound, speech and music. Indeed, the term 'listening public' for a while became interchangeable with the idea of the radio audience.

Listening in the Air

Radio technology was also first presented to the public in demonstrations and exhibitions. There was inevitably wonder and awe at the science that enabled sound to travel without wires through the 'ether', but by the 1920s there was also a widespread sense that a great potential would be wasted if this new technology were not deployed to properly *public* ends. This meant fully exploiting radio's reach, its flexibility, its indiscriminacy, its immediacy and its liveness – to become, in effect, more than just a wireless gramophone.

A few months after the BBC first went on air, for example, an article in *The Daily Mirror* reflected on the *public* potential of being able to 'overhear everything'. Speculating that the wireless microphone could soon go everywhere a newspaper reporter could go, so the 'listener-in' should soon be able to hear directly from the Houses of Parliament, the courts of justice, the universities and 'every other place where news of public interest is "created"' (Valdar 1923: 5). Some of this promise would eventually be realized, although broadcasting's access to established public events and institutions was anything but automatic. The paper's editorial, entitled 'The World Made One', expressed another common hope for the new broadcasting age: that the world would become smaller and less divisive through a new means of communication and understanding, and that, in time, a new spiritual bond would arise between peoples that would put an end to warfare. Although, sadly, such lofty hopes would prove dreadfully naïve, it was a characteristic expression of hope that the 'glowing white hot wireless enthusiasm'[8] could be harnessed to heal political wounds in the aftermath of a dreadful war, to speak to and for newly enfranchised populations and to bridge the prevailing social, regional and national divides. In the US, it was not uncommon to think radio could offer a means to integrate the myriad immigrant cultures or enhance a sense of common nationhood across a vast continent, though here the unifying potential of popular culture was more evidently part of the mix. Although there is plenty of historical evidence to suggest that American radio was just as capable of amplifying cultural divisions (Hilmes 1997; Douglas 1999; Doerksen 2005; Goodman 2011), the narrative of network radio as the great leveller during radio's 'golden age' has been very powerful. Writing in 1930, NBC President Merlin Aylesworth, for example, saw in radio a chance 'to preserve our now vast population from disintegrating into classes . . . We must know and honor the same heroes, love the same songs, enjoy the same sports, realize our common interest in our national problems' (in Boddy 2004: 19). And in Germany, where political divisions were heightened by the consequences of defeat and economic turmoil, the 'father' of public broadcasting, Hans Bredow, hoped to use the radio to 'bring together the different classes of the people separated by political and religious differences, and forge them into a spiritually united listening community' (in Dussel 2004: 52). Similarly Albert Einstein, in opening the 1930 Berlin radio exhibition, praised the curiosity and inventiveness of the technicians who had given the world this machine that could contribute to the reconciliation of peoples (in Hay 1975: xi).

And all this was to be achieved by the act of communal listening, listening as a shared experience with political consequence. It is indeed remarkable how swiftly the notion of the listening radio public was extended to encompass whole populations, regardless of the relatively small number of people who could initially 'listen in'. Somehow the combination of an indiscriminate address sent into the ether, with the unknowability of an audience using the apparently universal and natural skill of listening, effected the conflation of the limited numbers of 'listeners-in' with the all-embracing fiction of 'the listening public'. This necessary fiction was produced and reproduced for both listeners and readers in the public sphere and could be usefully deployed for political and commercial ends. It certainly underpinned the appropriation of the airwaves as a public service in the UK and Germany, and it served as a tempting bait for commercial sponsors in both the US and Europe.

Only gradually did the need arise to test the 'truth' of that fiction with audience research. Even in the US, advertising sales were at first based on (highly gendered) suppositions about the audience combined with basic demographic statistics rather than dedicated audience research. The first formal ratings system and telephone surveys were launched only in 1929 and more qualititative research only got under way in the 1930s, most notably by Paul Lazarsfeld and his colleagues at Columbia. Meanwhile, the BBC under John Reith, with its remit for cultural leadership, was especially reluctant to engage in any listener research lest the Corporation fall prey to giving the audience what it professed it wanted, rather than what it might not yet know it needed. The question would be aired from time to time within the Corporation because, as one internal memo put it, it was inevitable that programme makers who have 'no appreciable reaction from the public, no applauses, no hisses' should from time to time 'lose faith in their own autocracy'.[9] And yet the view that won out was that the radio had 'so many publics (and no Public)' that faith in any kind of statistical levelling to find 'the average listener' would be misplaced.[10] Nor was there anything to be gained by knowing the size of an audience for a particular programme, because 'every broadcast had the same target – the entire population' (Silvey 1974: 185).

As with the phonograph before it, then, broadcasting found a public among the contrasting versions of the public that were already circulating. In other words, radio's listening public was cross-referenced with the already established commercial, literary, theatrical, phonographic and political publics, and these operated variously at 'national, sub-national, pre-national and trans-national levels' (Hilmes 2012: 13). And, it is worth pointing out, it existed *alongside* those continuing publics, and was the subject of intense public scrutiny and occasional opprobrium within those other spheres. But those other publics were limited and contained, identifiable by numbers assembled or copies sold. As Reith saw it, the radio audience was not *a* public, but *the* public, and broadcasters had to acknowledge it included the *unwilling* audience as well as the willing.[11]

This explains in part why broadcasters were so often unconvinced that listeners knew *how* to listen, a feeling compounded by the invisibility and inaudibility of an audience whose reactions were impossible to gauge. Since the public address was 'indiscriminate', the public might itself be 'indiscriminating' in its listening, which would be bad for the listener, bad for the medium and, by extension, bad for public life. The cultivation of the listener's ear was implicit in the propagation of different programming techniques and genres (explored by Susan Douglas (1999) in her 'archaeology of radio listening'), and in the efforts of educationalists to inculcate attentive and appreciative listening to counteract the temptation of distracted listening (Tebutt 2009; Goodman 2010). The BBC even considered founding listeners' 'guilds', 'to train the listener to listen intelligently and to raise his standard of appreciation'.[12] Although this was clearly an operation in cultivating 'good' taste to mirror that of the cultural elites, there was, at root, a sense of a project with a *public* dimension. In much the same way as literacy had to be taught and nurtured for the public good as well as for individual edification, so too did this newly public form of listening demand new skills of selectivity and attention. While broadcasters slowly learned to speak in a 'familiar' tone of voice suitable to the domestic conditions of reception, so too did listeners have to learn how to hear that institutional and public voice as speaking to them alone while at the same time understanding it still as an impersonal *public* address (Peters 2010: 128).

In a light-hearted yet quietly misogynist piece in 1924, *The Daily Mirror* recognized the value of the wireless in enhancing people's capacity to listen, and without much ado made a connection between the social skills of listening and the world of public affairs:

> One of the merits of 'wireless' is that it encourages the habit of *listening* – unlike the telephone, which merely increases talkativeness. They tell us that the strain of this attentiveness is developing a wrinkled 'radio face' in women. All of us – not only women – are bad listeners in these days. We want to be heard first. We all talk together. [. . .] Yet social success really depends on the faculty of keeping quiet [. . .]. This useful habit is trained by listening in. [. . .] The power of attention will remain and carry the ambitious listener – who knows? – perhaps even to the highest office in the State.[13]

In radio's infancy, listening-in was such a novelty that, perhaps for the first time, listening itself became a matter for celebrity gossip, as columnists reported how various stars of stage and screen were installing receivers in their homes and dressing-rooms in order that they might 'listen-in' and, of course, be *seen* to be listening in.[14] Listening became in the 1920s a fashionable status symbol, as it would be in different guises over the decades, through the public visibility of transistor radios and ghettoblasters to the iconic white earphones and wires of the iPod. Listening, therefore, achieved a new *visibility* in relation to the new technologies of sound, an iconic activity in its own respect, hauled out of obscurity, but also hived off from its 'normal' interrelationship with the other senses.

Listening with Images

This new visibility of listening was a feature of a very particular moment in modern media culture, where of the two leading media of modern communication – radio and film – one communicated without image, the other without sound (or at least, without synchronized sound). Frederic Jameson saw this 'autonomization' of the senses as 'a response to, but also in mimetic rivalry of, the alienating effects of a rationalized, commodified world' (in Connor 1997: 219). But then sound came to the movies, and image came to radio in the form of television, but image-less radio survived where silent film did not (at least in the mainstream). It would be tempting to make an argument about the self-sufficiency of sound over image, the preference for hearing-without-seeing over seeing-without-hearing. But visual arts often flourish without recourse to a soundtrack and many sonic arts are combined with visual stimulation. Radio probably survived (which means people actively continued to invest in it, promote, support and listen to it) because listening-without-looking meant music and the worlds conjured by the spoken word in the imagination could be woven into the patterns of everyday life, accompanying domestic and mobile routines and providing incidental companionship. But it might also have had something to do with the elective affinity between listening and a pluralistic, public sensibility.

Listening publics are not constituted in relation to media that deal only in sound. The modernization of listening is also part of the story of audiovisual media, although judging by much of the scholarship on cinema and television it would be easy to think this history was all about spectatorship, or at best a visual experience accompanied by a soundtrack. It is perfectly commonplace to talk about 'seeing a film' or 'watching television', but it ought also to be commonsensical that 'listening' does not happen only when there is nothing to look at. Listening without seeing might in some sense be the apotheosis of modern listening – the normalization of listening to 'absent' sounds via technologies of recording and transmission – but it was certainly in part the desire to reconnect listening to looking that lay behind the various innovations in audiovisual media.

A decade after announcing his phonograph, Edison famously informed the Patents Office that he was 'experimenting upon an instrument which does for the Eye what the Phonograph does for the Ear'. He would capture the visual world in motion as he had captured the movement of sound – and exploit the commercial opportunities that would follow. In recording movement, and playing it back 'in real time', the kinetograph, like the phonograph before it, promised to capture time itself – or rather to overlay a recording of time past in time present. It is this relationship to time as *duration* that reveals the *phonographic* heritage of the movies above and beyond the introduction of a soundtrack (Feaster 2009). The *synchronization* of sound and image, however, faced challenges both technical and cultural. First, the projection of images was a problem more easily solved than the projection (amplification) of recorded sound. There were continual attempts to market sound film using phonographic technology via a panoply of competing devices – the *Biophone, Cinematophone, Animatophone, Synchroscope* and *Vivaphone* among them, but most were either too expensive or unreliable to become commercially viable. But part of their failure was that the listening public, attuned to the individualized acoustic experience of domestic gramophones and phonograph parlours, was unable to 'overlook' the limitations of projected sound in public auditoria. Meanwhile, we have come to know this period as the age of silent film.

But no films were ever screened in silence. The films themselves may have been mute, but the screening was often accompanied by a lecturer, live or recorded musical accompaniment, or even actors playing out the dialogue behind the screen. From around 1908 there were also various mechanical systems for producing sound effects like bells, sirens and horses' hooves in time with the action. These bore such names as *Noiseograph, Soundograph, Dramagraph* and the *Excelsior Sound Effects Cabinet*. The two biggest machines, the American *Kinematophone Machine* and the British *Allefex*, could each produce over 50 such sound effects (Jossé 1984: 48).

There were also noisy interventions on the part of the audience. The 'live' sounds created in the auditorium emphasized the collectivity of the viewing experience producing a sense of 'immediacy and participation' that 'actualised the image' (Hansen 1991: 43), and diminished the gap between the illusion on the screen and the location in which it was viewed. In short, the sounds of the silent cinema acknowledged that the public was made up, naturally, of spectators who were also always already listeners, and that the sense of public participation, the sense of a public event unfolding in the present rather than the witnessing of a past event recorded on film, was bound up as much in the listening as in the viewing experience. As an advert for the *Soundograph* boasted, 'It will put life and realism in your pictures.'[15]

So the sound of silent film was much more complex and varied than the simple piano accompaniment we tend to associate it with today. With competing venues showing the same film reels, enterprising exhibitors sought to stand out from the crowd by the quality and creativity of their 'live sound'. The nickelodeon theatres, for example, that were so popular in the decade or so from 1905, set the stage for a carnivalesque soundscape of competing sonic traditions:

> Out front, ballyhoo music competed with an eager spieler, while inside a live piano battled audience remarks from time to time interrupted by an

> operator's announcement, an illustrated song, or mechanical music (Altman 2004: 390).

Altman recounts how moral and music reformers sought to impose order on this unruly cacophony, and succeeded, at least for a while, in standardizing film sound by organizing it into complementary features of the programme. Indeed it was in the attempts to control and manage the sound of silent cinema that 'film exhibition found its first stability, and cinema thereby its initial identity' (2004: 390). Along with changes in narrative form and with architectural changes mimicking the bourgeois theatres of old, the control of cinema's soundscape was another way of imposing respectable order on a disorderly audience (Gunning 1986; Uricchio and Pearson 1993). It was an audience, moreover, made up of people – including women – normally excluded from established publics. The new strictures of silence that sound film imposed on the audience not only curtailed the role of local exhibitors but helped to foil the potential to develop an alternative public sphere (Hansen 1991: 99).

The efforts to impose respectable order on the nickelodeon audience had another unintended but significant effect. In relentlessly publicizing the results of their statistical analyses of the audience, the reformers routinized 'the representation of a new form of public-ness and produced a viable mediating fiction of the public organized around and through this new mode of address' (Shimpach 2007: 137). So this new mass public, dispersed in theatres across the country, was represented back to itself – albeit as 'a problem' – enabling patrons to imagine themselves as participating in a wider public formation. It was in this process of being discursively constituted that members of the audience achieved that 'self-alienation' that is a prerequisite for participation in the public sphere (Warner 1992). Paradoxically, cinema goers were constituted as a public in the process of their literal silencing, in the process of being interpellated, in some sense, as a *listening* public.

Developments in optical sound recording led to a new wave of synchronized sound films in the early 1920s – by the European *Photophone* and American *Phonofilm* companies, for example. Despite enthusiasm at the demonstration screenings, commentators seemed to think it would be better suited to documentary than entertainment, because of the heightened realism that sound brought to the experience.[16] *The Guardian*, for example, concluded that 'For those who go to the Kinema seeking a dreamland, the spoken word might only mean sad disillusion – a quick awakening to the world of hard, unromantic fact.'[17] Right through the

1920s, sound cinema was widely regarded as unlikely to be more than a passing fad, and certainly not one that would threaten the supremacy and artistry of silent film. There was a reluctance on the part of established studios to invest in sound, and it was only when the struggling Warner Bros. company picked up an unwanted patent on the grounds they 'had nothing to lose', and had an unexpected success with *The Jazz Singer*, that prospects for the sound film changed significantly. The misgivings had come from various directions: economic, for the introduction of dialogue would damage the transnational film trade; aesthetic, for the introduction of sound might still the fluid movement of the image; and even political – Eisenstein and Pudovkin famously feared synchronized sound would lead to the *inertia* of the montage technique, undermining the radical potential of asynchronous, contrapuntal sound (Thompson 1980: 115). There were also misgivings about the quality of the sound reproduction. Many spectators were disappointed as listeners, dubbing the new films not 'talkies', but 'squalkies'.[18]

However, sound film did eventually catch on, of course, bringing with it new ways of listening, and an audiovisual experience that instituted 'a more commanding authority over the observer' (Crary 1989: 102), even though the coincidence of 'sound with image, of voice with figure' was always already the condition of unmediated experience. One new effect was the acoustic 'close-up', the technique of isolating, magnifying and interpreting individual sounds to produce a heightened sense of realism and a reordered relationship with the acoustic environment off-screen.[19] This new forensic attention to the noise of the world, thanks to its association with optical impressions, would train the ear to make order out of chaos, to distinguish individual voices within the cacophony. For Siegfried Kracauer, this new way of listening was not just a matter of individual apperception, but had more public consequences. In a review of an early sound film screened at the Gloria Film-Palast in Frankfurt in October 1928, he reflected on the capacity of the new technology to 'redeem' the 'spontaneous sounds of the street'. The street is a recurring figure in Kracauer's work, and it often stands in for a faceless alienation. The redemption of the sounds of the street meant revealing, or rediscovering, the collective, anonymous sounds that surround us without our active acknowledgement:

> Reclaimed as an audible presence, they would actively change the audience's perception of *a shared world* over and beyond what the silent film had already contributed in making 'accessible to our consciousness the life of lights and shadows' (Barnouw 1994: 130, my italics).

Here is an auditory equivalent to Benjamin's (1936/1992a: 230) later formulation of the 'optical unconscious', with the microphone in place of the
camera exploring a space filled with the unconscious, 'shocking' the audience into a more active apprehension of the world as a vivid and shared
acoustic environment that transcended national, partisan or linguistic
boundaries. New narrative techniques, exemplified already in *The Jazz
Singer*, also invited audiences to eavesdrop on intimate conversations and
exchanges projected into public space, turning spectators into 'a group of
auditory-voyeurs intent on hearing sounds that are not meant for us'
(Altman 1995: 68). Except the sounds of such intimate conversations *were*
meant for the listening public, however much they were inscribed diageti-
cally as private. This is the double articulation of mediated talk that would
have been familiar to filmgoers who were already radio listeners. This is a
pattern repeated throughout the history of film sound, with each innovation taken up only to the extent that it could 'satisfy the needs created by
the other sound practices to which potential consumers are accustomed',
whether from broadcast sound, home-based music systems or mobile and
gaming environments (Altman 1995: 72).

In classical Hollywood cinema, a unified soundtrack was fed through
loudspeakers situated behind the screen, helping the impression that sound
derived from, and was at the service of, the image. Developments in stereo
and surroundsound were later deployed in the service of creating spatial
fidelity, but increasingly multiple channels have been used for different
filmic elements – typically a monoaural channel for dialogue, stereo for
music and surroundsound for effects. The abiding intention is to maximize
identification with the film, to immerse the audience *inside* the filmic space,
not just before it, in front of a screen. The development of more sophisticated sound design and playback arguably requires the audience to perform
ever more demanding and complex auditory tasks. In terms that echo the
excitement of new powers of audition noted in the early days of sound
film, Gianluca Sergi (n.d.) has described the enhanced sensory perception
afforded by the latest digital developments in cinema sound:

> This powerful, sensual involvement with this three-dimensional (sonic) space
> is clearly designed to heighten the cinematic experience and provide audi-
> ences with a constant source of pleasure. The Hollywood listener is bestowed
> with an aural experience which elevates him/her to a state which may be
> defined as the *super-listener*, a being (not to be found in nature) able to hear
> sounds that in reality would not be audible or would sound substantially
> duller. This is a new breed of spectators who can expect screen objects to fly
> above their heads into (and out of) the auditorium.

The recurrent celebration of new forms of immersive reality is the subject of a separate chapter, but it also features in the following account of how listening figures in the construction of a public for the other dominant audiovisual form of the twentieth century, namely television.

Almost as soon as sound broadcasting had begun, it was widely expected that 'image radio', the marriage of cinema and radio, would inevitably follow. The arrival of broadcasting led to another wave of experiments in 'converging' different media forms, for example, the Manchester station 5N0 experimented with broadcasting cinema orchestras on the air, and loudspeakers were commonly set up in cinemas so viewers of silent films could listen to a simultaneous radio broadcast of accompanying music or even dialogue performed in a radio studio.[20] Despite some 'quite successful' attempts, such as a cine-broadcast of *Robin Hood* in London in 1923,[21] and the promise, inevitably, of 'lending great realism to the screen',[22] the practice clearly never really caught on – although interestingly enough, the 'broadcasting' of live theatrical and televisual events is now once again a feature of cinema programmes, exploiting the collective audience experience as a selling point in an era of audiovisual abundance and ubiquitous personal media.

Because it was the image that was new, and because the idea of 'the listener' was already well-established in relation to sound radio, the audiences for television when it finally took off were called 'lookers-in' and then 'viewers', as if, like the movies, television was beginning life as a silent affair. There was very little mention of sound, though there was discussion about the difference between 'listening' and 'looking'. Radio critics in particular feared television would undermine people's imaginative faculties, that listeners would no longer 'visualize' for themselves. Others hoped it might put an end to the dread 'background listening', since it was assumed background viewing would be impossible (Gorham 1946). But if television was very obviously a kind of radio developed by broadcasting corporations, the introduction of images to the wireless was also widely compared to the introduction of sound to the movies, a comparison born of memory and experience, rather than institutional context. Again, it was predicted this new audiovisual realism would be best suited to 'recording actual events'.[23] After the 'purely auditory art' of radio, television 'with its objective restraints on perception will seem literal-minded' (Cantril and Allport 1935: 262).

After long years of expectation, experimentation and delay, television can be said to have 'arrived' in the 1950s, as reflected in numbers of services launched, sets sold, licences granted, time spent watching, and its increasingly important place in popular culture. And, of course, its arrival did 'impact' on other, more established media forms, although to present it in these terms is to reduce complex intermedial relations to the language of competition. This is reflected in the common description of the *listening* public giving ground to the *viewing* public during this transitional period.[24] But apart from overlooking demographic and other differences in changing patterns of media consumption, and the limited information provided by bare quantitative data, what is missing most significantly in these contemporary accounts, and the way in which historians continue to represent this phenomenon, is that the television public was, *of course*, also listening. In its dominant form, television, for all it is listed as a part of visual culture, did not go through a 'silent' phase as cinema had done before it.[25] Indeed, composer and film critic Michel Chion (1994: 159) insists the image remains 'optional' in television, and that 'the properly televisual is the image as something extra'.

Despite being labelled as a device for *seeing* at a distance right from the start, and despite the audience being described as 'lookers-in', it is clear television was always expected to have sound, and, indeed, that the sound came *first*. The prevailing idea was to illustrate talks and performances rather than add a soundtrack to visual footage. In short, television was widely expected and understood to be radio with pictures (Hilmes 2008: 153), and reviews of early television often commented on whether the pictures were really necessary or desirable.[26] In fact, in the 1930s, before TV sets were commonplace, television was simultaneously broadcast to radio receivers in audio form and, as one review caustically suggested, 'nothing is likely to be missed by the unsighted multitude'.[27]

Certainly during the 1950s, radio was more often than not called 'sound-radio' in the UK press, a term that implies that television is radio too, indeed radio without qualification.[28] The quintessence of radio is the wireless transmission of sound *and* vision. What all this points to, apart from anything else, is the limitation of identifying publics in relation to particular media or texts. The separate construction of radio listeners, television viewers and cinema goers obscures the otherwise obvious fact that any individual or group can be all of these things over the course of a day, a week, a year or a lifetime, and that the *experience* of these various media, and other forms of communication besides, is not absolute, but relational. If we began our media histories not with a preconceived notion of media technologies, or even of media audiences, but with an ambition to think about the experience of media available to particular people in particular times and places, then we might indeed find new questions to ask and new stories to tell. To consider the cultural practice of listening to the media necessarily breaks down those medium-specific boundaries.

Listening was clearly an important part of the experience of television, and certainly engineers, producers, designers, artists and audiences were all intimately aware of the importance of sound to the televisual experience. So what accounts for the almost complete elision of the act of *listening* from contemporary and retrospective discussions of television consumption? It is, of course, just one more example of the rapacious tendency of 'visual culture' to subsume all modes of symbolic representation. In fact, sound meets image throughout media history, and yet their histories have too often been told as separate stories. In terms of television, its heritage as radio with pictures, rather than broadcast cinema (the 'tele-talkie'), enabled the listening relation to be taken for granted, arguably in fact to be the *primary* televisual experience. For many years the relatively poor quality of the image and the small size of the screen, in comparison to what people had come to know in the cinema, would mean that the visual experience was playing catch-up to the auditory in the realism stakes. The quality of the television image is something that characterizes technological and marketing discourses from the very early days to the current incarnation of high definition and 3D screens. There tends to be less attention to audio quality, although the introduction of stereophony during the 1950s and 'home cinema sound' are important exceptions. A later chapter will pick up on the discourses of realism that lie behind this notion of 'quality'.

Famously, the cinema industry, fearing the loss of audiences to the convenience of the small domestic screen, began in the 1950s to experiment with new formats that promised ever more immersive qualities – *Technicolor*, *Cinemascope*, 3-D and stereophonic sound. A dramatic, if short-lived example was *Cinerama*, an experiment in curved widescreen cinema, using three projectors and a seven-track directional sound system that was intended to fill the cinema goer's entire field of vision and audition. But the 'deepies', as they were nicknamed, were not the only audiovisual medium appealing to sensory plenitude during this period. Televisions, too, were marketed on the same sort of idea, albeit on a suitably domesticated scale. Pye, for example, introduced its 'Solid Sound' technology to televisions in 1958, advertising it as an innovation bringing sound 'to fill every corner of the room [. . .] adding startling depth and "solidness" . . . and a "breathtaking new realism"'.[29]

It is not surprising that it is in the manipulation of sound more than image that such claims to immersion are made in relation to audiovisual media. Acoustic space is by definition immersive, as sound surrounds and pervades the body. Sound is always already 3D, always experienced viscerally in the here and now. The image, by contrast, is two dimensional and conceived of as separate, fixed and distanced from the body. It was in the

1950s with the rise of television that Marshall McLuhan was beginning to develop his ideas about the immersive, mythic communication of electronic and spherical acoustic space. Meanwhile, Habermas was working on his thesis about the decline of a public forged in the abstracted, linear and disembodied culture of print, that would later in translation accidentally be ascribed the properties of a sphere. This accidental meeting of these two ideas is productive for thinking about the listening public, and for illuminating historical debates as new media found their public roles.

By way of almost arbitrary illustration, take the BBC's 1957 'New Deal' for radio listeners – the Corporation's response to the declining radio audience and the need to re-direct licence fee money towards the costs of television.[30] The idea was to cement audience loyalty by making each of the three national services more distinctive: the Light Service was to become 'lighter', the Home Service 'homelier', and the Third Programme, well, it wasn't clear. The plans for the Third were not announced straightaway, but there were rumours of cutbacks and shortened hours. Immediately, despite this deliberately 'highbrow' station attracting a tiny fraction of the total audience, the great and the good mobilized to protest against 'the diminished Third' on the grounds that the BBC had a public duty to broadcast to 'serious listeners'. The Sound Broadcasting Society sent a delegation of luminaries to lobby the Director General, with Vaughan Williams representing music, Laurence Olivier drama, and T.S. Eliot the spoken word. Perhaps as a result, the changes to the Third Programme were rather minimal in the end – and the decline in radio audiences barely affected.

This is just one fleeting incarnation of a recurrent debate about broadcasting and other media – about the serious and the popular, about dumbing down and declining standards in relation to some mythical golden age. And it plays out pretty neatly along predictable class lines, expressed in terms of particular taste formations. But it is also a debate formed around distinctive understandings of *listening*. 'Serious' listening, as demanded by the Third Programme, was attentive and discriminating – the product of accumulated cultural capital and the expression of a certain form of cultural labour. Otherwise listening was passive, secondary, instinctive and undemanding. Serious listening, the sort elevated to the highest status by the culture was, in fact, a form of *literary* culture. Popular listening, by contrast, was mundane, accessible to all, more about relaxation and escapism than intellectual labour. In other words, serious listening was about engaging with a *text*; popular listening was an *immersive* experience, it was all about *context*. The more immersive the experience, the less like a literary experience it became. Here is one explanation for the agitated anxieties about the debilitating effects of immersive media, the leading example of which during this period was television. Looked at from this perspective, it is arguably less interesting to think about the impact that television as an upstart medium was having on radio, the press and cinema, but the way in which television was emerging into a culture that was still fundamentally organized, influenced and valorized by the sensibilities of print. For the defenders of the Third Programme, the more listening was like reading, the more the ear functioned as an eye, the better.

By the same token, the denigration of popular listening, and of immersive media in general, was part of the entrenched understanding of auditory, experiential perception as passive and uncritical. Indeed, the fear of mass communication itself is at root a fear of a public rendered silent and 'passive', occupying the role not of speaker, but of listener. As the arguments and evidence presented in this book are intended to show, however, falling silent to listen is not a sign of passivity, nor an act of submission, but is an active part of the communication process. Rethinking the public sphere as an auditorium, with all the non-linear qualities of resonant space, offers a productive way of rethinking those established boundaries and hierarchies associated with the print-based model to include those things like involvement, experience, simultaneity, collectivity and globalism that McLuhan associated with immersive electronic culture.

The invention of new listening publics in relation to the new sound media of phonography and wireless and that were extended by the talkies and television and into contemporary convergent media culture was, in other words, caught up in the tensions between normative ideals of publicness associated with the bourgeois reading public and newer forms of mediated publicness associated with the cinema and mass culture and, perhaps archetypally, with television. The tensions are productive, and do not, I think, need to be 'resolved'. But certainly the widespread elision of listening from accounts of television's growing dominance in the 1950s seems to be symptomatic of a failure to recognize the radical implications of expanded forms of mediated perception during this most conservative of decades.

Expanded Listening

To speak of expanded and immersive media in relation to early television is to appropriate terms that have arisen in relation to the most recent configuration of media technologies – digital, online, mobile and multimedia. It is beyond the scope of this chapter to offer more than a brief glimpse of some of these newer technologies, but it is clear that many of the motifs from the history of when older media were new continue to echo in the contemporary media scene. Frances Dyson (2007: 3) has recently provided a rich analysis of new media sound that also identifies the links with the old:

> new media represents an accumulation of the auditive technologies of the past; a realization of the telepresence first offered by the telephone, a computational form of the inscriptive techniques of the phonograph and tape recorder, an appropriation of the ethereal aspirations of radio, and an embrace of film sound's spatiality.

Given all this, it is possible that despite the prominence of screens in this new media age, listening is an increasingly pertinent way of thinking about our relationship with the media. But beyond these textual characteristics, contemporary ways of experiencing and interacting with the electronic media can also be traced through an auditory lineage. Recorded, broadcast and telephonic sound went mobile long before the screened image, forms of audience interaction from the vox pop to the phone-in have been staples of radio broadcasts since the 1930s, and 'user-generated content' has been a feature of both phonography and radio technology in the analogue era, from home recording and DXing, through mix tapes, citizen band and pirate radio.

Many people would have had their first encounter with digital technologies as listeners to audio formats like the CD or digital radio. Otherwise, however, sound was a latecomer to computer-mediated communication, save for the 'equipment sound' of beeps and whirrs and background hum. Of the main interfaces for sound on personal computers and online, the earliest was streaming audio that emerged only in the mid 1990s, gradually to be joined by mp3 files, file sharing, podcasting and user-publishing sites. Sound itself is made visible for the purposes of editing and manipulation on screen, 'embedded in a textual-graphical-visual' interface (Nyre 2008: 34).[31] But alongside the residual visuality of computer culture is the parallel phenomenon of a growing 'global headphone culture', which has been described as the provisional culmination of the 'mastery of listening' developed over decades in relation to mediated sound (Nye 2011: 64). More generally, media sound now accompanies great realms of experience in public and private spaces both on- and offline. It can fill a stadium or be channelled through an earphone as the most intimate experience. It can be produced, manipulated and distributed by ever growing numbers of people in a bewildering variety of applications and is part of everyday global, local and interpersonal communication networks.

To the extent that the all new media are about 'remediation' (Bolter and Grusin 1999), perhaps the most significant difference in relation to the constitution of listening publics has been the capacity to share files in private, public and hybrid spaces. It is already more than a decade since Steve Jones (2000: 217) argued that in relation to music, 'recording sound matters less and less, and distributing it matters more and more'. The 'intensely social and collaborative' (Goggin 2011: 74) ways in which music and other audio/visual material is now shared and enjoyed via mobile and online media is at one level simply the latest expression of active and sociable listening practices channelled through successive new media. Recognizing this contests the interpretation of headphone culture as relentlessly individuating and privatizing. Moreover, inasmuch as the detached observation of older media corresponded to the 'essential relations of the eye', the 'return' to interaction can be seen to correspond rather to the relations of speaking and listening.

But more significantly, there is a case for saying that despite the continued prevalence of written text, the immediacy, interactivity and pervasiveness of texting, messaging, tweeting etc. makes 'listening', or perhaps, rather, 'secondary listening' the most apposite metaphor for the perceptive mode more generally in the current media age. These micro messages aspire to the immediacy and interactivity of talk, and that supposes a listening response. In fact, the proliferation of fragmentary and ephemeral media messages in both visual, audio and audiovisual form has long since been described as producing an 'auditory mode of receiving and processing information' (Ong 1982: 13). More recently, writing about new ways of researching and writing in the age of Google, commentators mourn the loss of 'structured thought' in the face of the 'associative glut' of linking one thing to another (in Loy 2007: 253). Here is a distant echo of Socrates' disillusion with the written word – the new medium censured for undermining established modes of thought. While the promise of a permanent, absolute and ubiquitous online archive might be the apotheosis of Socrates' fear of the redundancy of memory, it is not the silencing of discourse that is being mourned here, but a crisis in the linear, visual logic of the print age in relation to a resurgent resonant, acoustic logic of the electronic age.

Finally, the convergence of once disparate media in singular hand-held devices that are used for both labour and leisure purposes and that are ubiquitous in both public and private spaces further complicates the ideological distinctions drawn between active and passive, public and private listening. There is a sense in which the state of permanent receptivity that characterizes the contemporary culture of mobile and social media can be understood as a culture that is constantly keeping an ear out for the next call or text or tweet – 'listening out' for connection with the world. The political and ethical consequences of inhabiting this condition will be explored in later chapters, but the next section sets out first to amplify some of these aspects of the modernization of listening in the construction of listening publics.

Listening in the Age of Spectacle

3   Listening in Good Faith: Recording, Representation and the Real

Listening to the 8 a.m. news bulletin on the 'flagship' BBC radio *Today* programme on 28 March 2008, there was a hilarious moment that soon went viral when the newsreader, Charlotte Green, 'corpsed' in uncontrollable giggles while reading an obituary.[1] It was the previous report that had set her off – the sound of the world's first recording of the human voice. It dated to seventeen years before the invention of the phonograph, and twenty-eight years before the otherwise oldest surviving playable recording.[2] The voice singing 'Au clair de la lune' had been recorded on 9 April 1860 by Édouard-Léon Scott de Martinville on his 'phonoautograph', a device that etched sound waves on smoke-blackened paper, but was not capable of playing them back. This graphical inscription had now been translated into a ten-second digital audio clip by the 'First Sounds' research group, and presented to the Association for Recorded Sound Collections at Stanford. The *New York Times* (27 March) described the result:

> the anonymous vocalist, probably female [and possibly Scott's daughter], can be heard against a hissing, crackling background din. The voice, muffled but audible, sings [. . .] a lilting 11-note melody — a ghostly tune, drifting out of the sonic murk.

That's not how the *Today* producer heard it, commenting into Green's earpiece as the piece was playing that it sounded like a bee buzzing in a bottle – an arguably more accurate description. For audio historians this recording represents a moment of the highest significance in the story of sound media; for the contemporary listener it was literally a laughable technological failure. It was laughable for not sounding like a voice in song – for not sounding *like the real thing*.

Listening for Real

The expectation that recordings will sound like 'the real thing' runs like a red thread through the history of mediated sound and underpins the construction of listening publics in the media age. Sound recording would open up a radically new realm of representational practices which would take many forms, but it was the *mimetic* qualities of the new technology that were first seized upon, either in terms of reproducing the 'original' sound as nearly as possible, or in reproducing the 'original' listening experience. Inasmuch as a public is an imagined community reflected back to itself, that reflection must be recognizable, apparently transparent and trustworthy. The history of audiorealism, then, so often told in terms of technology, aesthetics or taste, can also be understood as constitutive of a new form of *public* experience, involving new forms of listening for the real – however defined – and listening *past* the processes of mediation.

Every new medium has been attended by claims that it allows reality to be differently, more persuasively and more completely 'recorded'. Characteristically it will be claimed the new representations mark a radical departure from those available via older technologies; that they are in various ways superior and represent another stage in the inevitable march of progress; and that they allow a more direct access to reality. Media history of course doesn't simply repeat itself but 'our culture still speaks about new communication technologies in remarkably familiar ways' (Spigel 1992: 182). Certainly the discourses of realism that have clustered around sound technologies, from the phonograph to digital audio, are in turn deeply embedded in familiar and powerful discourses of technological determinism, ineluctable progress and realist aesthetics. That the debates tend to focus on the science or technics of 'reproduction' serves to disguise how much they are also caught up in the art of representation and the conventions of listening. The dominance of the realist discourse is particularly remarkable in relation to new audio media because it runs alongside the other prevalent claim that digital audio, like other non-analogue technologies, is endlessly manipulable and therefore poses a challenge to established epistemological categories, including the codes of realism.

The modern media's fascination with realism finds its roots in the eighteenth century, when the processes of modernization began to undermine the stable and 'knowable communities' which had characterized most people's lived experience. This is the period which gave rise to new forms of social representation – from the novel to social statistics, from the encyclopedia to the newspaper; all forms which transcended the knowledge available to first-hand experience (Peters 1997). These new forms in all their variety and invention, whether presented as narrative or as information, or as something inbetween, were all somehow concerned with the documentation and representation of 'actualities' – contemporary events taking place in different places at the same time – that reflected the social world back to itself. The newspaper is a prime example – organizing its content by date according to narrative principles of miscellaneity and comprehensiveness. There need not be, indeed there rarely is, any connection between one story and the next, other than it having occurred in the same time frame.

The new media of film and phonograph separated out sounds and sights in 'real' time, as they unfolded in the world (unlike the retrospective reporting of print and other visual arts). This is what Niklaus Luhmann called *realzeitliche Gleichzeitigkeit*, or real time simultaneity (1996: 79). Sound recordings also unfolded in real time at the point of playback, however distant that was in time from the originating sound event. Or, to put it more poetically, '[t]he stream of time could be bottled and stored for later use' (Peters 1999: 144). The storage of sound, however, does not render the *perception* of sound any less evanescent, notwithstanding the possibility of repetition or reversal. This tendency of sound to disappear – or rather, to dissipate into space – this sense of movement and fleetingness, means that listening is always also caught up *in the moment*; it is an active disposition, always straining toward the present tense, a sense of presence. Phonography tapped into deep-seated desires about letting time stand still, about becoming immortal – although ironically the commercial application of the technology, in achieving the mass production of serially interchangeable 'hits', far from guaranteeing 'immortality', produced a new ephemerality in the marketplace (LeMahieu 1988: 89; Ross 2008: 50).

The rise of modernity, then, marked the beginning of a continuing fascination with realist representations of the entire social horizon of experience from the extraordinary to the mundane. What is particularly salient is that these new realist forms of reflexive representation emerged as part of the same nexus that produced the modern public sphere. Political discourse echoed technical advances in verisimilitude, promising 'real representation' and 'direct experience'. Discourses of realism thus surrounded the introduction of the new recording technologies and their later grafting on to electrical media of transmission in the form of broadcasting. The apparent connection to 'the real' was part of the appeal for audiences, and part of their hold over them. As Rick Altman (1992: 30) has put it, 'Between the illusion of reproduction and the reality of representation lies the discursive power of recorded sound'.

Lisa Gitelman (2006: 26–57) has provided a meticulous account of the way Edison's invention was *publicized* via a series of exhibitions across the US, in which its powers of mimicry were extolled. According to the exhibition literature accompanying the first demonstration in April 1878, Edison's assistant 'sung and shouted and whistled and crowed' into the mouthpiece and then, as the next day's *Washington Star* reported, 'the same sounds floated out upon the air faint but distinct' (Gitelman 2006: 31–2). Hundreds of exhibitions by the Edison Speaking Phonography Company followed. Usually, after an edifying explanation and demonstrations of the working principles of phonography, members of the public were invited to speak or sing or make any noise they liked into the machine, to hear 'themselves' back, often keeping the tinfoils as material mementoes or curiosities to show to friends and family.

Edison boasted that his phonograph could reproduce sounds, 'with all their original characteristics at will' (1878: 530). With no discrimination it picked up any noise within its range, including 'the messy glissandi and dissonances of the natural world' (Armstrong 2005: 1).[3] Although the phonograph was named for its ability to 'write sounds', it was not experienced only, or even primarily, as a transcription device. The 'living' sounds it produced inspired anthropomorphized accounts of its mimicry, such as this from *Harper's Weekly* in March 1878:

> This little instrument records the utterances of the human voice, and like a faithless confidante repeats every secret confided to it whenever requested to do so. It will talk, sing, whistle, cough, sneeze, or perform any other acoustic feat. With charming impartiality it will express itself in the divine strains of a lyric goddess, or use the startling vernacular of a street Arab (in Heumann 1998: n.p.).

Its technical indiscriminacy allowed phonography to be understood as an egalitarian medium, ready to give voice to all and sundry – the hierarchies of taste and class preserved only in the accompanying commentaries. The mystery of the recording process and its uncanny ability to capture the idiosyncrasies and accidents of all forms of expression occupied commentators for decades to come. In its automated relation to the arbitrary, the random, the transitory and the irrational, it marked the dawn of 'sonic modernity', a break with the musical traditions of transcribing and reproducing sound (Kahn 2002: 180). It was precisely this inscription of the accidental, the reproductions of human frailties and imperfections that was so fascinating – and so frustrating for recording artists. Minute details, fleeting sounds, could be amplified both literally and figuratively, attracting a level of attention never possible before. Where art had sought to aestheticize and improve upon nature, this new artifice made a virtue of reproducing nature 'in the real'. Here was a representational system without system, seemingly without any preconceived categories of selection or aesthetic priority. This radical shift in representational convention 'effectively reversed the rational hierarchy between the essential and inessential, between

substance and accident' (Lastra 2000: 46). The phonograph, like the photograph before it, was apparently imbued with the scientific – *and public*
– virtue of disinterested objectivity. Its relation to the 'real' seemed to be
one of a passive and diligent recorder, a talking machine that would simply
tell it like it was.

Phonography as Public Record

From the outset it was assumed phonography would have a role in docu-
menting public life. Speaking to the *Scientific American* in 1877, Edison
forecast the uses to which he envisaged his invention could be put:

> for taking dictation, for taking testimony in court, for reporting speeches,
> for the reproduction of vocal music, for teaching languages [. . .] for corre-
> spondence, for civil and military orders [. . .] for the distribution of the songs
> of great singers, sermons and speeches, the words of great men and women
> (in Kittler 1999: 78).

Music is notably rather underplayed in this list. It has been suggested its
relegation at this early juncture was to do with poor sound quality (Chanan
1995: 3), although it is only from the perspective of current recording
practice that it is possible to talk of 'relegation' in this way (Sterne 2003:
202–4). What is more striking about Edison's list, composed at the very
dawn of recorded sound, is how much of it is devoted to intervening in the
public sphere. Edison (1878: 534) was motivated by the desire to preserve
sound for posterity:

> to preserve for future generations the voices as well as the words of our
> Washingtons, our Lincolns, our Gladstones, etc., and to have them give us
> their 'greatest effort,' in every town and hamlet in the country.

The voices of the great and the good were thus to be recorded in the
public interest, although there was a commercial interest too, with voices
sold as souvenirs – and at a premium when a celebrated voice 'had been
stilled'. The Columbia Phonograph Company distributed the dying words
of Pope Leo XIII in September 1905, but was at pains to point out in its
advertising that he was 'aged and feeble' so the length and volume of the
recording was not the same as their customers could expect from their
entertainment records.[4] In November 1910 the Gramophone Company
took out an advert in *The Times*, announcing in bold type, 'Tolstoy's Last

Message', available for 3/6s. In copy which exploited the company's trademark of 'His Master's Voice' to merge the voice of the master writer with the voice of the company's gramophone, the advert declared:

> A master mind has passed on – but the living voice, so often raised in the cause of right, is with us still. The great philosopher took care his message should not die, and left, in the shape of a wonderful Gramophone record – spoken by himself in English – an epitome of his philosophy, as a legacy to the English-speaking world. *His own words – his own voice – spoken in English – spoken by the Gramophone.*[5]

The promise of hearing voices of the past was not met with universal enthusiasm. The first response of the *Manchester Guardian* on hearing of Edison's invention was 'That it should be possible to make a man's words live literally for ever, is terrible' (21 January 1878: 5). Even a quarter of a century later, in response to a campaign to have the British Museum archive the voices of the famous, a columnist railed sardonically against the prospect:

> Hard enough is life in our time, but one trembles to think of the lot of our unfortunate descendants. Not only will they have the speakers of their own day, but the bottled up oratory of past generations. Are the echoes of the fiscal controversy ever to ring down the corridors of time? Are our present MPs fit to go cackling through the centuries? Is the comic singer who has wearied us to torment our posterity? Our grandchildren won't comprehend the meaning of that delightful phrase 'the silence of the tomb'.[6]

As an instrument that could store a voice for posterity, the phonograph was quickly adopted by anthropologists and linguists to put the words, voices and sounds of cultures at home and abroad literally *on record*, cataloguing and classifying them in pioneering sound archives (Rühr 2008: 51–2).[7] The great advantage for social scientists interested in language was the technological ability to reproduce the *glossolalia* erased in written transcriptions. Michel de Certeau (1996: 29–30) uses this term to describe how the 'bodily noises, quotations of delinquent sounds, and fragments of others' voices' erupt into ordinary conversation, disrupting 'discursive' expression. As sound recording and reproduction became more established, developing its own sense of institutionalized authority, so too did it increasingly follow this logic of suppressing the glossolalia of everyday speech, surrendering to the standards of scripted discourse. The more authoritative and institutionalized discourse becomes in literate cultures, for example in political, religious and academic circles, the less tolerated become the hesitations, tics and 'drifting sounds' of mundane conversational speech.

Discourse in this sense tries to free itself from the fragility of dialogue, from these 'noises of otherness', a process in which the interlocutor 'is removed to a distance, transformed into an audience'. The technological possibility of 'retakes' and editing underscored this logic, in a doubling of the technical search for perfection. And yet, it is precisely this potential to represent *embodied* speech in the public sphere that is so radical a move.

Such was the power of the idea of transparent phonographic reproduction that listeners did not at first seem too troubled by the 'reality gap' that is all too apparent to ears accustomed to more modern recordings. Indeed, early audiences were enthusiastic about the distortions of the sound of 'real' sound produced either accidentally by the machine or intentionally by running the recording backwards or at a different speed (Lawrence 1991: 13). There was also a certain egalitarian accessibility inasmuch as listening to recordings did not seem to require any particular scientific, technical or musical training of the ear. In its infancy, then, the very fact of the recording and the thrill of experiencing it was privileged over the 'quality' or content of the recording. Soon enough, though, the reproductive quality of musical recordings in particular came under increasing scrutiny.[8]

Learning Mediated Listening

Despite relentless advertising about the 'true', 'perfect' or 'faultless' qualities of sound (terms found in almost any advertising copy for phonographs and gramophones after 1900), recordings were often panned as 'tinny' or 'canned' by music critics. The Edison Company responded by working hard to persuade the public via advertising and on-stage 'Tone Tests' that the quality of their recordings could compare with live recitals (Thompson 2002: 237; Sterne 2003: 261–6). These public sound tests and other gramophone concerts indicate the lively public interest in the new technology and its claims for audiorealism, and are just one example of successive 'high-fidelity spectacles', that were expressions of a 'longstanding love of the technological sublime' (Barry 2010: 117). On the other hand, they can also be read as evidence of the extraordinary *effort* required to persuade the public of the fidelity of these sounds, which might indicate that the relationship between copy and source was never quite transparent. Although it is doubtful audiences were ever fully persuaded of the fidelity promised, these public events did help legitimate the comparison between recording and live performance in the minds of the general audience (Thompson 1995, 2002: 238). They are also an intriguing early example of collective critical listening to mediated sound in public space.

The efforts to persuade listeners of 'sound fidelity', a term that was coined as early as 1878, are evidence that it was as much about 'faith in the social function and organisation of machines' as the recognizability of the repro-duction (Sterne 2003: 221–2, 219). Nevertheless, the pioneers of phonog-raphy, both technicians and listeners, were certainly driven by the quest for a 'true' sound, more faithful to the original source. The sense that recorded sound is not a copy or an *image* of a sound, but the sound itself reproduced, resonates through many critical accounts of audio and audiovisual media. Phonography seemed to be like photography in appearing not to encode the world into other signs but to have an *immediate* relationship with the real, authenticated by an indexical relationship with the object itself. But it is rather misleading to think of sound recording in relation to an 'object', since sound is produced in the relationship between objects and unfolds over time, as a sound 'event', not as a moment 'in' time, as with a photo-graph. The sound event also unfolds in space, and with recording there is the doubling of space – that in which the sound event originally occurred and that in which it is played back. Indeed, sound recording has been hailed as a more complete reproductive medium than film or photography, which renders the visible world in only two dimensions, whereas sound is repro-duced in all its three-dimensional vitality. Certainly it has long since been argued that visual space is accepted as 'real' only when it is accompanied by sound to give it depth (Balasz 1931/1970). Jean-Louis Baudry (1976: 110), for example, argued that it is cinema's use of sound, which cannot be rendered figuratively (the listener hears the sound itself, not an *image* of the sound), that is the ultimate guarantor of cinematic realism. Sounds in film are 'reproduced and not copied. Only their source of emission may partake of illusion; their *reality* cannot' (my italics). This is an insight exploited in all sorts of audiovisual production, including new forms of 'immersive media'. Recent research into the experience of video games, for example, indicates that improved image quality has no effect on the players' sense of presence (embodied realism), whereas 'sound quality almost universally impacted' (Skalski and Whitbred 2010: 67).

Recording, in principle and – especially with the development of electri-cal recording – in practice, captured not only the specific sound source, but also the sounds of the space surrounding: the ambient sound. This trait would lead to two 'traditions' of sound recording – those that strove to reproduce sound in the original context, and those that strove for the clarity of a sound object isolated in an anechoic chamber. Thus discourses of sound 'quality' developed alongside those of 'fidelity', albeit always tempered by discourses of convenience and cost. Here are different orders of sonic reality being contested, different measures of realism at work, but both convinced of the ability and *desirability* of realistic and transparent acoustic reproduction. And yet there were and are several caveats to this view of three-dimensional sound as being necessarily realistic. The first was the profoundly unnatural phenomenon of disembodied sounds and voices separated from their originating source in time and space (Connor 2000). In its first editorial about the 'phonegraph', the *Manchester Guardian* (21 January 1878), for example, acknowledged that it 'would certainly not be credible were not everything nowadays credible, for science, which was thought to be the weapon of scepticism, threatens to make us sceptical of nothing so much as of the evidence of our senses'. A further editorial, occasioned by the granting of an export licence to the UK some months later (22 April 1878), was still more circumspect about the uncanny powers of the new machine:

> the voice is certainly somewhat muffled and 'minified' (whatever that might mean) when returned from 'the iron tongue of the phonograph'. Still, the result is quite near enough, and, indeed, a good deal too near for our liking. Nothing so much belongs to a person, is so characteristic, so much a part of his inner self, as his voice and intonation. To recall these is almost to recall the spirit that breathed in them. It is not merely uncanny; it is sacrilegious. [. . .] We have no desire to see Mr Edison burnt at the stake, but we are not sure we can say the same of his invention.

Until the modern age, the disembodied voice belonged either to the realm of the sacred, the magical or the supernatural. The quest for audiorealism was at least in part motivated by a nostalgia for the real, a desire to envelop these uncanny experiences in the cloak of authenticity and the simulation of presence – in short, to 'close the obvious gaps of distance, disembodiment, and dissemination' (Peters 1999: 211).

A second caveat about the transparent reality of sound recording is that, as the Tone Tests showed, the 'fit' between the original sound event and its reproduction was not necessarily self-evident, but one that listeners had to learn, both as an audile technique and as a matter of faith. The new technical cultures of sound reproduction drew on older narrative tropes to bolster the construction of 'male technocratic expertise' in the telegraphic and engineering professions. These narratives routinely featured 'the alien naif who mistakes mimetic representation for reality' (Gitelman 1999: 266), that is to say, those people, often marked by class, race, age or gender, who misapprehended the technicality of the new devices and thought the machines contained the orchestra or the speaker themselves. This is a trope that figures particularly prominently in received ethnographic accounts of natives' encounters with Western media technologies. Thus, however 'real' the representation, the discourses of audiorealism still rest on assuming there is a skill in recognizing the 'mastery' of the reproductive technology, and not being fooled by it.

A third caveat is that, however advanced the recording technology, the sound reproduced 'always carries some record of the recording process, superimposed on the sound event itself' (Altman 1992: 26). This is necessarily the case either because of the idiosyncrasies of the recording machinery or the processes of amplification, filtering, equalization, noise reduction, compression and so on. The 'original' sound event might be – indeed in studio situations invariably would be – constructed to accommodate the limitations of the technology. Many 'real' events had to be re-staged under studio conditions for technical, practical or political reasons. And singers, speakers and musicians had to adapt their performances for the recording horn of the phonograph, or later the microphone – perhaps keeping still where they might have moved during a live performance, perhaps extending or editing their performance to fit the duration of the foil or the disc, and so on. Moreover, the repeated listening that recording enabled, allowed for new analytical scrutiny of sound, and allowed performers to encounter and learn from their own performances and those that had gone before (Katz 2010). Furthermore, the new forms of public intimacy that the microphone and the loudspeaker enabled, both in recording and transmission, inspired the development of new types of performance in both the entertainment and political fields, with famous examples including the microphone-savvy 'crooners' and the audience-savvy 'fireside chat'. These sorts of *productions* are already working to an abstracted sense of what a 'faithful' rendition of a live performance might be.

Finally, as Adorno recognized (1934/1990), the very mechanical nature of the inscription meant that sound could be severed from temporality, that a sound could be inscribed without it ever having been 'sounded out'. In this way, sound recording, as inscription, need not bear an indexical relation to the real, at least *a priori*, in much the same way as writing can record fictional, as well as factual events. In a move that could be seen to prefigure the possibilities of digital audio, Adorno recognizes that the phonograph needle could, in principle, produce, rather than simply reproduce a sound event. Moreover, the separation of sound from source allowed different ways of making music and speeches to travel across national, social and cultural borders, inspiring new hybrid genres and re-contextualized listening.

Recordings, then, are constructions as much as they are reconstructions. They are 'always representations, interpretations, partial narratives' (Altman 1992: 27). Indeed, the process of mediation eventually comes to upturn the very order of things. Unmediated sound is no longer measure of 'fidelity', but rather the 'new sound reality . . . supplants unmediated acoustical reality in strength, presence and impact' (Attali 1985: 103). Eventually, listening to mediated sound or sound 'as if mediated' becomes the predominant mode of listening. Thompson (2002: 3) notes that in the push for clear 'signal-like sounds' reverberation (the lingering over time of residual sound in a space) became an unwelcome noise to be eliminated by new engineering techniques that were designed to anonymize the location of the act of listening. This represents a largely invisible part of wider cultural and economic processes of rationalization and standardization, this time standardizing the consumption of sound and erasing the specificities of the space of reception.

In his extensive treatment of this problematic, Sterne (2003) critiques the 'ontologizing' of reproduced sound in accounts that invoke a distinction between 'original' and 'copy'. Such accounts rely on a sense of authentic 'face-to-face' presence and then mourn the consequent 'loss' of the real in the process of mediation – part of a melancholic reading of modern communication that will emerge in the discussion in chapter 8 about the elision of listening in formulations of the freedom of speech. In the most radical accounts, this 'loss' is rendered pathological, as in Murray Schafer's idea (1969) of 'schizophonia', a process in which sounds are increasingly ripped away from their 'organic' origins. Sterne (2003: 219), on the other hand, argues that a 'philosophy of mediation' tends to efface the *processes* of mediation: since the 'original' sound event is always already the result of mediation, the 'real' story, so to speak, is therefore not one of 'mediation', but of 'social relations among people, machines, practices and sounds'. In a later article, Sterne (2007) usefully suggests thinking of recording less in terms of 'mediation' than in terms of playing a musical instrument, since the human-technical interaction involved when a musician plays an instrument is not described in the same melancholic terms of alienation from the 'real'.

The fetish of transparent mediation evident in discourses of sound fidelity demanded a new kind of listening that listened *past* the process of mediation, as if accessing the 'real'. It demanded a kind of listening that involved a willing pretence to ignore the labour, the artifice, the materiality of the recording – and the listening – process. The transmission of sound over the airwaves seemed to hold out a still greater promise for a public mode of listening that was yet more transparent, yet more accessible, released as it was from the need for intermediate transcription. The development of broadcasting, then, was also steeped in the discourses of audiorealism.

Listening at a Distance

In 1887 Edward Bellamy published his celebrated novel, *Looking Backward*, in which the protagonist wakes up in the year 2000 in a technological and social utopia. In one scene he is astonished to find that the finest musical performances are transmitted according to individual timetables via phone lines to family homes. The utopian fantasy is a listening experience freed from the idiosyncrasies and inaccuracies of amateur players and from the disturbances of fellow concert goers. Seven years earlier music performed live in Zurich had been sent over telephone lines to a concert hall in Basel, 50 miles away. Similar events soon followed all over Europe (Chanan 1995: 26). The early hybridity of telephony and broadcasting is also evident in non-musical telephone services such as the Hungarian 'Telephone Hirmondó' company, founded in 1892, which broadcast scheduled information on stock prices, news and sport, as well as cultural events (Marvin 1988: 223–8). Telephonic broadcasts were still a feature even on the eve of radio broadcasting, some forty years later. In 1922, for example, the man who was to found the Muzak company, George O. Squier, applied for a US patent to transmit recorded music over the telephone in a bid to compete with the phonograph parlours and, later, the jukebox. Though the conquest of distance was the main concern for all these new services, questions of audiorealism and sound quality were always prevalent. In 1924, the local Munich press, for example, reported that a transmission of an opera performance via the telephone had been a great success, and indeed that the quality of the sound provided by the 100 microphones above the orchestra generated a better sound than was enjoyed by the audience in the hall – the only disadvantage being that the weaknesses of the performance stood out all the more clearly (Tosch 1987: 231–2).

It is fair to say that the search for transmission of sound over distance with as *little loss of realism* as possible has been a concern ever since those first telephone concerts. The goal has been to produce the impression of co-presence, as if there were shared space between the place of the sound production and place of its reproduction. The sound that was transported over distance should arrive undistorted, unchanged, and reverberate in the new space and, with eyes closed, be perceived as a *physical* relocation. Gradually the impression sought by sound engineers would be to transport the listener not just into a concert hall, but to the best seat in the stalls – a feat latterly achieved not by location recording but by programming a digital reverb unit to fabricate the acoustic characteristics of a particular space, either extant or imaginary. This translocation was part of the democratizing promise of the new technologies that allowed once elite culture to be heard by all and sundry – although old distinctions could be recuperated by reference to newly defined ones. So, for example, in its 1928 *Handbook* (85–6), the BBC was proud of its part in the 'democratization of music' by inviting its listeners into the most exclusive concert halls, but in the same breath worried that the listener 'should not confuse "tone" as broadcast, with its original'. In the absence of a technological solution to the fidelity gap, the BBC began staging concerts like the Proms in halls where listeners could get the 'real' thing.

Adorno's famous 1941 essay on the radio symphony ('an experiment in theory') turns on this notion in objecting to how the dynamic range of the publicly performed symphony was shrunk to fit the dimensions of the bourgeois interior of the domesticated listening public. He argued that the immersive quality of listening to symphonic sound in a public auditorium allowed a listener to escape the everyday 'serial' perception of time, while the dislocated and mediated version available to the radio listener was rooted immovably in quotidian experience. Add in the tendency for the radio to play only edited, fetishized highlights constantly repeated, and the listener's relationship to the radio could be nothing but passive, apolitical and regressive. While Adorno celebrates the 'simultaneous collective experience' of the concert hall, within which the listener is exhorted to attend to the 'immanent logic' of the symphonic work, the apparent isolation of the radio listener, combined with the machinations of the culture industry and the impoverished quality of the acoustic experience, contribute to his critical rejection of the radio and radio music. Adorno's critical listening practice rested, therefore, on notions of auratic presence and authenticity that could, implicitly, be technologically enabled and enhanced by the architectural technology of the concert hall, but which would be destroyed by the intervention of media technological representation and distribution. In other words, the ontological integrity of the artwork would be dangerously compromised under different technological and representational conditions. It was a particularly rigorous version of the audiorealism discourse, with a very particular critical intent, but in privileging the dynamic, immersive experience of listening, it did ironically share something with the motivations that drove the sound engineers working in the media industries he so abhorred.

It was during the 1920s, under the impetus of radio and electrical recording – and later that of the 'talkies' – that a paradigm shift occurred in the attitudes of recording engineers, from thinking about fidelity to a source, towards thinking in terms of creating an aural image (Chanan 1995: 55–70). In response to criticisms about the simple relay of 'flat' (that is to say, 'unnatural') sound from the acoustic vacuum of the studio – compared by some to Western pictorial art before the Renaissance 'discovery' of perspective (Schrage 2001: 239) – sound engineers, seeking to come closer to producing a more immersive sonic totality, had begun gradually to use multiple microphones, and to mix the sound from many channels. Studio recording was cheaper, more predictable and efficient, and so suited the pragmatic demands of the industry as well as fulfilling more abstract desires for 'realism'. In the new sound film, the realist demands of the narrative would outweigh the demands for spatial realism – for example, ensuring an actor's voice sounded the same between scenes regardless of location (Thompson 2002: 274). Similarly the general soundscape must be coherent and believable, so care is taken to create a naturalistic sonic ambience – the hum of a city, the sounds of the countryside, the background chatter of a pub – even if this means the representation is not 'authentic' as long as it fits with cultural and ideological expectations. The listening consumers of these 'aural images' were thus faced with a new spatial constellation that would also demand an adapted mode of listening, in that the spatial metaphors used in the production and critique of such works would translate into a bodily *experience* of this secondary spatial reality (Schrage 2001: 325–6).

The technology of acousmatic sound (sounds without a visible source) had to learn about perspective, a lesson that demanded attention to the relational position of objects in space, rather than an attention to the objects themselves. The various parameters of audio control available to sound engineers include relative loudness – to produce a sense of distance; stereo – to produce a sense of direction and movement; frequency – to produce a sense of both distance and movement; echo or quiet ambience – to produce a sense of openness; and reverberation – to produce a sense of the dimensions of indoor space (produced by the reflection, direction and absorption of sound).[9] With the arrival of the editorial control enabled by magnetic tape and later binary code, the primacy of the studio and its aesthetics was further embedded into the mainstream media system. Realist perspective in mediated sound had to be an artificial construction, made up of many parts and recombined to produce a new reality that was in some ways the sonic counterpart to visual modernism, although it was to become the industry norm. Still, there had been some initial resistance to multi-channel recording on the grounds that it demolished the individual and 'natural' perspective of a single pair of ears, instead producing a sonic blend that 'would be heard by a man with five or six very long ears, said ears extending in various directions' (Cass 1930, in Thompson 2002: 277). And controversy continues to attach to this paradox of 'artificial reality';

though the technical details may differ, the objections are consistently made on the grounds of such technological conceits being anti-realist. And yet, there is, of course, no universal standard of what is 'better' sound – witness the so-called 'analogue renaissance', that is, the preference of many consumers to listen to vinyl over CD, or producers to use older analogue microphones and recording devices to achieve particular effects.

Standards of sound quality are not defined only by taste and technology, but also by the marketplace. To give just some of the more significant examples, Alexander Graham Bell was able to promote his telephone despite technical deficiencies in sound fidelity, partly on the promise of later developments and partly because of how consumers 'trained' their ears to perceive the given reproduction as authentic and as good as it could be (Sterne 2003: 260–1). The introduction of FM radio with its 'better' reception was deliberately delayed in the US because of the competing interests from established AM stations and plans to keep the FM spectrum for the new medium of television. Similarly, the commercial digital radio multiplexes currently operating in the UK prioritize quantity of stations over quality, tending to operate at the minimum of 128 kbit/s when the regulatory authority 'expects' bit rates to be in excess of that, if not at the optimal 256 kbit/s suggested by DAB engineers that would be 'better than FM' (Lax 2007: 118). Perhaps the most pertinent example is the now ubiquitous use of psychoacoustic studies of 'auditory masking' that allows for 'data reduction' in digital recordings (removing those signals that are 'superfluous' to the reception of a realistic sound reproduction), a significant element in realizing the drive towards miniaturization and online accessibility of audio devices. The CD was promoted as 'perfect sound forever' but had been developed at below prevailing professional standards because of a corporate compromise between Sony, who wanted a disc small enough to fit into car stereos, and Philips, who wanted enough data storage capacity to store the whole of Beethoven's Ninth Symphony. Later generations of the technology were promoted as 'improvements' in sound quality, all the initial hype about perfection notwithstanding (Rothenbuhler and Peters, 1997: 250–1).

These sorts of compromises about 'good enough' technology hark back to the earliest days of radio when the very *imperfection* of the reception had been integral to the charm and appeal of listening – it was unpredictable, challenging and required certain levels of technical skill and patience. Early users had to concentrate on the differentiation of signal from noise. It was the immediacy of broadcasting, both temporal and communicative, that served to compensate for the distortions of the sound transmitted to the headsets of the earliest radio hams, some of whom seem to have looked forward to the 'perfection' of the radio with dismay, fearing there would then be 'no more fascination in it than there is in a phonograph or washing machine' (in Boddy 2004: 34). Even with the arrival of broadcasting and of loudspeakers, listeners would tend to sit close to the speakers (or horn) to receive as accurate a reception as possible. Reception was often poor or broke down completely. It was, therefore, precisely unlike the easy predictability of the phonograph. But the white noise of the airwaves perhaps carried its own signification of authenticity, as the magic of the act of reception initially exceeded the desire for any particular content.

Very soon, though, the radio makers did need to fill the airwaves with things to listen to, and the wireless entered the phase of being a great redistribution medium – books and newspapers were read out, plays and concerts relayed, lecturers and ministers invited to speak. The radio was enjoined to reproduce the reality of already existing cultures, albeit through the distorting lens of middle class or commercial bias. There was also a manifest gender bias that was expressed in various ways, including the question of sound quality. Since voices with a higher pitch suffered from distortion in the process of conversion of sound waves to electrical signals, this technical limitation was quickly translated into the maxim that women's voices were unsuitable for broadcasting – and for phonography before it (Lacey 1996: 198–206; Gitelman 2006: 70–1). Similar arguments were used about regional accents. Technological excuses were often just a disguise for straightforward prejudice.

In all sound media, the drive for realism is supported by the invisibility of sound. If the aim was a certain transparency of reproduction, to make the mediating machinery 'disappear', then the fact that it was not necessary constantly to look upon the machine could only reinforce this sense of being in the presence of the originating sound. As early as May 1924, John Reith was exhorting radio listeners to 'camouflage' their receiving equipment since looking at it made listeners more likely to 'come to the conclusion that the sound is metallic and unsatisfying' (in Scannell and Cardiff 1991: 360). Listeners were required to be complicit in the completion of the 'transparency effect' of the new media, learning to trust and accept mechanically reproduced sounds as real. Phonographs were sold with changeable needles to allow listeners to vary the 'tone' of different records according to taste or mood, to allow them, in other words, to 'play' the phonograph like an instrument, to 'craft' a sound in collaboration with the manufacturer – an art that audiophiles have pursued ever since with each new generation of technology (Sterne 2007: 11). The 'pay-off' for the audiophile has been described as a pseudo-religious moment of transcendence in which 'the medium disappears [and] there is the possibility of a communion' when we 'break through to the other side' (Rothenbuhler and

Peters 1997: 253). By taking an active part in the production of the media-tized soundscape, the audiophile enacts a rejection of the passified, femi-nized role of listener as consumer.[10] In the transparency of its representation and the privatized nature of its reception, the gramophone, and later the radio, seemed to offer an even closer connection to the real, to the eternal, both because of and *despite* the mechanical intervention.

Listeners were reported to prefer the tonal quality of sounds coming over the airwaves to those inscribed on discs and cylinders, perhaps because of the greater frequency spectrum or the better amplification (Sterne 2003: 276), or perhaps simply because of the sense of intimacy and involvement that liveness conveyed. In early reports of broadcasts from public places or from places far distant, the fact that the sounds came through loud and clear was habitually more a matter of report than was the ostensible content. Take this *Daily Mirror* report from 24 April 1924 on the first time the King's voice was heard on the British airwaves:

> Radio made history yesterday when it carried with absolute clearness every syllable of the royal speeches at Wembley [at the British Empire Exhibition] to millions of listeners throughout the United Kingdom, the Dominions and in foreign lands. [. . .] the King's speech had been heard distinctly all over the British Isles and there had been no interruption [. . .] It was as though one were standing beside the royal group, so wonderful was the clarity of the spoken word.

The *Mirror* had also arranged for loudspeakers to be installed in the Royal Albert Hall where 10,000 people gathered to listen together to the event. Other cities did likewise. A listener described to the *Radio Times* his experi-ence in Leeds where 18 loudspeakers were:

> perched at the feet of [the statue of] Queen Victoria herself [. . .] it was impossible, what with the grunt of passing trams and all the sneezing and coughing (it was a cold morning), to catch every word the King said, but we heard his resonant voice [. . .] The loudspeakers, the statue, the Town Hall itself, faded from our consciousness (in Briggs 1981: 24).

This ability of sound to produce this sense of 'being there' was underscored by the indiscriminacy of the microphone in picking up all sounds in its range. The CBS man in London in the 1930s, César Saerchinger, recalled the thrill when covering an important political conference, in knowing his listeners, via the microphone, 'could pick up, from the conference table direct, the speeches, the rumble of voices, even the whispers and rustle of papers' (in Bliss 1991: 72). Clarity of tone here translates into a sense of 'real' proximity to the event. This is then easily exchanged for a sense of proximity to the centre of authority, a sense that, when shared with countless others, translates into a sense of belonging and unity with the 'mediated centre' (Couldry 2003: 47). The collapse of distance achieved through the realism of sound transmission, particularly when carried live, is presented simultaneously as the collapsing of really existing hierarchies and social boundaries.

Contemporary discourses of audiorealism – and the idea that technological progress will somehow get us closer to the 'real' – can be traced back to the beginnings of recorded and broadcast sound, which themselves were caught up in the wider discourses of realism and representation in the nineteenth and early twentieth centuries. But to find connections is not necessarily to say there is nothing new. For a start, it should be clear from all this that the concepts of sound quality and sound fidelity shift over time, which suggests that audiorealism could be defined simply as the prevailing level of an acceptable semblance of reality. This level of acceptance is generated somewhere between technical expertise, creative imagination and the market. As Friedrich Kittler (1999: 2) put it, our sense of how real we perceive a representation to be at any particular time or place is the result of how a 'compromise between engineers and salespeople regulates how poor the sound from a TV set can be, how fuzzy movie images can be, or how much a beloved voice on the telephone can be filtered.' There is and can be no 'perfect' representation in sound, although new software and new genres repeatedly seem driven by this nostalgia for the real; certainly the marketing men seem to want to keep the dream alive, as companies continue to compete with each other to sell 'unprecedented realism' to the listening public.

The continuing faith that there is something real, natural, authentic on the 'other side' of the recording is all the more remarkable in the era of digital recording whose signs are symbolic rather than indexical, when sound has become raw and interchangeable information. In relation to the digital arts more generally, Lev Manovich (2001: 208–10) has used the term 'metarealism' to mark a move away from the old-style realism of the analogue era. Although there is a surface realism, he argues the new realism 'incorporates its own critique inside itself'. It does not offer a total illusion because the possibility of interactivity and manipulation has introduced an element of control and the power to deconstruct the illusion. There is an oscillation between knowingly giving in to the illusion and the active suspension of the illusion. 'The user invests in the illusion precisely because she is given control over it.' While there is clearly a technological aspect to this argument, Manovich is careful to avoid the pitfalls of technological determinism, arguing that this oscillation is a structural feature of many aspects of modern society.

The notion of 'metarealism' is a useful one, especially as it focuses our attention on the different experiential moments operating during any engagement with interactive media, the shifts in modes of perception from absorption to distraction, the shifts in disposition from passive to active, from abandonment to control. But as Manovich acknowledges, these oscillations are not produced only by digital technologies, and it is certainly possible to see the antecedents in the history of sound media. Manovich prioritizes the visual dimension of the multimedia applications, the shifts between cinematic type illusions and multiple windows of text, for example; but the user of digital media is also a listener, oscillating between knowingly investing in the illusion of audiorealism and actively suspending it. But in various ways, and to different degrees, this has always been the case, as listeners to early sound media were 'trained' in how to give in to the illusion, and encouraged in various ways to partake in the construction and manipulation of the illusion.

In the end, many of the applications of digital audio can be seen to share in the same desire that has predominated throughout the last century of recorded and broadcast sound to transcend the limits of representation, to generate an apparently 'authentic' acoustic experience and to achieve the real. It is at turns a desire born of nostalgia, commercial incentive, aesthetic ideals and professional pride. It is also born of 'common sense', both in terms of a shared sense of perception and in terms of shared assumptions about the dominant applications of each new generation of media that build on prevailing patterns of reception.

Realist discourses about text and technology were bound up in the construction of listening publics inasmuch as those publics found the sounds of the public sphere 'faithfully' represented back to them, in form, if not necessarily in content. Representations in sound, so radically new and uncanny, were multiply coded as trustworthy and authoritative and became part of a new 'habitus', a disposition towards mediated sound as reliably real that allowed public life legitimately to be played out before a listening public.

4   Listening Amid the Noise of Modernity

If the promise of perfectible sound has characterized much of the public discourse about mediated sound, then running through those debates is the problem of *noise* – noise as disturbance and interference, as sound out of control. Emerging into a soundscape that was already louder, more complex and intrusive than before (Schafer 1977/1994), the new sound media paradoxically contributed to the cacophony while at the same time promising radically new forms of control for the listener. Sound technologies were seen as contributing to sensory overload and sickness, but also as potential palliatives. This chapter reviews some of the historical and critical debates about noise and social control – debates that repeatedly turn on listeners' negotiation of public spaces and the identification of noise as a marker of social distinctions – to argue that readings of the 'noise' of modernity have historically been filtered through the 'phonographic imagination' – a term that endeavours to capture the modern sense of listener empowerment and control.

The inability to close our ears to the sounds around us seems to make hearing a more sensitive sense than vision, more vulnerable to the impositions of the external world. Certainly this 'incapacity' tends to figure prominently in the discourses about noise as an irritant, a nuisance, a pollutant. Noise is immaterial, yet it can invade the body and colonize the mind. Expressions of anxiety about noise are therefore particularly acute and persistent. Yet the sense of hearing is a cultivated sense, and recourse to simple biological attributes conceals more than it reveals. Sensitivity to sound varies through time, across cultures and between classes, and so the ways in which the soundscape is perceived and managed says much about the structuring of social relations. As Steven Connor (2003) puts it, 'All sound is an attempt to occupy space, to make oneself heard at the cost of others. Sound has power.'

Noise is commonly defined as untamed, disordered, inarticulate sound, or sound that intrudes or interferes, and those that produce noise are habitually labelled 'uncivilized'. But all sound is produced by 'some more or less violent disturbance' (Connor 2002) and the distinction between sound and noise is an arbitrary one. Jacques Attali (1985) argued that sound simply represents the social organization of noise, a move that highlights both the primacy and pervasiveness of noise and, more importantly, signals the possibility of control and resistance that is bound up with the management of noise.

The technological transformation of the acoustic landscape around the turn of the twentieth century included not only new forms of sound-based communication, but also the noise associated with new machinery in factories and offices, in cities and the countryside. There is evidence of complaints about noise throughout history, but complaints escalated from the 1870s (Bijsterveld 2008: 1), though this was as much to do with a change in sensibilities as a change in the material environment. As the modern world became safer, more rationalized and predictable, so too did the reported sensitivities of its inhabitants become heightened – witness the range of movements like temperance campaigns, garden city projects, naturism and eugenics alongside noise abatement campaigns that were responses to the irritations, complexities and sensual excesses of modern living.

It was the noise and smell and bustle of urban life that was the source of most social and medical complaints about the strains and stresses of modern living. The metropolis subjected people to a barrage of stimuli that assaulted all the senses, and from which the individual had to retreat via a variety of defensive strategies (Simmel 1903/2002). These were emotional responses, automatic rather than intentional, involving a withdrawal into oneself (a reserved attitude) – or an ambivalence towards the world (a blasé attitude). Critical attention following Simmel has focused on the visual overload of the city, the looking away from the invasive 'gaze' of countless strangers – a practice of 'civil inattention' (Goffmann 1966: 87) or 'polite estrangement' (Giddens 1990: 81). For Simmel, 'the eye has a uniquely sociological function', the mutual glance being the purest instance of reciprocity. And yet he was also keenly aware of the acoustic excesses of the city, arguing that it was precisely the metaphorical deafness produced in a deafening environment that made the city so confusing and stressful to inhabit. A world without hearing was more perplexing than a world without seeing. A world without hearing undermined community and communication.

The city, so closely bound up with the idea of the crowd, is also bound up with the idea of noise, since the voice of the crowd is indistinguishable as anything other than noise. Moreover, the very proliferation and proximity of insistent and generalized noise was something entirely different from how sounds historically had had a close and transparent relationship with their point of origin, whether human, animal or environmental. The leading historian of noise, Hillel Schwartz (1995: 6; 2011), has identified this shift in the understanding of noise as occurring between about 1860 and 1930:

> Where before noise had been defined vaguely as the failure of certain tones to cohabit peacefully, and where before noise had been felt as something intermittent, soon it would be defined psychologically as unwanted sound and it would be felt as something constant. Modernity, it seemed, and seems, disturbs the peace.

The soundscape into which modernity burst, while not necessarily tranquil, had nonetheless been largely ordered, understood and immediate. Noise in the main would have been localized, temporary, and identifiable. The noises of modernity, by contrast, while sometimes celebrated as the sounds of progress, were often characterized as chaotic, and contributing to the loss of a sense of place and community or as intrusions into a pastoral ideal (Marx 1964/2000). Where distinct sounds convey information and meaning, the indeterminate and homogeneous noise of the modern city stands for anti-information and meaninglessness. Modern noise was also read as disruptive of the established social order, the noises of industrialization and mechanization associated with the unruly and uncivilized mass, in contrast to the studied quietude of the bourgeois and intellectual elites.

The Phonographic Imagination

In many retrospective accounts of this shift in how noise was understood, much is made of how sound is ripped from its secure and organic location in time and space. It is represented as a radical shift in the history of sense perception in shattering the once stable connection between sound and vision. From this perspective, noise, far from being simply an irritating side-effect of modernization, comes to stand at the very heart of the re-ordering of modern perception, with all that implies for the construction and reconstruction of identities, social relations, representation and cultural practices. Into this already fragmenting auditory environment burst the media technologies of sound transmission, recording, amplification and broadcasting, which made still more real the disassociation of sound from time and place and body. But it is actually these new technologies – or, rather, the understanding of these new technologies, the telephone and the phonograph in particular – that crystallized and popularized this idea of the disembodiment of sound; because for all that contemporary commentaries and complainants speak of the cacophony of the city, the noises are more often than not exhaustively listed in association with the machines or vehicles or street hawkers that produce them. The concern at the time seems more often to be about the abundance of noise and the loss of all tranquillity, rather than the sense of disembodiment or disassociation of sound from its environment that the critical theorists write about.

Of course, most of the contemporary accounts of the discomforting noise of modernity were, by definition, generally written by professional writers and critics who, perhaps more than most, are likely to crave peace and quiet in pursuit of their craft. Moreover, it seems these formulations were informed retrospectively by what we might call a *phonographic imagination*; that is to say, the separating of sound from time, place and body – has been read *into* the modern metropolis, alerting critics to the broader transformations in the sounds of the city. The phonograph does not just 'write sounds', it rewrites sound history. It is not just a timely piece of technology that fits the auditory dislocations of modernity; it is a conceptual tool that allowed critics to 'pick up' the nuances of modern acoustic perception, just as the phonograph's needle picked up sounds.

Lest this sounds too trite, it is worth pointing out that this phonographic imagination is not tied in a simplistic way to Edison's patented machine. Kittler (1999: 33), for example, has attempted to trace how the phonograph was *prefigured* in the cultural and literary imagination, to the extent that 'All concepts of trace [. . .] are based on Edison's simple idea. The trace preceding all writing, the trace of pure difference still open between reading and writing, is simply a gramophone needle'. Still more emphatically, Douglas Kahn (2001: 16) provides an expansive definition of 'phonography' that clusters around, but is not determined by, the invention of the phonograph as a physical object:

> all mechanical, optical, electrical, digital, genetic, psychotechnic, mnemonic, and conceptual means of sound recording as both technological means, empirical fact, and metaphorical incorporation, including nineteenth-century machines prior to the invention of the phonograph.

This is an example of how technology 'can reveal the dream world of society' (Gunning 1991: 185). The capturing of sound had long been the stuff of human myth and fantasy, but it became less fantastical once the visual world could be photographed. Both scientific and popular discourses about this and other technological possibilities flourished throughout the nineteenth century, and public discussions of both sorts helped to shape and define the eventual materialization of the new representational technologies (Lastra 2000: 16–18; Boddy 2004: 7–15). Close readings of the public history of the phonograph also lend weight to the notion of a phonographic imagination prefiguring (and therefore serving to shape) the specific technology. Gitelman (2006: 29) is clear that in its interrogation and extension of textual practices, 'Edison's invention was less a causal agent of change than it was fully symptomatic of its time'. To give just one example, she describes how audiences at public demonstrations of the tinfoil phonograph in 1878 were self-consciously participating in a new public formation around a cutting-edge technology, and yet the choices of, and responses to, the things that people chose to record – including body sounds, nursery rhymes, popular songs and poetry – were at the same time an exercise in displaying and maintaining prevailing cultural hierarchies of taste. Moreover, the things they chose to record were, more often than not, the sorts of things that were *already* used to repeating:

> They repeated bits that were already often repeated: a prayer, a lyric, a snippet from a common vocabulary of quotations (from Shakespeare), or a piece from a common past (from the nursery). They mimicked to the machine they knew would mimic them mimicking. They made themselves fully its subjects, recording themselves by phonograph at the same time that they acknowledged its rote 'memory' by comparing it to theirs (Gitelman 2006: 35).

As more historical work is done to recover the aural past, it becomes clear that to generalize about noise would be foolhardy. Not all technologically produced noise was considered disruptive of a natural, pastoral ideal. Manmade sounds could be controlled, organized and patterned in contrast to the unruly sounds of nature (Jackson 1968), and so the production of noise could itself become a sign of progress, industry and reason. Mark M. Smith (2001: 139) has described how, in antebellum America, the opening up of the western frontier was associated with the quashing of the 'sporadic, unpredictable noise' of nature and tradition with the 'rhythmic, ordered sound of progress'. Jennifer Stoever (2007: 29) argues that, in this context in particular, noise 'frequently functions as an aural substitute for and marker of "race".' Similarly, in the cities the sounds of the workplace could connote the virtues of industry, order and the work ethic, and their silencing be associated with economic depression. So noise in modernity could be directly associated with *progress*, a positive reading of 'noise' that drew on the long-standing association of loudness with authority, strength, masculinity and power. It was only towards the end of the nineteenth century that there came to be a widespread distinction between 'productive' and 'unproductive' or 'unnecessary' noise, replacing the earlier simple association of noise with progress with a more differentiated idea that began to see progress in terms of noise *control* – the dampening of noise in engines and machinery and domestic appliances coming to signify greater efficiency and rationalization (Smith 2003: 27). The definition of certain sounds as noise and the value judgements associated with those definitions are always an expression of power and status.

It was around the turn of the twentieth century, with a new array of technological means of controlling and manipulating sound, and represented through the phonographic imagination, that noise abatement societies began to appear across Europe and North America (Bijisterveld 2008; Thompson 2002: 2–5; Goodyear 2012). The European societies tended to be elitist and fairly ineffectual. Noise was associated with the 'vulgarity' of particular classes, so reformers concentrated on training offending classes to restrain their noisemaking; in other words, that everybody should develop the requisite middle class sense of *propriety* – the proper containment of privately owned commodities like gramophones and radios within private space. Record enthusiasts argued that commercial recordings at least made an ordered and professional intrusion into the common soundscape. As *The Talking Machine & Cinematograph Chronicle* put it in June 1905, 'what sane person could with truth say that it was not infinitely superior to the efforts of the boarding house vocalist and pianist?' The Gramophone Company even managed to make a virtue out of the disturbance factor, producing an advert in 1915 that carried the following copy:

> 'There should be music in every home *excepting the one next door*' says a saucy new song. As a matter of cold fact it is often the desire-to-possess engendered by the sweet strains that filter through from 'His Master's Voice' gramophone 'next door' that starts a man out to leave £20 or so at the music-shop in exchange for 'his-very-own' model of 'His Master's Voice' Gramophone.[1]

Meanwhile, campaigners against noise focused on public education and influencing public opinion (Bijisterveld 2008: 92). There was talk of the 'right to silence' and the criminalization of certain kinds of anti-social sounds, particularly at night or in close proximity to domestic dwellings. But in reality, the hope was for a thorough re-education of unruly and socially disruptive behaviour. Debates focused on the *etiquette* of listening so as not to disturb other people; that is, how to act as a private citizen within a public listening space that was bifurcated between the space of the imagined public constructed through sound and the embodied sonic space of the immediate community.

American noise abatement campaigns tended to be more populist and to look to technological solutions. They tended to stress not the uncivilized aspects of noise, but its inefficiency. Noise levels and their effects had to be *measured* and *rationalized*, particularly in the workplace, but also in the home and in shared public spaces. The advances made by acoustic engineering to embrace purer, signal-generated sound revolutionized the architecture of public buildings (Thompson 2002) – a 'silencing of space' that echoed the modern social injunction on audiences in public spaces to listen in silent and individualized contemplation (Johnson 1995: 282). It is a tradition that eventually connects with contemporary techniques of 'anti-noise' including noise-cancelling technologies (Bassett 2011). In various ways, the general public, with its modernized, commodified listening skills, was becoming increasingly aware of the possibility, desirability and practicality of deploying new sound media to reshape and control their own private and local environments, and potentially banish, or at least overlay, certain types of noise. As Sterne (2003: 21) puts it, 'the collectivized isolation of listeners could also become a proper strategy for containing noise and bringing acoustic order to a chaotic milieu'.

If it is not until the turn of the twentieth century that the noise of modernity becomes a widely articulated crisis, the question arises whether the new sound media provide a key, or at least a clue to the articulation of this crisis. Sound, or noise, by its nature, had always been unruly – hard to contain spatially, and impossible to transpose over either space or time. First the telephone and then even more so the phonograph, by overthrowing the embeddedness and ephemerality of sound, held out the promise of an unprecedented and imperial mastery over the sonic environment, in the here and now, but also, perhaps, in the future and elsewhere. Sound became ripe for control in the abstract, but more particularly in specific everyday situations. Early gramophones relied on handcranked mechanisms that allowed listeners playful opportunities to speed up or slow down what they were listening to, or, for the first time in history, to hear a sound or a word played backwards. Listeners have repeatedly been sold new and improved forms of control, from volume controls to graphic equalizers to audio editing software. So the phonograph and its attendant and successor technologies potentially transformed the ways in which individuals and communities came to believe they could control who and what they listened to, and how they listened to it. This had consequences for the degree of self-determination and the degree of tolerance with which listeners inhabited their acoustic world. This was an attractive proposition, as the marketing for the phonographic industry recognized. Advertising copy for the Gramophone in 1909, to give just one example among many, carried the phrase 'A Gramophone in the Home means that you have *at your command* all that is best and latest in the world of music [my italics].'[2]

This 'command' of sound was to be achieved not least through *ownership*, of the gramophone, of the records and, by implication, of the sounds themselves. Phonographic technology heralded a new stage in the commodification of sound, turning sounds into something that could be bought and sold and owned in new ways, thereby suggesting a *re-valuation* of the sonic landscape. Where sound had always been ethereal, abstract and transitory, recorded sound acquired the form of a tangible physical object. Copyright of words and music had always thus far inhered in the manuscript or score, not in performance, since a performance had never before been recordable or publishable. Although this was to change, of course, there is a fascinating report from 1888, shortly after the introduction of the 'perfected phonograph' into the UK, which demonstrates an interesting period of transition. The *Manchester Guardian* story told how a machine had been used to 'steal music':

> During the performance [in New York] of Gilbert and Sullivan's new opera 'The Yeomen of the Guard', one of the audience attracted attention by the singularity of his manner and movements. An investigation was made, and resulted in the discovery that he was the agent of a rival theatrical manager armed with a phonograph by means of which he was intending to steal the music of the opera. The machine required to tell its own tale, and it gave a perfect reproduction of the unpublished score.[3]

Aside from the amusing image this conjures up of someone trying to conceal a bulky phonograph about their person, this story of commercial espionage dates back to phonography designed for transcription rather than reproduction. The recording itself had no commercial value – the sound quality achieved would hardly have impressed – but the phonograph was used as a shorthand device to reproduce the *score*, not the theatrical production, the voices of the singers or the ambience of the event. Before long, however, sound would be commodified. Records provided 'the first means of musical presentation that can be possessed as a thing' (Adorno 1934/1990: 58) and would be collected, like stamps and photographs, in albums.

This promise of the disciplining of sound by capturing and owning it to some extent counters the more prevalent understanding of the new sound media as disciplinary technologies. Since the primary engagement with the new technology was as *listeners* rather than as producers of sound and voice, they have been seen as continuing and deepening the transformation of the public audience from a noisy, participative collective, to a mute collection of individualized consumers subjected to the discipline of silence and restraint – a transformation gradually effected since the seventeenth century by the labelling of working-class audiences as 'rowdy' and disreputable by theatrical elites who had begun increasingly to valorize an inwardly-turned listening-as-appreciation as opposed to a more distracted mode of attention (Sennett 1978; Johnson 1995: 51–70). These classed – and gendered – discourses circulating around the control of sound and listening resonate throughout the public discussions about the 'proper' use of new sound media and complicate the notion of listening as simply or inevitably passive and subjugated. They also find their echo in contemporary descriptions of new ways to personalize acoustic space afforded by the increasingly accessible possibilities of digital manipulation and distribution of sound.

Media, Noise and Silence

Listeners to phonographs and later wirelesses generally retreated from public space to consume the new acoustic commodities, but recorded sound also began to permeate public space in controlled and uncontrolled ways. The adoption of recorded and broadcast sound in pubs, cafes and clubs was both swift and pervasive. By 1910 in Germany, for example, it was reported that 'Today one can barely find any public house where there is no talking machine or other mechanical musical instrument providing entertainment for its guests', even 'in the smallest and most remote village' (in Ross 2006: 26). The noisiness of the city, and the steady colonization of public space by privatized sound, began to mean a premium was put on peace and quiet, and silence too was to become a newly precious commodity.

To many critics the new media seemed to threaten the peace of both private home and public space. It is striking how many of the theorists who have been so influential in media and cultural studies mourned the loss or degradation of quietude, particularly in places of public association. The colonization of public space by media sound was lamented, for example, by Siegfried Kracauer (1924/1995: 133), who in 1924 wrote that 'Even in the café, where one wants to roll up into a ball like a porcupine and become aware of one's insignificance, an imposing loudspeaker effaces every trace of private existence'. His friend Adorno (1991: 58) echoed these sentiments, bemoaning the amplification of sound in even 'the smallest nightclubs [. . .] until it becomes literally unbearable: everything is to sound like the radio'. Radio in these formulations becomes coterminous with noise. Paradoxically, it becomes offensive as noise for so-called 'discerning' ears, precisely because of broadcasting's middle-brow logic that was produced by a desire to obey the 'law of maximum inoffensiveness' which was itself a product of the ubiquitous availability of radio in every sort of public and private situation (Miller 1992). The dialectic between public and private, objective and subjective experience plays out in the encounter with the pervasiveness of acousmatic sound – sound divorced from its apparent point of origin by technical means. It is a struggle between the sense of a private individual self and a sense of a community, acoustically signified.

The association of silence, or *stillness*, with the idea of 'contemplation' has a long history in philosophical thought (Tester 1995; Bramen 2007; see also chapter 8). The loss of time and space without sound was a threat to the life of the mind itself. The new technologies, as they drowned out the silences, were accused of driving out private thoughts. To quote Kracauer again (1924/1995: 333):

> Since many people feel compelled to broadcast, one finds oneself in a state of permanent receptivity, constantly pregnant with London, the Eiffel Tower, and Berlin [. . .] one becomes a playground for worldwide noises that, regardless of their own potentially objective boredom, do not even grant one's modest right to personal boredom.

This could almost be a description of the current experience of constant connection and incessant tweeting and messaging, where permanent receptivity is experienced in more than simple communicational terms (Bassett 2011: 280). If media technologies fill public and, increasingly, private spaces with distractions from the spectre of boredom, or *Langeweile*, then they are an assault on *experience* itself, as we see in the following extract from Benjamin's essay, 'The Storyteller' (1936/1992b: 90):

> If sleep is the apogee of physical relaxation, boredom is the apogee of mental relaxation. Boredom is the dream bird that hatches the egg of experience. A rustling in the leaves drives him away. His nesting places – the activities that are intimately associated with boredom – are already extinct in the cities and are declining in the country as well. With this, the gift for listening is lost and the community of listeners disappears.

Here is a suggestion that experience resides in the openness and community of listening, in listening out for the unexpected and undirected, rather than listening in to privatized and commodified sound. The idea that listeners needed a break from the continual flow of stimulation was certainly something that resonated more widely. Rather than filling the remotest corners of the country with the throbbing hum of the metropolis why, wondered one sceptic known as John O'London, could the silences of Nature not be broadcast to counteract the noisiness of modern urban life? He would 'set up his aerial tomorrow', he promised, 'if, in the heart of London, I could hear the cattle lowing on remote hills' (Whitten 1924). Reith (1924b) himself replied, assuring him that soon 'the liquid notes of the nightingales shall be borne in mystic aether waves to the home of the jaded town-dweller'. Two months later, on 19 May 1924, the BBC's first live outside broadcast featured the musician Beatrice Harrison playing the cello in her wooded garden, joined by a nightingale, as if in a duet. The broadcast, attracting some 50,000 letters of appreciation, was repeated annually for the next 12 years.[4] It was also relayed for CBS, winning praise for 'the most interesting broadcast of 1932' (in Edwards 2004: n.p). It is tempting to see this nightingale as a Reithian dreambird, hoping to hatch the egg of experience. The radio could not broadcast silence itself, for that would have signalled technological failure and a loss of control, but for Reith (1924a: 221) the song of the nightingale was the next best thing:

> The sound of the nightingale has been heard over all the country, on highland moors and in the tenements of great towns. Milton has said that when the nightingale sang, silence was pleased. So in the song of the nightingale we have broadcast something of the silence which all of us in this busy world unconsciously crave and urgently need.

There was in general a greater tolerance for silence in the elevating schedules of a public broadcaster devoted to the listener's self-improvement. Where commercial broadcasters provided a seamless flow the better to keep the listener caught in their nets, the BBC of the 1920s and 1930s positively endorsed periods of silence (fifteen minutes or so) between programmes precisely to allow listeners to switch off, or to contemplate what they had just heard or were about to hear.[5] Only the ticking of the studio clock was audible to reassure listeners that there had been no breakdown in the signal. There was some public consternation at these breaks – the editor of *Amplion Magazine*, for example, urged the BBC to speed up its 'stage management' – although the *Radio Times* published a letter from a listener who held such complainants to be 'Shylocks' for begrudging the BBC staff and artistes 'five or ten minutes respite at half-time'.[6] In his 1933 book, *Shall I Listen?*, the BBC's own radio critic, Filson Young, bewailed the 'sinister thumping of the silence signal', precisely because 'rhythm in this naked form is far from the peaceful and negative thing that we connect with the ideas of silence. The ticking sound, especially as slow as this, is to some people an unpleasant reminder that the seconds of their lives are beating away' (Young

1933: 256–7). On the other hand, he was also forthright in his criticism of those listeners who could not bear the silences, and thought them a waste of time:

> Such people are afraid of silence, just as they are afraid of solitude. What they are really afraid of is themselves, and of Life; they wish continually to be escaping from both. They do not wish to be thought at. They do not wish to play or sing; they wish to be played or sung at (263).

He went on to encourage listeners to make the best use of the silences:

> Silence would be wasted if it merely represented a blank, and something negative. It is a positive thing in itself; it is a definite opportunity to sit without the distraction of voice and sound, and think the thoughts that are within oneself [. . .] it would certainly be a poor way of spending an evening to think only the thoughts that are supplied by other people or suggested by what they were doing (264).

This is just one example of how public service broadcasters sought to overcome the fear that radio's mass address would somehow standardize taste and thought. In the absence of feedback channels, the broadcasters had a duty to fall silent to let the listeners fill in the gaps. Silence was granted a new status in the flow of transmitted sound. The very *possibility* of filling empty space with mechanically reproduced sound in principle changed the status of that silence, rendering it unfulfilled though it had not been wanting before. As John Durham Peters (2004: 194) puts it, 'the lesson of media history as philosophy of history is the retroactive redescription of the previous standard as limited'.

Of course, as a quintessentially modern phenomenon, noise is necessarily caught up in dialectical contradiction. While it is true that, for some, silence amid the noise was to become a precious commodity, it is also true that for others the new availability of controllable sound was eagerly deployed to drown out the remaining silences. Silence can connote peace, but also terror, loneliness and death. Kant could not think of anything worse than to lose the power of hearing: 'even in the midst of company to be damned to isolation' (in Jütte 2000: 128). Technology could bring the sociability of sound into the silence, and banish the loneliness of being lost in a noisy crowd. Even the silence of the dead had been compromised by the new technologies of sound recording; 'where once total silence was only possible in death, now the dead continue to speak, sing, make noise and pollute the body politic, leading to an eerie epistemological rupture' (Weiss 1995: 78).

While some mourned the loss of community and concentration, others found inspiration precisely in the modern cacophony, Futurism's Art of Noises being only the most famous example.[7] Noise was raised up as an aesthetic and critical strategy in its own right, as productive as it is destructive:

> Noise destroys and horrifies. But order and flat repetition are in the vicinity of death. Noise nourishes a new order. Organization, life and intelligent thought live between order and noise, between disorder and perfect harmony (Serres 1982: 127).

If our reaction to noise is a bodily, primal one, if it is experienced as a disturbance of the norm, then it offers the potential to escape from the cognitive and cultural structures that we inhabit. It is not my intention here to embark on a summary of artistic modernism's multifarious encounters with noise, so I will simply quote the leading historian of sonic modernism, Douglas Kahn (2001: 21), who captures why noise has proved so enthralling to so many:

> Where better to hear and feel unexpected licks than on the complexity and unpredictability called noise? Where better to imagine ontological riches in the raw? What better way to test authoritarian tolerance than with a raucous rage or arresting ridicule, and how better to bring attention to things without bringing things to attention? Where better to lose wayward thoughts, attempt to lose thought altogether (if only to give it a rest, and find thoughts where none might have existed? Where better to find damn near anything?).

So, modern discourses about noise played out along the fault lines of social control and the organization of space, and were intertwined with debates about perception, experience and creativity. They also intertwined importantly with discourses about both body and mind.

Sounds in Body and Mind

The third broad line of attack on the noise of modern life mobilized on the grounds of health, first in relation to damage or loss of hearing, but later also in relation to the impact on the nerves, specifically with the new disorder of 'neurasthenia' widely diagnosed in the late nineteenth and early twentieth centuries. The new media were also widely associated (metaphorically as much as anecdotally) with mental as well as bodily affliction, particularly in terms of 'hearing voices' and the 'schizophrenic' subjectivity of listeners tuning in to forms of mediated speech that were at once personable and impersonal (Peters 2010).

One of the earliest examples of an intervention against noise on health grounds came in 1888 from the German Union for Public Healthcare, which passed a resolution for greater protection of ears and nose against noise and stink caused by commercial and industrial processes (Jütte 2000: 199). It was targeted mainly at workers in industry, but women working as telephonists were also vulnerable to impaired hearing and a range of nervous complaints, including giddiness, aural hallucinations, hyperactivity and depressive episodes (221–2). The following year a new clinical condition known as 'traumatic neurosis' was diagnosed (coinciding, not coincidentally, with new accident insurance legislation), in which patients complained of 'nervous shock' associated with technological apparatuses such as the telephone (Killen 2006: 202–3).

New technologies are frequently accompanied by new complaints, fears and illnesses, such as railway spine and electric allergy – or the current fears about the effects of mobile phones and their masts. But the acute aggregation of new technologies and new stresses of urban living at the turn of the twentieth century fuelled the identification of new disorders associated with the assault on the senses. The telegraph, in particular, was a common metaphor for how the nervous system transmitted impulses, becoming part of the popular imaginary, fuelling notions of bodily susceptibility to the modern proliferation of electrical signals (Otis 2002; Picker 2003: 84–90; Killen 2006: 204). In general, though, it is striking how central the vulnerability to *noise* is to many of these diagnoses (although perhaps not surprising given 'noise' has its roots in the Latin *nausea*). Exposure to uncontrollable noise is commonly said to play on the nerves, and the noises of modernity were certainly integral to the diagnoses of *neurasthenia* around the turn of the twentieth century.

Neurasthenia was a condition 'characterized by feelings of fatigue and lassitude, with vague physical symptoms' (OED), bringing together the new concerns of psychiatry and neurology as a description of the effects of the dislocating experience – the *malaise* – of modern urban life (Hofstra and Porter 2001). The term was popularized by American neurologist George Miller Beard who ascribed the cause of neurasthenia to 'wireless telegraphy, science, steam power, newspapers and the education of women; in other words modern civilisation' (Beard 1880, in Petrie and Wessely 2002: 691). His German counterpart, Wilhelm Heinrich Erb, whose work was cited extensively by Freud in his writing on sexual morality and modern nervous illnesses, similarly ascribed the condition to the 'unmeasurable rise in traffic' and the 'global net of telegraph and telephone wires' which made even trips designed for rest and recovery a stressful experience (Erb 1893, in Jütte 2000: 200). In turning to the distractions of technology as a remedy for these technologically-induced complaints, Erb argued that a spiral of nervous decline was set in motion: 'the weakened nerves seek refreshment in stronger stimuli, in heavily spiced pleasures, so that they become even more fatigued' (in Zielinski 1999: 84). Again, class and gender biases shaped the diagnoses, with the middle classes and women more likely to be deemed vulnerable to the stresses and strains of modern living. As a diagnosis it caught on because of how it connected physical and emotional symptoms with the changing social and environmental conditions, and corresponded with prevailing assumptions about the impact of the noise and bustle of modern life on the nerves. This meant it was a potentially hugely widespread condition: 'Who today is not neurasthenic?' asked a psychiatrist in 1900 (in Schrage 2001: 63).

Key to the diagnosis of all these conditions was the notion of 'shock', whether from some specific external agent – such as a mechanical jolt as in the case of railway injuries, an electric shock in the case of telephone operators – or from the traumatizing shocks of the experience of modern life itself. Only in the period following the First World War, with the bitter and politicized debate about war neuroses did diagnoses of shock turn to psychological rather than neurological or, indeed, material, explanations (Crouthamel 2003: 163–5; Killen 2006: 214). Meanwhile, neurasthenic patients were considered 'casualties of modernity' and the cure was to retreat from modern life to spas and sanatoria, to more traditional forms of occupation, or to the anaesthetic refuge of opium and other narcotics. The diagnosis, however, was as much a cultural as a medical one, and the decline in its prevalence by the 1930s can be attributed to the fact that urban living, office work, modern media – and, indeed, the presence of women in public life – had become more commonplace and less anxiety-provoking (Schuster 2003). Moreover, the popularization of psychoanalysis in the early twentieth century also offered a new explanation and treatment for psychosomatic disorders.

Meanwhile, the modern *malaise* remained intimately bound up with the introduction and dissemination of the new media, especially those that manipulated sound – the telegraph, the phonograph, the telephone and the radio. But if some associated the new sound media with sickness, others found in them potential cures. Radio promised not only music to soothe fractured nerves, but the possibility of 'radiodiagnosis' – medical attention or advice at a distance (Sterne 1924). The development of psychoanalysis itself, the 'talking cure' that contributed to sounding the death knell of neurasthenia as a diagnosis, had affinities with both phonography and telephony. The phonograph was used in early psychiatric sessions, but the limited duration of cylinders meant patients had to be implored to speak quickly, only emphasizing the effects of stuttering and other signs of *Wortsalat* (Kittler 1995: 300). But the connection was also metaphorical. Freud, for example, closed out all visual stimulation (except the idea of dream images) in his psychoanalytic sessions, constituting them purely as a *Hörwelt*, a listening world. The conversation proceeded without eye contact, like a *telephonic* conversation, and the psychoanalyst's notes aspired to *phonographic* fidelity (Kittler 1995: 360). Barthes (1985: 252) cites Freud's advice to fellow practitioners in 1912 as exemplary of a new and entirely modern type of listening:

> The analyst should bend his own unconscious like a receptive organ towards the emerging unconscious of the patient, must be as the receiver of the telephone to the disc. As the receiver transmutes the electric vibrations induced by the sound waves back again into sound waves, so is the physician's unconscious mind able to reconstruct the patient's unconscious which has directed his associations, from the communications derived from it.

Barthes described this as a quintessentially *modern* type of listening that endeavoured not to focus or preselect what was listened to, but to be calmly attentive to all that is heard. This was a form of 'listening out' that blurred the conventional divide between hearing as a physiological activity and listening as a psychological act, and which put the listening subject in a state of receptivity and interchange with the environment.

But it was not just metaphorically that the new sound technologies seemed to offer the promise of a cure for the ills of modernity. The power of radio, with its connection to the mysterious 'ether' in particular inspired tales of healing, both spiritual and physical.[8] The ether was held to offer contact with the dead and a cure for the cancerous (Miller 1992; Sconce 2000). There were reports of miracle healings. In London in 1923, the 2LO station announcer, Arthur Burrows who, with his 'perfect' wireless voice was known to younger listeners as 'Uncle Arthur', was reported to have 'facilitated the recovery' of a little girl who was seriously ill, as his broadcasts of fairy tales were relayed to her hospital bed by telephone.[9] The 1924 case of a Bavarian boy, deaf and dumb since birth who, on donning some headphones, suddenly began to show, to the amazement of his family, that he could perceive the music that was playing (Tosch 1987: 203). Such stories were common enough for them to be satirized – in 1924 the satirical magazine *Simplicissmus* told the story of a lame Jewish boy who was told by the Rabbi to listen to a blessing over the radio at a particular time. Not noticing that the receiver was tuned to a different frequency, it was the Pope's voice that came across the airwaves, apparently shocking the boy back into rude health (Tosch 1987: 203).

If the media were not quite able to cure the ills of modern life, they could at least provide an analgesic. There are any number of commentators from both the Left and the Right who bemoaned the abuse of music in particular as a means of distraction, or as aural wallpaper, to numb the alienation or disguise the boredom of modern life. In 1930, a German philosopher, Johannes Maria Verweyen, even diagnosed the uncritical surrender to radio in this way as a type of affliction in itself, to which he gave the name 'radioitis'. Very often the consumption of mass-mediated culture has been described as an addiction, and one to which women, children and the working classes are assumed to be particularly susceptible (Rosenhaft, 1996; Winn 2002). George O. Squier, on the other hand, having patented the transmission of music over the telephone in 1922, saw this desire for a wall of sound as a business opportunity, and founded the Muzak company (Jones and Schumacher 1992; Lanza 2004).[10] From transmitting 'wired radio' to businesses, the company went on to become synonymous with piped music in public places, producing a background designed to stimulate certain behaviours, usually some form of greater efficiency on the part of workers or consumers (LaBelle 2010: 170–9). The company described its service as 'planned music', and it is this association with control and conformity as much as the colonization of the soundscape with functional music that has attracted so much critical attention, even being accused of 'putting a whole nation to sleep' (Holly Near, in Love 2002: 84).

References to the use of sound as an analgesic, a narcotic, an anasethetic or a cultural sleeping pill are usually associated with a critique of mass culture and a nostalgia for authenticity. But a more sophisticated account of the use of media as a guard against the modern condition is suggested by Benjamin's work on phantasmagoria, and it helps draw together some of the threads so far. In Benjamin's terms, the new sound media opened up a 'phantasmagoric' space in the auditory realm. Benjamin learned from Freud that:

> consciousness acts as a shield protecting the organism against stimuli [. . .] by preventing their retention, their impress as memory. [. . .] The problem is that under [. . .] the daily shocks of the modern world – response to stimuli *without* thinking has become necessary for survival. This overstimulation of the senses, their bombardment with shock experiences and fragmentary sensations had to be countered with mimesis as a defensive reflex, like the

automatic smile on the face of passersby, an adaptation to the world rather than incorporating the world as a form of empowerment (Buck-Morss 1998: 388–9).

These self-anaesthetizing techniques of the body were largely automatic (although gradually backed up by an 'elaborate technics' of anaesthetics, both medical and narcotic) to numb the impact of reality. But these various compensatory techniques were complemented by the growing potential for phantasmagoric effects in the new media, from the magic lantern through panoramas, dioramas, pleasure piers, wax museums to the cinema itself. These phantasmagoria work on the senses physiologically the same as any stimuli, but they work in a compensatory or anaesthetic way through having been produced in an artificial and controlled environment under conditions of collective reception. Benjamin wrote primarily about the expansion of phantasmagoric forms into the public spaces of the city and the cinema, and although visual forms dominated what Buck-Morss calls the 'phantasmagoric sensorium of modernity', Benjamin did also engage with the city as 'a landscape of noisy life' (Gilloch 1996: 7). It seems productive to consider the new sound media as having opened up just such a phantasmagoric space in the auditory realm, a parallel sonic environment which offers a 'natural' sensory experience in a denaturalized setting and one that is experienced by individuals but which is available to all. Representation by definition invokes a dialectic of simultaneous non-presence and presence, but the reconstitution of the sound event in three-dimensional space disguises the dialectic more effectively as our bodies *inhabit* this acoustic space, this artificial reality. The artificial sound overlays the local sound and is experienced simultaneously. There is an enforced proximity to the sound event that lessens the possibility for distanciation or detachment, heightening the phantasmagoric effect. The political implication of all this is that 'sensory addiction to a compensatory reality becomes a means of social control' (Buck-Morss 1998: 395). It is a paradox still playing out in the way individual listeners turn to branded devices and corporate websites to create an experience of auditory autonomy through their loudspeakers and headphones.

Mediation, Representation and History

This desire to control sound as a compensatory reality is not simply about controlling the choice of sound, or the conditions of listening, but also control of sound quality and audiorealism that was the subject of the previous chapter. It is arguably noise, or at least the desire to banish noise, that has driven many of the technological innovations in sound reproduction and transmission. Noise in this instance is defined as traces of the act of mediation that might disturb the illusion of a direct and faithful reproduction of the originating sound. But noise is defined only in the ear of the beholder. By now, the almost complete digital elimination of static, signal interference, degradation, hiss, pops and the other 'noises' of reproduction have instilled a kind of nostalgia among both producers and consumers for the recording techniques of the past, for example in contrasting the 'warmth' of vinyl or the characteristic signature of analogue radio with the sterility or 'coldness' of digital audio. Many recordings now include varieties of disturbance that could technically be avoided, but are included for aesthetic reasons, and there are even some very sophisticated playback technologies that allow an individual consumer to overlay a digital recording with so-called 'vintage' or 'retro' acoustics, in other words, overlaying it with *noise*.

Noise here provides 'warmth' and 'character', something apparently 'real' or 'expressive' in place of the intangibility and soulnessness of the digital. It seems to hark back to an early advertising slogan of the Gramophone Company, 'The Living Tone'.[11] What appears as nostalgia for apparently more 'primitive' modes of recording – above and beyond what is, ostensibly, the *content* of the recording – actually allows us to see that without noise there is, in effect, *no* recording, as noise is the marker of difference between the original and the copy.

It appears the localized noise generated at the point of reception grounds the listener in a particular time and place and acknowledges the separation of the original and the representation. Noise embeds the listener in a particular location as opposed to the 'non-place' of a perfectly noiseless recording or transmission. It restores the listener's located *experience* to the mediated event. By directing attention to the technological process of mediation, noise also highlights the process of *re-presentation*. Noise 'compels us to experience the reproduction rather than the original, the document rather than the event' (Link 2001: 39). This, of course, could be described as a more 'authentic' or 'real' engagement with the originating sound than that offered by conventional discourses of audiorealism which aspire to the real precisely by removing all trace of the means of reproduction. So, without noise, there is no distanciation, no perspective. Having said that, without the distancing perspective of time, we may not be able to recognize the noisiness and disturbance of contemporary (media) technologies because we look *past* the disturbance to the non-material *meaning* (witness the way the cracks and whistles of older media only become obvious in retrospect). Noise is 'always present yet only recognized after the fact' (Hainge 2005: 9).

The same is true not only for the material traces of reproduction, but also the historical specificity of the moment of production. The phonograph again is emblematic. Here was a technology hailed from the beginning for its remarkable sound fidelity, its apparent transparency. Like photography before it, phonography had seemed marvellous in its ability for 'Nature' to reproduce itself, as if it were an autographic art unreliant on human artistry (Lastra 2000: 22–3). And yet, not only do the recordings sound dim and 'imperfect' to contemporary listeners, the localized and partisan decisions about *what* and *who* to record are also more plainly evident in hindsight, belonging to a particular moment in gender, race and other social relations, bound up with particular concerns about status, authority and propriety, and expressions of particular modes of address and entertainment that disturb modern sensibilities and expectations.

Of course 'noise' in this sense is not restricted to sound media alone, but comes to stand for any disturbance or excess in the process of mediation, something that takes on particular significance in thinking about media in and as history. Media representations that were once feted for their realism look or sound quaintly archaic with the passage of time and the shifting of both technological and interpretative criteria. 'By distancing us from the event, noise tends toward the quality of memory' (Link 2001: 39). Lisa Gitelman (2006: 4–7), too, makes a similar point in her analysis of media as 'historical subjects'. The fact that old media seem 'unacceptably unreal' is a clue that media are 'functionally integral to a sense of pastness'. We have access to the past only through the processes and technologies of mediation, but those processes and technologies are themselves historically contingent. It is the 'noise' in the system, the material reminders of the act of re-presentation, that is the most direct way we are alerted to the media as framing devices of the past. Noise, in other words, *disturbs* the 'structural amnesia' inherent in processes of representation.

Noise, then, far from being just an irritating side-effect of modernity, actually offers a different perspective on modern life and the sound of media within it. Putting noise back into the history of the media offers a way to put the history of the media back into social history, back into the history of the senses and of aesthetics. To put it in terms of an acoustic analogy, 'though it is often the case that signal overwhelms noise, it is noise that binds the signal, that serves as a medium, a baseline, a plane of relief against which signal stands out' (Evens 2005: 14–15). In many ways, the confrontations and negotiations that listeners have with the noises of modernity, in public and in private, are confrontations with modern life itself.

5   Listening Live: The Politics and Experience of the Radiogenic

'At the beginning of radio was boredom.' In 1930 these were the words with which Hans Flesch, one of the most influential pioneers of public broadcasting in Germany, reflected on the early days of the medium.[1] But, he went on, because it had 'entered in a dazzling and charming technological mask, only a few people noticed.' The trouble with radio, as far as Flesch was concerned, was that this potentially revolutionary new medium was only being used to transmit music 'from musty concert halls', outmoded lectures, and, in a rather dismissive reference to the Woman's Hour, 'the pickling of legions of gherkins' (in Dahl 1983: 113).

Two years later in his famous radio theory, Brecht (1932/1967: 127) echoed this dismay about how the radio was encumbered by a parasitic dependency on already existing political and cultural forms and practices. Among the remedies he proposed was a new form of drama designed to exploit the potentials that radio offered as a medium of *communication* rather than simply as a means of distribution. He argued that it was the listeners that had to teach the radio how to speak as radio, or more precisely,

> what obliges radio to abandon its one-sidedness is precisely the fact that since the radio has nothing to say it must be taught to speak by the public, a public interested in realizing its publicness (Mowitt 2011: 61).

That same year, Walter Benjamin (1932/1972) too got engaged in the debate about finding a mode of broadcasting that was appropriate to the new technology. Just as Brecht had claimed 'the public was not waiting for the radio, the radio was waiting for its public', so too for Benjamin the stuff of radio was inextricably bound up with the radio public that was constituted with every broadcast. He called for a radio practice which should correspond not only to the technology, but also to the demands of a public which was the contemporary of its technology. More than just the aggregate of listeners, this listening public embodied a new reality which transcended the mere transmission of information.[2]

These are just a few of the better-known interventions in a widespread debate in the formative years of radio about the potential of *radiogenic* forms; that is, broadcasts that recognized, celebrated and exploited radio's 'essential' qualities. Dissatisfied with radio as a peddlar of second-rate *ersatz* culture, critics called for new forms that were *properly* radio, that exploited those properties that made radio distinct from what had gone before. It was a call for a form of textual production – which would explicitly problematize the acoustic reorganization of sensory experience and legitimize sound broadcasting as art. It was also a call for forms of broadcasting that properly acknowledged and engaged radio's distant, dispersed and domesticated audience – its listening publics.

This chapter explores the content and context of this debate about radiogenic forms, with a particular focus on the German case which provides a particularly vivid context within which questions of radio form came to the fore. In the febrile cultural and political climate of Weimar Germany, artists, technicians, politicians, critics and others conducted lively and often embittered debates about the most appropriate form, content and listening practices for the radio, until they gave way under the new regime to the proclamation of propaganda as the one true radiogenic form.

The term *radiogenic* is not one that has passed into common parlance, even among radio specialists, though controversy over the status of internet radio *as radio* suggests the issue is still 'live'. Alan Beck has argued that the way 'the radiogenic' currently circulates is threefold: to describe texts that are ideally or specially suited to radio, or that utilize to the maximum the distinctive qualities of radio, or that display an optimum aesthetic use of sound. The term 'radiogenic' in this aesthetic sense then embraces a contradiction that 'points to both display and concealing, the artful and the art-within-the-art' (Beck 1999).

Radiogénie in this sense aspires to parallel the better known *photogénie*, a term associated with the French impressionist film director, Louis Delluc, that was relatively quickly adopted into debates in the English-speaking world about the 'essence' of cinema. The 'photogenic' relates to the poetical, uncanny or sublime properties of an image captured by photography that have their *genesis* in the meeting of artistry with a particular media form. In the same way, the 'radiogenic' refers to those aspects that are only evident in the recording and broadcasting of sound and that reveal or express an encounter with some sort of truth. Nowadays the term 'photogenic' has been more widely adopted as an adjective for a subject that appears aesthetically pleasing when photographed – a much more restricted application of the term, the meaning of which is now conveyed by the term 'filmic'. *Photogénie* in its original sense includes the capturing of fleeting and spontaneous moments, like a particular facial expression, or exposing familiar actions to the scrutiny of slow motion. It also alludes to the sense of the uncanny in the dissecting and embalming of the flow of images over time.[3] The disembodiment of radiogenic voices represents a similarly uncanny moment, the ether described as 'a *necropolis* riddled with dead voices, the voices of the dead, and dead air – all cut off from their originary bodies' (Weiss 1995: 79) leading to a mad *Totentanz* in our ears, while Kittler (1999: 3) could even claim that 'death is primarily a radio topic'. Yet these statements, however suggestive – or macabre – seem to be at odds with another of the apparently 'essential' characteristics of radio identified from the beginning, that of its very liveness.

For Delluc's fellow director, Jean Epstein, the photogenic was a key term that alluded both to the aesthetic properties of film, and also to the sensibilities of an audience able to appreciate the artistry of cinema (Farmer 2010). It is a two-fold approach that is reflected in similar debates about early radio and that moves the term beyond simple essentialism towards a shifting definition produced in the encounter between material and cultural conditions of production and reception. The idea of radio's liveness, for example, is grounded somewhere between the textual, the technological and the listening public. Rather than the pursuit of some idea of 'essential' film or 'pure' radio, the techniques discovered by experimentation, with the specific language and materiality of film or radio under changing and specific conditions, would reveal more than just new aesthetic practices, but new forms of perception and therefore new forms of engagement with the world. With the arrival of synchronized sound, for example, Epstein extended his understanding of the photogenic to include *phonogénie* as the parallel phenomenon in sound. The phonogenic was identified in those moments where the microphone went beyond its limited apprenticeship in reproducing realist sound, allowing instead, by creative manipulation and collage, for the perception of truths beyond the normal faculties of the ear (in Abel 1988: 66–8). It was similar hopes and ambitions that drove many artists to explore the specific language of radio – the radiogenic.

The word 'radiogenic' seems to have been imported into English from the French, according to a *Radio Times* article in 1930, although debates about 'wireless art' go back to the very earliest days of broadcasting.[4] Similarly, the words '*Radiogenie*' and '*radiogen*' appear in German, although it is the adjectives *funkisch* (or also *funkgemäß*, *funkeigen* and *funkgerecht*) which are most characteristic of these debates through the 1920s and beyond. Underlying discussions about radio's potential during its first decade was the recognition that an 'artificial reality' was being constructed through a new acoustic space, a space that was *subjectively* perceived or reconstructed imaginatively by individual listeners, but that had some *objective* (and *intersubjective*) reality in its simultaneous and dispersed consumption by a multitude of such individual listeners. The structuring hypothesis of the radio discourses of the 1920s was that since this dimension of reality was technologically generated, then the effects could be strategically employed on a number of levels: first, as an experiential response to the consequences of modernization; second, as an intervention in political debates; and finally, as aesthetic experimentation in the age of technology (Schrage 2001: 171). It is in this last sense, the realm of aesthetics, and it is to these debates, and the extent to which they were shaped by conceptualizations of the listening public, that we now turn.

Radiogenic Experiments

The radio of the Weimar Republic, particularly its drama, is feted for its experimental resistance to the 'realism' or 'naturalism' that dominated the schedules elsewhere. In fact, most programming during this period in Germany was culturally conservative, but there were significant spaces carved out for more experimental work in which sound montages and the manipulation of voices, music and noise came to the fore (Schrage 2001: 232–5; Gilfillan 2009). Hans Flesch, for example, was interested in the intellectualizing character of radio and freeing sound from its traditional connections with the world of the real – including the synthetic production of sounds that presaged developments in electronic music later in the twentieth century. The archetypal example of early radiogenic experimentalism was Flesch's 'study for a broadcast grotesque', *Zauberei auf dem Sender* (Magic on the Radio), broadcast in Frankfurt in 1924, just months after the station first went on air.[5] Flesch is widely considered one of the first producers to recognize how the act of broadcasting to a distant and disaggregated public changed the nature of what was broadcast (Schivelbusch 1982: 65; Hörburger 1977). 'Magic on the Radio' is the self-reflexive story of a fairy-tale teller and a magician trying to take over the *already* institutionalized airwaves, the characters interrupting the apparently genuine announcer in a move that foreshadowed Orson Welles' famous use of the same trick in *War of the Worlds* over a decade later. The play's ambition was the melding of art and technology in a satirical exploration of the acoustic possibilities of illusionist aesthetics in a live and public medium. It was playing with the form of radio at a time when radio was still being formed.

From the start, debates about which kinds of aesthetic strategies were best – or even exclusively – suited to radio tended to centre on the specific problematic of producing narratives, whether factual or fictional, through the medium of sound alone. This was challenge enough for radio as a *reproductive* medium – translating literature, lectures and stage plays into broadcast form. Some were already oral forms, but the new question was how to translate the *aura* of the performance and the personality of a dis-embodied voice to a multitude of strangers.

Even music until a few decades before had always been experienced as an embodied performance in shared space. The predominance of music on the airwaves could, as Alfred Döblin (1930: 8) conjectured, be explained by the ontological fit between this universalizing medium and the most universal of all the arts. For others it was due to the ontological fit between recorded, mechanized music and the radio machine (Jolowicz 1932: 71). Others again, though, found recorded music offended against radio's essence as a medium of *live* performance. But beyond the transmission of music, or the relay of already existing cultural forms, the key debates centred on the challenge for radio to produce new, specifically *radiogenic* artforms.

The challenge came not least because institutional, cultural and, in certain circumstances, commercial pressures meant the schedules were immediately filled with *reproductions*. Quite apart from the fact that Weimar radio was encircled with restrictive regulations and defensive conservatism among suspicious cultural elites, the very relentlessness of the schedule – the self-imposed requirement to fill almost all day every day with material – also mitigated against innovation. Incidentally, this very profusion, the drive to provide non-stop output, could be another of the distinguishing features of broadcasting, though some observers hoped radio's very transience and immediacy meant it would lend itself more than other media to improvisa-tion and innovation.

In 1925, Brecht's musical collaborator, Kurt Weill (1925: 1627), called for an 'absolute radio art' that aspired to 'unimaginably extend acoustic expression'.[6] These sentiments were later echoed by Rudolf Arnheim (1933/1979: 24) who argued the radio would come into its own only when, like film, it had passed through the primitive stage of wanting to reproduce reality in favour of a more creative and appropriate technique of acoustic montage. Indeed, when pioneers of the radio play such as Breslau's Walter Bischoff were looking for a genuinely radiogenic (*funkisch*) means of expres-sion for the 'theatre of the millions', they studied film and phonography as examples of how technology could be used to produce new forms of art.[7] That such ambitions to match the creativity and specificity of film were hard to meet is testified by the fact that in 1927 not one of the 1,177 entries to a competition for a radiogenic (*funkgerecht*) play run by the German national broadcasting company was considered worthy of the prize (Pinthus 1975: 64).

Perhaps the most famous example in this tradition is Walter Ruttmann's *Weekend*, an 'audio-film' commissioned by Flesch, premiered at the Berlin Radio Exhibition in 1928 (which incidentally included the first public demonstration of television in Germany) and broadcast on the Berliner Funkstunde in 1930.[8] This short, eleven-minute 'film' was an acoustic montage of words, musical fragments and sounds 'depicting' the urban landscape of Berlin over the course of a weekend. The piece followed on from his enormously influential film *Berlin: Symphony of a City* (1927), a visual montage tellingly given a title that referred to the orchestration into five 'movements' of urban sounds, as well as images and movement, and that spoke to the musical qualities of filmic art. Ruttmann was greatly influenced by Dziga Vertov's notion of the 'Kino-Eye', most famously realized in another of the great 'city-films', *Man with a Movie Camera*. Vertov, too, had wanted to create a montage of the city in sound, and in 1916 had even set up a 'Laboratory of Hearing' to produce documentary and musical-literary audio montages, but he was frustrated at the impossibility of recording all the complexity of the sounds around him and fatefully turned his attention from the ear to the eye (Kahn 1992: 10). Almost a decade later, in 1925, Vertov revisited this idea of *Radiopravda*, 'radio truth', newly encouraged by the possibilities of sound recording on film which would enable the reproduction of 'every rustle, every whisper, the sound of a waterfall, a public speaker's address', and which could be worked into an acoustic montage of working life. This could then, he proposed, be broadcast as a 'radio-newspaper' with the aim to 'organise' the workers' listening and develop a 'radio-ear' that would promote an auditory bond among the international proletariat (Vertov 1925/1984). This documentary zeal was proposed as an explicit rejection of the more prevalent engagement with radiogenic ideas for purely aesthetic ends.

However, it might also be said that some advocates of radiogenic art that required 'a new ear' were less interested in providing an art for the people, than in the people accommodating themselves to the new radio art. Certainly radiogenic experiments were by no means universally welcomed by listeners, with newspaper reviews referring to such experimental montages as Alfred Braun's *World Journey through a Working Day*, a bricolage of the sounds of a working day across the globe, as 'an aberration of the true purpose of radio'.[9] While the ambition was for the listener's experience of time and place to be intercut into the acoustic reconstruction of a global geography of shared acoustic experience, the modernist dissonance and fragmentation came across to some listeners as no more than 'superfluous sound effects'.[10] The left-wing press was more enthusiastic, though; *Vorwärts*, for example, praised it as a skilful song of working-class heroes.[11]

The following year, another play (incidentally the earliest extant recording of a German radio play), *Dead Man*, by 'worker-poet' Karl August Düppengießer that took unemployment as its theme, self-knowingly featured the voice of a Berlin listener who complained the broadcast was nothing special since they might as well have simply put the microphone out in the street, which would have produced the same effect. This 'listener' aspired to speak for others in the audience who were tired of relentless realism, those who did not want a 'poor copy' of the street, but wanted to be 'elevated' by artistry (Döhl 1982: 15). However much these particular sentiments were put in the fictional listener's mouth to underscore the playwright's point of view, representations of listeners back to themselves were widely deployed in various ways in this period in the attempt to create a sense of 'presence' in terms of time and place with the wider public of listeners that was somewhere between the real and the imagined.

In the UK, the leading exponent of 'radiogenic' production was Lance Sieveking, most notably his monumental *Kaleidoscope* features, the first of which, in 1928, was subtitled '*A Rhythm, Representing the Life of Man from Cradle to Grave*'. This experiment in sound was constructed live on air, involving over a hundred personnel across seven or eight studios, coordinated via the innovative 'Dramatic Control Panel', a technical 'instrument' that allowed the orchestration of different inputs and microphone arrangements (Fisher 2002: 77; Sieveking 1934: 17–23). Sieveking's book on *The Stuff of Radio* (1934) tellingly includes an appendix of extracts from plays 'too purely Radio to be printed for reading', while the title of the first chapter, 'Ghastly impermanence of the medium' suggests that liveness was not something to be celebrated in and of itself. This kind of 'feature', an arrangement of themed sounds without a plot, as Sieveking described it, came to be known in Germany by the late 1920s as the *Hörspiel*, literally an 'audio play', often thought of as an 'acoustic film', which was a piece designed for the ear alone as opposed to the *Sendespiel* ('broadcast play') which was the simple relay of a piece of theatre.

Radio was not a visual medium, but producers were very aware listeners would conjure up images in their mind's eye in response to acoustic cues, while at the same time being liberated from the tyranny of the image. Radio playwrights also speculated on the development of a new art of listening. For Walter Bischoff (1926: 73–4), the modern urban ear had been degraded to the point of being little more than a warning device. He saw the task of radio to restore to the ear its lost sensitivity for the tone colour, breath and pitch of the spoken word. In a similar vein, Theodor Csokor hoped 'to awaken *a perspectival sense and way of thinking via the ear*' (in Schrage 2001: 246). In short, for some critics and practitioners excited by the arrival of this new medium, radio represented the possibility of a creative emancipation of the art of listening, although others cautioned against expecting too sudden an overthrow of long-acquired habits.

With notable exceptions like these, however, German radio drama departments for the most part played it safe. Nervous broadcasters wanted to demonstrate radio could be a worthy transmitter of the best of German culture, with the occasional nod to more popular genres like crime, science fiction and the western. Elsewhere in the schedules, the dominant style in this period has been described as '*dozierend*', or pontificating (Ross 2008: 97). This most modern means of communication was commandeered to meet traditional ends, part of a wider move of 'defensive modernization' common in the Weimar Republic (Führer 1996: 777).

As in the UK, radio listeners were broadly considered in need of cultural uplift and integration into the cultural status quo. The broadcasters often called on the services of the leading writers of the day – Thomas Mann, Arnold Zweig, Alfred Döblin – asking them to read from their works. But eventually the drive for radiogenic innovation came precisely from this literary establishment, with a conference in Kassel in 1929 to discuss the 'problem' of literature and radio. Döblin, the author of *Berlin Alexanderplatz* – itself arguably a radiophonic novel – co-founded the 'League of Free Radio Authors' that championed the *Worthörspiel* as a literary expression of *Neue Sachlichkeit*, the 'New Objectivity' that was a dominant aesthetic in the visual arts in Weimar Germany (Dahl 1983: 110; Gay 1969). Döblin saw journalism and music as simply reproduced by radio, while his own field of literature was *transformed* in the process of broadcasting, because it restored the spoken, *living* aspect of language to a tradition that had been cast deaf and dumb by the dominance of print. Even though this living language was distorted by the artificial and depersonalizing one-sidedness of the exchange, the celebrated author welcomed radio's incentive to write literature for the masses rather than a coterie of literary elites. In other words, the peculiarities of the new medium promised to have a reviving and democratizing effect on the literary form.

In 1928, the Czech modernist, Karel Teige called for a 'radiogenic poetry', a poetry made out of sound and noise just as film made poetry out of movement and light. Significantly, however, the *auditorium* in which this radiogenic poetry would be heard was space itself and its public would be the international masses. Unbound by physical constraints, it would have far-reaching contemporary consequence. Here we begin to see a connection between the aesthetic dimension of *radiogénie*, the political and the experiential. Arno Schirokauer (1929: 1), the literary critic and radio playwright, made the connection more explicit still:

> At three million wirelesses, three million families, that is around nine million people, listen to the radio. The publicness of art has reached a stage that cannot be exceeded. Art has been socialised. It has been taken from private ownership into the ownership of all. The artist has become as public a person as the statesman.

Schirokauer's argument was that, while the printing press and the gramophone had made high culture available to the masses in the form of the copy, it was only with radio that the socialization of art could be perfected because of radio's intrinsically *public* nature. Just as the court had produced courtly art, and the bourgeoisie bourgeois art, so this mass medium should produce an artform for the millions. Schirokauer argued that radio's radical publicity would 'make the artist's existence political rather than private'.

Radiogenic Reportage

The impetus to aesthetic experimentation after the Kassell conference coincided with the onset of the Great Depression. As in the UK, 'a purely aesthetic concern with radio for its own sake was increasingly difficult to sustain as the clamour of the times grew louder' (Scannell in Crook 1999: 203). This led to 'a new style of social reportage' that took the microphone out of the studio to broadcast the voices of the general public, albeit that they were generally pre-scripted, pre-rehearsed or pre-digested to ensure against unexpected offence. The impetus behind this increase in 'actuality' programming was less to do with the possibilities of image-less representation than with the possibilities of liveness and simultaneity.

The thing that distinguished radio from other technologies that had preceded it was this extraordinary possibility of communicating simultaneously to vast numbers of people. Moreover, with the exception of the telephone, perhaps, unlike all other media at this time – that is to say, before radio was routinely recorded – radio functioned solely as a (re)-distribution system, not one of data storage. Where print, film and phonography captured cultural realities for posterity, radio lived in the moment. Once the radio waves had ebbed away, they left no trace, save in the memory of the listeners. It was this very transitoriness, this 'now-ness', that gave radio its own peculiar access to 'the real' (Cantril and Allport 1935: 259). Transcriptions of events in word and image were what other media had to offer. The radio's distinguishing quality and its attraction was to allow the listener 'to enter the stream of life as it is actually lived.' Liveness, then, rather than its acoustic form, was for many the irreducible essence of radio, and it carried a democratizing potential, as the simultaneity of its reception across geographical and social divides heightened and intensified a sense of common experience.

It seemed fitting that the technology to speak to the masses coincided with the rise of mass politics and the experience of urban living. Some saw a virtue in radio as the natural instrument of collectivist rather than individualist politics and experience (Gehrke 1930). It would bring the peoples of the earth closer together, a particularly heartfelt desire in the aftermath of the First World War. Indeed, so often were such claims made that one can legitimately speak of the mythologization of radio's democratic – and *public* – impulse. As early as 1924, Bredow proclaimed radio a 'worldwide auditorium' (in Dahl 1983: 103), while in 1927 the BBC adopted 'Nation Shall Speak Peace Unto Nation' as its motto. Within Germany, still reeling from defeat and inflation, Bredow's fear of stirring up political divisiveness prompted the architects of Weimar radio to keep it free of politics – a policy that was contentious even in the eyes of most of his contemporaries and arguably had dire consequences for the survival of the young Republic. It also had consequences for the debate about radiogenic artforms.

The daily provision of a varied diet of stories that were consumed in the home suggests radio shared more qualities with the newspaper than film, theatre or literature. Radio quickly came to be a 'talking newspaper', transmitting news and events with a speed and coverage the press could not match, although in Germany and elsewhere in Europe at least, the freedom of expression on the air was severely circumscribed by state regulation as well as by questions of taste and morality. Liveness was equated with participation. The European director of CBS, César Saerchinger, argued that American listeners were particularly keen to imagine themselves *participating* in a distant event as it unfolded, arguing:

> they were loath to sacrifice any part of such an experience for the sake of mere convenience. [. . .] They were willing to rise at 3 a.m. in order to do this, rather than listen to a mechanical repetition of the same event at a more convenient hour (Saerchinger 1934: 615).[12]

Even now, in this age of easy 'time-shifting', there are instances of this kind of 'appointment listening', but in general it is the case that broadcasting schedules came to be accommodated to the generalized routines of the average listening family, rather than the other way around. Indeed, the construction of 'liveness' is as much a matter of schedules being woven into the daily rhythms and 'habitus' of the household as it is to do with whether or not the sound was pre-recorded, while it is the possibility of the flow of broadcast being interrupted from outside that reinscribes the experience as *public* (Couldry 2004). Live radio, like life itself, is emergent, structured into routine as a way out of inherent chaos and unpredictability.

Even during these early years when live broadcast was the norm, it was not always possible to broadcast live, or rather, to broadcast live events and interviews at a time appropriate to audiences. Recording onto discs offered one way of 'conserving' liveness for later use, but it was a time-consuming process that often frustrated the public's expectation for instantaneous access to events. An important technical advance came with the use of film soundtrack, a much less cumbersome and time-consuming method of reproducing sound for radio, allowing time-shifting of just a few hours, rather than days, as well as easier editing and distribution.[13] Liveness loomed large in discussions of radio music, too, in the first decade of the medium. While it was possible to regard records as a fitting mechanized ingredient for the radio machine, a more common view was that such lifeless fare shortchanged the public. Fritz Ackermann, for example, argued that the gramophone brought 'the acoustic experience out of its aristocratic indi-viduation into civilization's democratic arena' (1932: 534), but a copy, however true, could only ever be a replacement, would always smack of the *decay* of the original. The radio, by contrast, brought an event to the ears of all without diminishing its originality. The record would always be beholden to the aristocratic heritage – only radio was truly democratic. Here is the privileging of 'liveness' as part of the realist aesthetic, something that came to be associated with the reportage as 'slice of reality'. Until the arrival of television, radio alone could deliver this sense of 'being right there, right now.'

Recording did, however, have a part to play in another kind of radiogenic reportage, by allowing a more intensive and complex montage of sounds. Again, Flesch was one of the leading advocates of this practice, particularly in his recording of public events to create a kind of audio chronicle, a museum of the airwaves.[14] Around the same time in the UK, Leslie Baily was making a name with his *Scrapbook* series on the BBC, in which he would present audio evocations of a particular year, appointing 'history to live itself again'. For Baily, though, while he worked to weave a tapestry in sound, he eschewed recordings, preferring to capture a sense of the 'imme-diacy of history' (Briggs 1981: 8–9). From an American perspective, if news reports could not be carried live, they should at least *dramatize* events and carry them as 'a "live" reproduction'. The most famous example of this genre, where 'liveness' was guaranteed by the performance rather than the event, was the weekly broadcast put out by CBS and *Time* magazine, 'The March of Time'. Saerchinger (1934: 615) described it as follows:

a lightning re-enactment, by live actors (with crowds, music, and noise effects as accessories) of a half-dozen or more of the week's outstanding events. These are strung together by musical interludes and characteristic fanfares, and each item is prefaced by a date-line and 'news-flash', pronounced by the narrator. Actors who study the voices and accents of the people in the news imperson- ate the chief characters, and such is the degree of realism they achieve that President Roosevelt has had to request the omission of the imitation of his own voice, as people had mistakenly believed that he actually took part in the broadcast!

Once again, the aesthetic and the public come together in the radiogenic debate. Even in outside broadcasts, where radio served its primary public service of extending access to listeners excluded from events by class or geography, there was an aesthetic and experiential dimension to these pro- grammes that was thought to be specific to the medium. This specificity was a combination of 'liveness', singularity and transience in the reproduc- tion of reality that should seek to deliver *moving* or *gripping* accounts of the events of the day – that is to say, reports that stimulated a certain emo- tional or experiential response (Palitzsch 1927/1994). Such broadcasts would produce an embodied sense of 'being there', which meant being at the heart of public affairs, at the heart of a shared public life.

The avant-garde composer, Paul Hindemith (and brother-in-law to Hans Flesch), was one of the driving forces behind the innovation of radio report- age on German radio.[15] Working with the celebrated reporter Paul Laven, in 1926, less than a year after the first outside broadcast in Germany (from the races in Berlin-Karlshorst), they developed what has been called a 'radiogenic reproduction of reality' (Schivelbusch 1982: 65), broadcast under the name, 'Disoriented Microphone'. A roving reporter simply let the microphone pick up the sounds of the streets of Frankfurt, its railway station and the docks. There was no script, and no sound effects; the micro- phone, in Laven's words, became its own studio to produce a 'play out of life'. The series ran for several years to great acclaim (Laven 1975: 17). Similar city portraits in sound were produced in Hamburg, where for the Director, Hans Bodenstedt, 'an athletic arena, a speaker's podium, class- room, factory, ship, zoo . . . the whole world [offered] itself as a studio' (in Cory 1992: 339).

The third form of reportage, to be added to the sports report and the actuality report, was the news report. Early in 1926 the first significant political event in Germany to be carried live over the airwaves – in a *Ring- sendung*, a national hook-up of all the regional stations – was the celebration in Cologne at the end of the occupation of the Ruhr. Here is an account from the journalist, critic and playwright Otto Palitzsch (1927/1994):

> Hundreds of thousands of people in the furthest towns and provinces took part in this celebration, with its speeches, the confused hubbub of voices, the echoes coming from the emotional city, the peals of the German Bell on the Rhein. The radio caught a unique occasion, a piece of history and passed it on as it was happening in reality.[16]

All these forms of reportage were considered to be ideal radiogenic forms, because the events and the coverage obeyed the same laws of singularity and transience. They were also directly involved in the debates about audio-realism that were the subject of an earlier chapter. Liveness and realism seemed to have an elective affinity, because of the meeting of the two meanings of *immediacy*, 'now-ness' and 'unmediated-ness'. The transmission of 'real-life' in real time continues to be the hallmark of both radio and television as 'public occasion', especially in those 'catastrophic' moments and media 'events', when the live broadcast functions as *witness* to history unfolding before a congregated public (Doane 1990; Dayan and Katz 1992).

Radiogenic Experience

The third aspect of *radiogénie* is the question of *experience*. While this would encompass some of the ways alluded to above in which certain programmes were deemed radiogenic because of their ability to elicit a certain visceral response in their listeners – so that they were moved, or gripped by what they heard – the meaning of 'experience' here is borrowed from the notion of a non-discursive dimension of the public sphere, as identified by Oskar Negt and Alexander Kluge (1993). This dimension, resolutely overlooked by Habermas in his analysis of the public sphere, is described as the 'social horizon of experience', in which experience is understood, as Miriam Hansen (1991: 12–13) explains,

> in the tradition of Adorno, Kracauer, and Benjamin: experience as that which mediates individual perception with social meaning, conscious with unconscious processes, loss of self with self-reflexivity; experience as the matrix of conflicting temporalities, of memory and hope, including the historical loss of these dimensions.

This historical loss refers to the 'disintegration and transformation' of the capacity for experience under the 'onslaught of industrialization, urbanization, and a modern culture of consumption'. Experience in this sense, then, encapsulates both individual perception and social meanings, including 'the collective experience of alienation, isolation and privatization' (Hansen 1993: 188). The radio in all its forms represented a distinctive recombination of individual sense perception and social reality, and thus redrew the social horizon of experience in bringing into being something that might be called the radio public. Radio was a site which both generated new experiences and enabled and encouraged reflection of those new experiences in and by the public.

It is hard to reconstruct the sense of wonder and awe surrounding the arrival of wireless broadcasts into the public domain. Radio was a sensation in both senses of the word: a marvel that aroused huge public interest as well as a medium that invited participation in a new sensory experience. Some wondered that the human spirit could embrace such novel sensations as the dislocation of hearing distant events alongside countless unseen fellows with such apparent ease. Otto Palitzsch (1927), for example, thought the fact 'that people haven't gone crazy in the face of such paradoxes is witness to their hardy constitution'. Writing just five years later, a psychologist was sanguine about the strain on the listening public, but that this 'mechanized distribution of impressions', despite being firmly anchored in social reality, 'would require a new psychological disposition if it was ever to become the sum of its parts' (Jolowicz 1932: 16). For Walter Benjamin, radio afforded 'unprecedented experiences of space and time' which would 'bring with them the dissolution of previously valid experiences of identity . . . and of politics' (Caygill 1998: 107).

The experience of listening to radio was also considered in the context of 'the sensorium of modern experience', and in particular in relation to the mechanization of work and culture. As Schirokauer (1929) put it, without developing forms and practices specific to the medium, broadcast culture would simply 'mummify' cultural traditions. Radio needed to respond *to the moment* and create modern entertainment that recognized the needs of workers whose ears had been 'tortured for eight long hours by the noise of machines', ears which were too tired and worn for the delicacies of cantatas and classical odes (Schirokauer 1929). This was not entirely a middle-class projection. The workers' radio movement too, considered radio to be potentially truly 'worker-friendly', a machine tool of the proletariat, albeit one that had to be wrested from the ownership of the bourgeoisie. The journals of the workers' radio movement were aware of the debates about radiogenic forms that featured so prominently in the middle-class papers, and indeed on occasion shared their drive for the development of radio-specific artforms, but more typically proclaimed that all artistic considerations should be subordinate to the wider struggle to achieve a workers' radio (Dahl 1983: 106–10).

It should be clear by now that the distinctions between the aesthetic, the political and the experiential are largely artificial, and certainly the boundaries between these categories in the radio debates of the inter-war period are only faintly drawn. However, to think through these categories separately does restore the political and experiential dimensions to an understanding of radiogenic forms that are most commonly understood in terms of formal aesthetics alone. Moreover, the collapsing of these distinctions would have profound implications for the constitution of the listening public, as becomes clear with an examination of radiogenic discourses in the service of a totalitarian regime.

Totalitarian Radiogenics

That the debates about the forms the new medium should take in Germany should have been so dominated by esoteric concerns was due at least in part to the overarching policy of keeping politics off the airwaves. It seems the attempt not to fall foul of the strict injunction against overtly political material might have led to creative energies being channelled into less contentious areas. The debates about radiogenic forms seem to have been particularly intense in that bitter political climate. Certainly Brecht's famous intervention in the debate – arguing that radio should be a medium of communication rather than simply one of distribution – has crystallized these questions for academics and practitioners of radio to the present day. But one of the obligations – and at the same time one of the potential pitfalls – for any historian of the Weimar Republic is to think through the relation to the catastrophic regime which followed it.

The relationship between technology, experience and politics was an ambivalent one, tending, as Benjamin recognized, in two directions: 'either in the intensification of democracy or in the use of the new technology for auratic ends, effectively subordinating politics to ritual' (Caygill 1998: 109). By the time Benjamin was making this analysis in the mid-1930s, the anti-democratic tendency was obviously in the ascendancy. With the rise to power of the Nazis, the discourse about radiogenic forms became more overtly politicized of course, but it also took some notable turns. The modernist experiments of Weimar radio were denounced as a Jewish pestilence, and the restructuring of personnel and programming undertaken as part of the wider *Gleichschaltung*, which included the incarceration of leading radio pioneers like Hans Flesch and Alfred Braun in KZ Oranienburg to await a show trial, was shamefully described as a cleansing process.[17] The debate about what forms were specifically suited to the radio did not go away, but took on an overtly ideological character based on a new equation: if the listening public equalled the German nation, then radio was the supreme instrument of propaganda. It was then but a short leap to see propaganda as the supreme purpose of radio; and for the question of *radiogénie*, the question of what forms were best suited to the radio, to be rephrased as the question of what forms were best suited to radio as propaganda. In a speech to the directors of the German radio stations two months after coming to power, the new Minister for Propaganda and Popular Enlightenment, Joseph Goebbels, made clear his vision of propaganda as a radiogenic form:

> I am convinced that the radio, too, has its own art and its own cultural form. One should not believe that one can simply transmit that which takes place elsewhere in creative life.

The radio was to use 'all means and methods to convey the new way of thinking to the ears of the masses' in a way that reflected the 'tempo and temporality of modern life', but in a distorted echo of Flesch's sentiment, 'above all, it should not be boring'.[18] Some of the themes were familiar from the earlier period, albeit directed for different ends – the rejection of second-hand culture, the preference for live and lively presentation, the invocation of a sense of collective listening, the demand to avoid boredom at all costs. The official view, expressed on the tenth anniversary of the first German broadcast, was that the radio only realized its destiny, its original and most radiogenic form (*seine urtümliche und funkeigenste Form*), when it brought the voice of the Führer into the homes, streets and squares of the listening millions.[19] In the mythologizing narrative of the take-over of power, National Socialism itself was declared to be a radiogenic political movement. According to the head of radio, Ernst Dreyer (1934: 103):

> We know the arrival of National Socialism was required to make any sense of the invention of radio [. . .] to make use of it as a spiritual instrument.

All that had gone before was, at least rhetorically, to be swept aside. A press release in December 1933 proclaimed the radio had a new objective, 'to mobilize the *Volk* in its entirety, to shake it up, to reconstitute it, to shape it: constantly to strive towards the creation of the new German'. The former slavish subservience to the theatre would be thrown out in favour of a *funkeigene Kunst*, a genuine broadcast artform. This would mean abandoning experimental attempts to render the unrepresentable in sound. Rather than trying to replace the visual, the new radio aesthetic would concentrate on deepening and perfecting the listener's relationship to the audible, so that the listener 'would not just see, but observe!' Rather than overloading the acoustic presentation of dramatic material, the new radio would involve simplifying and 'purifying' it, attending to the more melodic qualities of the spoken word.[20] Radio presentation had to give up its 'soulless, bloodless academic lecturing' and be made more enticing, more casual, more *radiogenic* (*funkentsprechend*) if the listener was to be successfully 'shackled' to the radio in its vital ideological work.[21] Once again, there was an injunction to take the microphone out of the studio, and not only to public events but 'to all those places in which life in all its manifold variety can be seen, and above all, heard.'[22] A familiar slogan of the period was, *Rundfunkhören heisst miterleben!* (Listening to the radio means sharing the experience!)

The archetypal *reportages* in the early years of the regime were the staged events celebrating the historic dates in the movement's history. A planning document for the broadcast of the first anniversary of the take-over of power on 30 January 1934 wrestled with the question of liveness. The torch-lit procession the previous year through the streets of Berlin and the Brandenburg Gate was to be repeated, but a live report, broadcast simultaneously on all transmitters – although preferable in principle – was deemed to be impractical. Recording the event did, however, bring other advantages, not least the possibility of interviewing members of the public without the preparation that would otherwise be necessary to ensure they were speaking the right script, so to speak. The repetitive nature of the procession also meant a recording could be cut together and broadcast that very night to give the appearance of liveness and, more importantly, could then be broadcast in the provinces and integrated into the local celebrations. The programme would belong to the newly coined genre of the *Großreportage*, the 'grand reportage', which was intended less as a commentary, but as a way of the event itself speaking directly to the listeners. Reporters should keep voiceovers to a minimum, as the sounds and speeches of the event should speak for themselves, with the songs of the Hitler Youth and the cheers of children to take priority in the final soundscape. The reporters were to be like 'directors', ensuring the acoustic build-up of tension and expectation from minute to minute until the point when the Führer came to speak. In this particular *Großreportage*, Goebbels himself would act as the final 'reporter', speaking from a window of the *Reichskanzlei*.[23]

The remit of Nazi *reportage* was for the reporter intuitively to exploit the listener's readiness for experience (*Erlebnisbereitschaft*).[24] The political vetting of voices on the radio was given a radiogenic gloss: the reporter had to convey genuine passion if the listener was to be moved, for the microphone would amplify any inauthenticity, and any sign of inauthenticity would break the connection with the listener. If the listener were moved, or 'held' by the sounds and voices coming from the radio, then the listener's imagination could be drafted in to work together for the greater cause. The ideal scenario was a participant reporter who could convey both the spirit and the message of the event and whose voice would resonate with *experience* and not just with ideas. If the reporter stood in the midst of events, then the listener was more likely to imagine himself in that position and be thus 'awoken' to action.

The use of multiple reporters for a single event was encouraged for both practical and radiogenic reasons. In the re-enactment of the torchlit procession, reporters would be stationed along the route in the capital – at the Großer Stern, the Brandenburg Gate, in the Wilhelmstraße and in the Chancellory. It was argued that the rapid switching between these various locations would realize the wish of any spectator at a public event – to move at ease, to be at the centre of events, to get the best view, the most genuine experience. Since the acoustic imagination was so powerful, it would only need the barest hint to produce this effect. The radio could learn from film reportage, where a close-up of marching boots could give a stronger impression than a long-shot of the marching column as a whole. The skilful radio reporter should be able to combine and convey the subjectivity of the participant with the objectivity of the observer; to provide vivid acoustic detail against a broader ideological backdrop; to connect the event to the stream of past events that flowed through the present into the future, thereby granting the listener the illusion of omnipresence across time and space. The reporter's words must act like an inner voice accompanying the events, offering short, sharply formed sentences that act like lightning bolts of illumination, and then seem to fold back into the event. The imagination did not need to be fed with chronological or carefully constructed narratives, and indeed the ruptures between segments could afford to be quite abrupt, since it would serve to keep up the listener's interest if it was left to their own creative independence to make the necessary connections.

Above all, the new form of national socialist reportage had to rid itself of any vestige of the neutrality of the 'liberal epoch', together with any sense of the listener as 'critical'. All coverage would be directed by the Party, with an emphasis on ideological value and servicing the Party will. By the same token, the Party would thereby become *sinnerfuellt und sinngestaltend* – more meaningful and able to shape how meaning was made. There would be 'no place for neutrality, where people could pause and reflect on their experience', but rather an engaged reporting style where the listener would be caught up in the call for action. If this seemed to make the reporter's task more difficult than before – since every word would have to be weighed up for its effectiveness as a call for action – it would in fact come more easily to those who were conscious of their place in the fate of the nation. The national socialist reportage would no longer, therefore, simply be a report, but would in itself be a political action, and could, indeed, turn any event into a political action on behalf of the Party. By the same token, according to Hadamowsky, the listener had no right to criticize the radio on aesthetic grounds. The only criteria for critical judgement should be whether the programme was entertaining, up-to-date, of an appropriate standard, and whether it offered the listener ideological schooling, inspiration and incentive to action.[25]

Only radio offered the possibility of affecting the nation as a whole, proclaiming a unified message from a totalitarian regime. By extension, the *Volksgemeinschaft* was also proclaimed to be particularly well-suited to the radio. As an editorial in the leading radio journal of the day declared in the hyperbole characteristic of the *Machtergreifung*:

> It is no exaggeration to say that Germany is the land of radio. In no other land does radio enjoy such a position in public life, such political significance, such a life-forming capability. No nation is mentally so attuned to radio, spiritually so ripe for it, intellectually so fertile, nor able to find in it the direct expression of its life as the German people (Kemritz 1934: 433).

In the totalitarian imagination, it was as if the nation, or at least a racially defined version of the nation, was itself a radiogenic entity, and which finally collapsed any remaining distinction between politics, aesthetics and experience.

Ways of Listening

6 The Privatization of the Listening Public

Listening publics in the age before modern media had to assemble in public space. The media of phonography and broadcasting for the first time allowed listening publics to be constituted by citizens in the comfort of their own homes, or within other privatized soundscapes. Although the idea of using either phonographic or radio technology for home entertainment was surprisingly slow to dawn,[1] the privatization of the listening public – from the domestication of the gramophone to the ubiquity of personal mobile media – has been a constant if paradoxical motif across the long twentieth century, extending the reach of public listening, but apparently defining it as individuated, dispersed and disempowered.

Privatization is a complex word that at turns encapsulates a spatial metaphor, an economic strategy, a psychological disposition and a withdrawal from the political sphere of public life. Indeed, the idea of the public is necessarily conceived in opposition to the private. And yet this is evidently extremely problematic in the age of modern media. Public and private are not terms that can any longer – if they ever could – be simply opposed to one another, but exist in fluid and mutable relation to each other, producing hybrid forms and spaces that resist simple categorization. In fact, the public/private distinction can be reproduced repeatedly by projecting it onto narrower or broader contexts, or indeed on 'different social "objects" – activities, identities, institutions, spaces and interactions – that can be further categorized into private and public parts' (Gal 2002: 81). From different perspectives the same phenomenon can be justifiably described as *either* public *or* private, or *both/and*; for example, a radio station that is described as 'private' in economic terms, might be described as belonging to the 'public' sphere of communication and paid labour. A 'private' opinion expressed on that station becomes 'public', although it might be listened to in the privacy of a car on a public highway. The fractal character of the distinction allows us, encourages us, to experience the dichotomy as 'stable and continuous' even in the face of all the changes to the content of the distinction. We tend to collapse the embedded distinctions because of the persistence and ubiquity of the central opposition, and so we fall into the trap of thinking there is only one shifting boundary to worry about, as the proliferation of embedded distinctions escape our attention.[2]

Overpowering Passivity

The reading public was constituted as a dispersed and privatized public in the age of print, the 'mass ceremony' of reading the daily morning paper being performed, as Benedict Anderson (1983/2006: 35–6) evocatively described it, 'in silent privacy, in the lair of the skull', by readers confident of sharing in an imagined community 'visibly rooted in everyday life'. The re-sounding of the public sphere through new media technologies further entrenched the privatized modern public, characteristically encountering public life within domestic space.

'Publics' are widely contrasted with 'audiences' along axes that divide public from private, active from passive and, significantly, speaking from listening. That the modern mass media – and radio in particular – relied on *listening* that took place stereotypically in the private sphere of the home was a double whammy that gave rise to the expression of widespread cultural anxieties from all directions about the passivity of audiences unable to speak up. During the formative years of broadcasting, this passivity was understood by some as being imposed on the listener by the mass address that spoke to no-one as someone, and everyone as anyone, denying the possibility of active engagement, personal development or equality of response. Others bemoaned the superficiality and banality of radio programming as being no more than the reflection of the passive acquiescence of an audience that did not know how to demand anything better. The danger – or, for those with a commercial or an ideological battle to wage, the promise – was the prospect of the mass of passive listeners who were gullible, suggestible, malleable, impressionable, compliant.

Even those who celebrated the positive benefits of broadcasting and its potential for spreading ideas and creating communities of listeners, whether for the benefit of commercial clients, for educational reasons, for propaganda purposes or just for the general cultural good, all would as often as not assume that the default position of the listener was one of passivity out of which they had to be jolted. This might have been couched in terms of a training of the ear, or the development of a listening culture. It might even include the advice to switch off, in order to listen all the more attentively to programmes deliberately chosen rather than passively let the unrelenting radio waves wash indiscriminately over the entire day. Or it might have been evident at the level of textual experimentation – finding new ways to stimulate and entice, using forms of direct or intimate address – or by finding ways to get listeners to do more than 'just' listen – by becoming part of a studio audience, part of a vox pop, a participant in a competition, or by encouraging them to write in, collect cigarette cards, join a fan club. A favourite strategy would be the invitation to the listener at home to 'join' already existing public audiences with the relay of plays and music from theatres and concert halls or to involve a 'live' studio audience in an attempt to integrate the remote and isolated listener into a more collective experience.[3] All these various 'audience effects' (Peters 1997: 14) were deployed precisely to represent a sense of the public back to itself, a sense of collectivity, of participation, of inclusion in a (usually) national conversation and public experience.

And yet this strategy of inclusion could backfire, with listeners at times reporting feeling precisely *excluded* from the main event happening elsewhere, relegated to the position of eavesdropper; so alternatively, there also developed a range of techniques to try to persuade the listener they were in fact in an intimate dialogue with the broadcast voice, a privatized exchange that wilfully ignored the reality of the public dynamic (Peters 2010: 125–7). These specific textual strategies to make the listener feel 'at home' in this imported public soundscape were underscored by the practice that gradually became the norm of matching the schedules to archetypal domestic, familial routines. This radio audience has been described as 'less of a public and more of a group of mute receptors . . . a collection of people reacting *individually* rather than collectively' (Levine 1988: 195), disciplined and 'docile' listeners in a space, 'drastically separate not only from that of the performer but from the fellow public as well' (Hilmes 1997: 186). There were gratifications to compensate for these 'privations', of course. Apart from textual pleasures, the radio offered an escape from 'the crowding and shoving, the unwanted advances, the noise, the often foul smells of small theaters' in favour of the 'security, ease, and privacy of the home during listening hours' (Douglas 1999: 65). This cosy vision of a *domesticated* audience was used as an enticement in advertising copy that commonly drew on literally *familiar* images to represent the otherwise unimaginable audience situated uneasily between the public and the private (Currid 2006: 39).

For critics on the Left, all textual ploys to produce the *effect* of a public simply disguised the neutering of the genuine public potential of radio technology; and anchoring reception in the domestic sphere derailed the potential for a radical reconfiguration of the nascent radio public. And yet, while it is indeed possible to read the domesticated audience as a mass audience tamed and disciplined, the privatization of the listening public had obvious affinities with the privatized reading public which was understood not as passive, but as actively engaged in critical reason and the development of public opinion. A passage in *The Listener*, reviewing the first decade of broadcasting, illustrates how the paradoxical characteristic of a passified but active listening audience was part of critcial discourse right from the start:

> The programme reaches the listener in the quiet of his own home: he receives it as an individual, protected from the emotions which are so easily aroused in mass audiences. Broadcasting is indeed inhibited in its own nature from playing upon or playing down to the emotions of its five million listeners in the mass.[4]

Now the idea of a 'passive' audience has long since been pretty well discarded in the field of media and cultural studies. The idea of the 'active audience' that replaced it was developed out of studies of the *television* audience (as well as about readers of newspapers, novels and romances), and television and film still dominate reception studies. Of course this is partly to do with academic fashion, funding regimes, and simply the prominence of audiovisual media in contemporary society. But it is surely also in part to do with a residual privileging of the 'active' eye over the 'passive' ear and the ongoing association, however implicitly perceived, of radio as the paradigmatic medium of the age of 'mass' communication.

Even when listening is attended to as an *activity*, it is not necessarily as an activity with public intent or consequences. Sterne (2003: 155) emphasizes the 'individuation of acoustic space' of the modernized 'audile technique' with its roots in the science of acoustics, the medical stethoscope and the Morse telegraph. This disciplining of the auditory body, this modern 'training of the ear', exerted a powerful, if subtle, influence on the development of radio listening (particularly in the days of headsets when listeners had to concentrate on continuously adjusting the receiver to hold a frequency). The desire for acoustic sovereignty coincided with the other economic and political pressures that led to the development of an individualized and privatized audience – pressures to maximize the sale of technical goods and pressures to suppress the radical political potential of the new communications media. If modernized listening is all about individuation, no matter what the conditions of reception, whether in a family group, a public place or alone, the modern disciplinary technique always serves to separate listeners, privatizing and individualizing their listening experience. But listening is not just an acoustic, embodied experience, it is also a cognitive activity, and one that inhabits a space of intersubjectivity. It follows, then, that there is a social or public horizon of experience that subtends the individuated acoustic experience.

Privatized Listening in Public Space

Most people's first encounter with sound recording would, in fact, have been either at public demonstrations or, from around the 1890s, in the enormously popular 'phonograph parlors' located in train stations, hotels and other public places (Sterne 2003: 196–209). The parlours would feature numerous machines, each set to play a different recording listened to via headphones or hearing tubes for the individual patron, enabling a kind of privatized and commoditized listening in public space (Kenney 2003: 23–30; Sterne 2003, 201–6; Gitelman 2006: 47–8). Kenney (2003: 26) reconstructs the experience of the parlours – frequented by a wide social mix of visitors – as follows:

> Coin-ops provided the opportunity for masses of individuals in crowded public places to escape into a few intensely focused moments of bright, optimistic, and ultimately reassuring urbane musical entertainment that also contained a variety of revealing commentaries about the modern urban world.

The confusion of terms here – masses, individuals, crowds, publics – indicates the confusing status of this new experience of mediated sound. These new machines occupied liminal spaces, neither entirely public, nor entirely private; neither entirely new, nor entirely familiar. They harked back to familiar 'cheap amusements' while promising entry into a brave new technological future. They were also an expression of what Boddy (2004: 14) has called 'a sustained crisis in the cultural definitions of public and private space'. He summarizes the 'striking irreconcilable topographies' of this period, including:

> Schivelbusch's public railway carriage appointed in the deeply upholstered style of the bourgeois living room, Benjamin's urban arcade presenting the street as furnished interior, and the domestic living room itself penetrated by the new industrial artifacts of the telephone, the stereopticon, and the magic lantern.

The phonograph clearly fits into this picture by bringing the sounds and voices of public celebrities into the home, and in creating a private listening space in a traditionally public and shared environment. The listening experience enabled a retreat into personal reverie while at the same time providing connection to a public world of sound. This privatization of the soundscape in public space is highly resonant of later devices, such as the Walkman or the iPod (Bull 2000, 2007; Weber 2008; Bergh and DeNora 2009). It would be easy, if not necessarily persuasive, to trace a simple teleological line between the past and the present, but the very fact that this kind of public-private listening fades in and out as a dominant cultural practice indicates that the history is much more complex.

Technological constraints play their part in this history, but technologies are adapted and adopted in relation to consumer demands and social needs and in relation to public regulation. In Britain, for example, the attempt to introduce 'penny-in-the-slot' machines into British pubs ran up against a ban, and by 1905 were already reported to be a thing of the past.[5] Where 'great crowds' had once visited phonograph shops with up to 100 machines lining the walls with a varied and changing programme of records, brilliantly illuminated at night and taking 'astonishing sums', the novelty had worn off more quickly than in the American parlours where phonographs were supplemented by other novel forms of entertainment, like the kinetoscope, or 'on the Continent' where plushly appointed listening rooms were organized more like sound libraries where selections of music could be called up from a catalogue and played through a listening tube from the collection stored in an adjacent room.[6]

Individuated listening in public space, while popular, did not become a mass phenomenon during this period, and indeed for much of the twentieth century remained a rather specialist niche, for example listening booths in record stores. In place of hearing tubes and headphones, loudspeakers came to the fore in public places, creating soundscapes designed to be shared, while at the same time machines were developed for the domestic market, enabling privatized listening in private space.

With loudspeakers, recorded sound entered public space in a variety of ways – in gramophone concerts, advertising, or in sociable spaces like cafes and pubs. It was also taken into the open air. By 1914 portable gramophones were being advertised with images commonly displaying well-to-do couples and families gathered to listen in some idyllic rural setting.[7] These apparently straightforward scenes contain a surprising degree of complexity. Their gramophone has allowed them to transport a little bit of home into public space, to claim a new space temporarily as their own, perhaps – and yet the means to do that would be by playing a recording of some public performance. It has remained a common trope ever since, though the technologies have changed: sounds created in public places are appropriated as privatized commodities and then used to recolonize public space in the image of the private home.

The idea of using the gramophone to transport a little bit of home to the world around you was even taken to the trenches of the First World War, where, in those most barbarous conditions, in that most lethal sound-scape, the gramophone offered some pretence of control over the environment and some sort of comfort. The record companies at the same time profited from increased sales of patriotic and sentimental music for the frontline and the home front, as well as promoting machines for both drawing rooms and dug-outs. There is a distinctly romanticized sketch of soldiers at the front listening to 'His Master's Voice' in an advert from the Gramophone Company in early 1918. The text reads:

> The brave men who are facing the perils and hardships of war in the trenches need a relaxation which takes their mind away from the mud and shells for a little while. [. . .] The music from the London theatres and Concert Halls faithfully recorded on 'His Master's Voice' by the original artists refreshes their war-tired minds and makes good old Blightey seem nearer.'[8]

Although they are sitting at the entrance to a trench, with barbed wire in the background, they look as relaxed and jovial as any of the other contemporary characters depicted in advertising for 'al fresco' listening, as the gramophone music transports them back to the national homestead.

Radio, too, quickly found its place as a portable entertainment, used to accompany picnics and car journeys and so on from the mid-1920s.[9] Indeed, one of the striking things about the popular illustrations of radio in magazines and advertising is the prevalence of images – alongside domestic family groups and glamorous women – of people listening in groups and listening in public places – for example, on picnics, in restaurants, on allotments and on the beach. Portability isn't quite the same as 'mobile', but the trends of miniaturization and mobility are certainly not peculiar to our own time. It was already reported as a 'craze' in the summer of 1923:

> We hear of the Nipper, the Midget, the Pigmy and the Lilliput, and now another is called the Butterfly, which is mounted as an ordinary finger ring! [. . .] If this craze for smallness continues, perhaps we may expect to see the hats of wireless enthusiasts adorned with multiple wire aerials, and policemen stationed to regulate the distance separating pedestrians so equipped, in order to avoid 'interference' or 'jamming'. If such a state of things ever comes about, a walk down the Strand should prove quite an exciting affair.[10]

If for some commentators the craze for miniaturization produced a comic vision of the future, for others it was a matter of poetic profundity:

Was there ever an invention so small in bulk and cost and so vast in scope and power as the wireless set? Almost it might be bounded in a nutshell, yet, in Hamlet's phrase, it is a king of infinite space (Brown 1925: 25).

This 'craze' for miniaturization has surfaced in different guises repeatedly over the years, most recently with the availability of mobile devices small and flexible enough to allow a personalized soundscape to be carried along as the user weaves through public and private spaces. These devices give the listener the impression of control, overlaying the ambient sonic environment with an intimate soundscape of their own choosing. At the same time, however, they are also choosing to submit to the far from intimate logic of the big corporations who provide the technology and the music, and to absent themselves from the very publicity, the *openness*, of public space. Michael Bull (2007: 67–8) describes how urban iPod users,

construct seamless auditory bubbles for themselves as they move through daily life communing with the products of the culture industry. In doing so users banish the contingency of daily life through immersing themselves within their very own private utopia in which they do not speak, but listen, silenced and silencing, through the spaces of the city, living in the continuous rhythm of unproblematic reception, shielded cognitively from the contingency of the world.

The story of listening to recorded music in public space through the twentieth century is the subject of much scholarship and is not something that can be pursued here except in the broadest of brushstrokes. The phonograph parlours lost their novelty as recorded music became more widely available in private homes and in other public spaces, and as 'jukeboxes' took over. These could offer punters a choice of recordings from a single machine, using loudspeakers to create a social sonic space – or to put it another way, to create the mood for dancing and social interaction. Dancing in public to recorded music, rather than in the presence of a live band, was at first an uncanny one that only slowly became common practice. It has long since become the norm of course, but it is interesting to note how, in contemporary DJ culture, expert listening becomes part of the performance, as DJs demonstrate their accumulated listening capital on stage as well as performing private headphone listening as they line up the next track (Nye 2011). And of course the qualities of recorded performance have long since changed the very stakes of 'authenticity' in live performance (Thornton 1996: 26–86).

Eventually, the presence of background music was to become the norm in many public spaces, migrating from places of convivial congregation like cafes and drinking establishments to more general social spaces like shops, factories, clinics, offices and public transport. Ergonomic studies in the 1930s had demonstrated mood music could enhance productivity, concentration and even levels of consumption. Music, often composed specially for the purpose by firms like the Muzak company, became exploited by public and private organizations as a form of social control in public space.

Listening, then, is not simply an activity that takes place in public spaces as in private ones, it can be used as a strategy to define and redefine public space from the inside and from the outside. These practices of privatization might suggest a retreat from public space, but there remains a public dimension because of the double articulation of mediation; that is to say, the sounds themselves still provide a connection with public culture. Phonographs, according to Kenney (2003: 54), 'far from promoting only "ceremonies of the solitary," paradoxically encouraged widely shared patterns of popular behavior, thought, emotion, and sensibility'. Here is a description of a social horizon of listening experience that potentially transcends the process of technical individuation and the commodification of acoustic space in public and private parlours. Kenney objects to Eisenberg's (1988) phrase, 'ceremonies of the solitary', because to focus on the domestic conditions of listening is to ignore the participatory and collective aspects of this new listening culture – listening in groups, listening in public, constructing communities of taste and fandom, heightening demand for public performances of privatized music. While the focus for Kenney is on music specifically, it is not hard to extend his argument that mediated listening could give rise to shared experience and new public cultures. The emergence of 'the modern listening subject' was not simply a story of audile individuation or the creation of 'auditory bubbles'. Rather, the modernization of listening needs to be understood precisely in this field of tension between the privatization of the listening body and the emergence of new forms of *intersubjective* auditory experience, and new forms of interpellating listeners as members of a public.

The experience of early radio hobbyists is a case in point. While the wireless was rapidly adopted by the military, commerce and shipping, there was a remarkable delay before it was exploited for public entertainment and information. For at least two decades after Marconi's first transmission in 1897, listening to the wireless meant tuning in via a self-assembled receiver-transmitter through primitive headsets to pick up whatever signals were being put out into the ether by other similarly isolated individuals. These hobbyists tended to be men and boys who would stereotypically secrete themselves away in attics, sheds and garages to 'fish' for signals. In this way they occupied an ambivalent and transitional space, secure in the traditional

domestic realm while playing with cutting-edge technology and imaginatively venturing across the airwaves of modernity. Metaphors of the pioneer,
the scientist and the adventurer valorized this 'listening-in' as a properly
masculine activity (Boddy 1994, 2004: 25–7).

The incentive for these listeners was not so much the act of listening *to*
what was received (at this point mainly dots and dashes rather than articu-
late voices or music), as listening *for* what was out there. In terms of an
'audile technique', it was as close as radio listening ever came to that specialized listening of the physician or the telegraph operator. But the sense of
there being others 'out there', engaged in the same activity, produced an
imagined community that can be seen as the beginnings of a new incarnation of a listening public. However dimly perceived, there was always what
Cantril and Allport (1935: 260) termed 'a consciousness of kind', stronger
than any produced by the written word because of the contemporaneity of
radio. Other people were out there at the same time engaged in a common
endeavour, engaged in a public communicative act, and pushing at the
limits of science, technology and imagination.

This sense of an imagined community was translated into more concrete
form with the establishment of radio clubs and wireless associations.
Although the seeds of these organizations with their multifarious publications were often sown by the electronics industry to stimulate trade, they
spoke to an existing sense of community and public-spirited endeavour.
This sense of connection that lay behind the solitary listening act is revealed
in the following extract from the recollections of a radio ham, published in
1923, about the early radio clubs that:

> came from the natural tendency to gather together and exchange experiences,
> information and knowledge. In this way the radio club became the meeting
> ground of the amateurs and presently there came into being a wonderful
> spirit of fraternity. One felt a queer little thrill at these early radio club meet-
> ings when he came face to face with a fellow he knew well in the air but
> whom he had never met (in Boddy 2004: 33).

This sense of community, of *fraternity*, in a technically demanding and
self-selecting enterprise meant that the rise of a more commodified, ready-
made and *easy* mode of listening associated with public broadcasting was
often met with pity or downright derision by many radio amateurs. From
the early 1920s, the radio set was to come down from the attic or in from
the garage and into the living room, its housing and controls designed for
a more 'feminine' taste and technical aptitude. One of the new watchwords
was 'convenience'; the radio could now conveniently accompany normal

domestic routines rather than be a separate activity. The exclusivity of the amateur radio clubs was gradually to be replaced by the radical openness, the *Öffentlichkeit*, of broadcasting's 'general public'.

A fundamental contradiction was here being played out – an active and interactive collectivity apparently being replaced by a more passive and domesticated audience in a process that nevertheless opened up wide new horizons of listening as public experience. Listeners to phonographs and later wirelesses generally retreated from public space to consume the new acoustic commodities. Privatized listening was promoted by capitalist interests, as it increased circulation and income from phonograph records and radio sets. Mechanical reproducibility and powerful transmitters meant identical copies could be sold or disseminated to dispersed and distant listeners, exploding the traditional sense of the audience sharing a single space for acoustic events, but bringing it closer to the characteristics of the reading public.

Domesticated Listening

Thomas Edison had first presented his phonograph in 1878. It was a sensation even if for a long time it could do no more than simply repeat, just once or twice, a few seconds of sound. The tinfoils were not transferable to other machines, and there was no possibility of duplication. In 1887 Tainter and Bell unveiled their 'Graphophone' with wax cylinders that could be pre-recorded and transferred between machines, but it was Emile Berliner who was quicker to identify the potential of the domestic market. A year later, he presented his 'Gramophone', a machine that incorporated a trio of radical innovations – the vibrations etched with acid onto a horizontal zinc disc in a spiral groove. By the early 1890s, he had also developed a duplication process and, when the hand crank was replaced by a reliable motor, the gramophone represented a marketable proposition – as a machine that played pre-recorded discs. Eventually, in 1896, Edison patented his 'Standard Phonograph', a sturdy cylinder model for home use, put on sale for $20.00 (Kenney 2003: 28). This lag of almost two decades from its invention as a transcription device is in itself a salutary reminder that there was nothing natural or inevitable about the delivery of recorded sound as home entertainment.

The domestication of recorded sound did then quickly tap into changes in the retail industry and the growing market for mass-produced and standardized goods. It also intersected with the emerging mass circulation of the popular press, the reconfiguration of the home as a site of leisure and consumption, and with the gradual professionalization of music-making.[11] 'Home entertainment' was coming to mean consuming products made for the home rather than home-made entertainments. It was on this last count that the cultural elites tended to resist the attractions of the gramophone. Playing a musical instrument at home was a necessary middle-class accomplishment, almost as important as literacy. Mechanized and 'internationalized' music was seen as a threat to domestic music, in both senses of the word (Ross 2008: 47–9).

In the UK, the Gramophone Company was quick to exploit the closing of public places of entertainment with the outbreak of war, and the popular misconception that it would all be over by Christmas, running an advert in December 1914 that asked:

> Will there be a Gramophone in *your* Home this Christmas? With town entertainments scarcer than ever, this world-popular instrument becomes indispensable. It is a veritable Home Theatre.[12]

By 1917, owning a gramophone was presented as a contribution to the war effort:

> The Director of National Service was right when he said that amusement was necessary. But in these days of trial, the best way is 'His Master's Voice' way – entertain in your own home. You save labour, time and money. [. . .] They love 'His Master's Voice' at the front – they will enjoy it when they come home.

At one level, this privatized, individuated mode of listening can be read as the transfer of control from the performer or producer of the sound event to the listener. The record could be listened to repeatedly, in fragments, as background accompaniment, at different times of the day or in different locations. The speed and volume of the playback was also brought increasingly within the control of the private listener. Much of the commercial development of new generations of audio equipment has been driven and sold on the promise of ever greater levels of control of the acoustic environment being passed on to the individual consumer. That control is also manifested in terms of the power of consumer demand and consumer choice in the range of recordings available.

The proliferation of recorded sound in everyday and domestic life has at the same time made these once radical new forms of listening banal, casual, unremarkable.

Where the phonograph had enabled a multitude of listeners to experience identical recordings in separate locations, the significant new dimension that public radio offered to each individual listener was, of course, the simultaneity of this experience with innumerable, absent others – 'a diaspora of simultaneous intimacies', in John Durham Peters' resonant phrase (1997: 14). This reconfiguration of the experience of time and space, and new imagined communities, rather than any aesthetic or acoustic quality, was for many the irreducible essence of radio, features that seemed to resonate with an era of urbanization and mass politics. Here was a new technology with the ability to relay events as they happened, matching the speed and tempo of modernity and the metropolis, but reaching into the deepest rural regions. Moreover, its disregard for physical and social boundaries and its easy accessibility (at least in principle) was widely embraced in the prevailing post-war mood of democratization and mass consumption. Indeed, far from perceiving radio as a quintessentially 'individualizing' medium of communication, many saw a virtue in radio as the natural instrument of collectivist politics and experience. It seemed inherently 'democratic', bringing people together in their dispersed domesticity with its all-embracing, indiscriminate, live address.

And yet, despite the utopian and 'collectivist' discourses that surrounded the emergence of radio, there arose the paradoxical situation of a predominately *privatized* modern public, characteristically encountering public life within domestic space. The BBC's 'National Radio Week' in 1930, designed to boost the number of listeners, used the rather telling slogan 'Go Home and Listen!'. Apart from the vague tone of admonishment conveyed by the phrase, it is a telling example, because this was a public corporation whose duty it was to 'inform, educate and entertain' *the public*, and which made it very clear that this should be achieved within the private home. But the imperative is also actively *to go and listen*, the implication that this is something that needs to be done self-consciously and with intent. The idea that people would simply go home, switch on and then simply 'hear' the radio as background to their everyday routines, rather than listen attentively, was anathema to the idea of public service broadcasting.

'Tap listening' was also widely debated as a problem within the commercial context of American broadcasting, as David Goodman (2010) has described. Despite it being evident that people who would leave the radio on all the time were actively *choosing* to use the stream of radio as a way to control their sonic environment – because it provided companionship, distraction or emotional involvement – this became refracted in various social commentaries as the listeners being 'out of control', susceptible to emotional and possibly other forms of influence, of abandoning their own sense of self and living instead through 'borrowed experience' (Herzog 1941). Women and children were (of course) the most vulnerable, but the irresolute use of radio for accompaniment carried with it the potential to feminize, infantilize and corrupt any and all who were not on their guard. The problem, in the end, always came down to the question of passivity – either too little attention to the material being broadcast, or too little resistance or critical distance from the emotional enticements coming from the loudspeaker.

Some critics therefore saw the radio as the very opposite of an individualizing medium, infecting the private space of the home with its public and blanket address. As early as 1924, the cultural philosopher Viktor Engelhardt could argue that 'the only means of defence is total resistance: switching off, removing the headphones, nothing else' (in Ross 2008: 182). This has been a constant refrain for critics of the numbing and isolating effects of broadcasting ever since, although for some even this response was deemed to be ineffective. Writing in 1960, Jean-Paul Sartre (1990: 271) summed up the contradictions and political implications of this privatization of the public as follows:

> When I listen to a broadcast, the relation between the broadcaster and myself is not a human one: in effect, I am passive in relation to what is being said, to the political commentary on the news, etc. This passivity, as an activity which develops on every level and over many years, can *to some extent* be resisted: I can write, protest, approve, congratulate, threaten, etc. But it must be noted that these activities will carry weight only if a majority (or a considerable minority) of listeners who do not know me do likewise.

Switching off would achieve 'absolutely nothing', since the inhuman radio voice would continue to echo through millions of homes and hold those still listening in abeyance:

> I will merely have rushed into the ineffective, abstract isolation of private life, objectively achieving nothing. I will not have negated the voice; I will have negated myself as an individual member of the gathering (Sartre 1990: 272).

For Sartre, the radio public was an indirect gathering based on absence, absence being defined as the impossibility of reciprocity rather than absence in a physical sense – he understood individuals on the telephone as being 'present' for each other, for example. Although it can be argued the *liveness* of broadcasting restores a sense of presence (Scannell 1996: 90), Sartre argued the 'absence' of the radio public had profound effects on the possibility of any kind of action (or *praxis* in his terms), resulting from it:

> The mere fact of *listening to the radio*, that is to say, of listening to a particular broadcast at a particular time, establishes a serial relation of *absence* between the different listeners (Sartre 1990: 271).

The listeners are constituted as a unity 'outside themselves' in the construct of the listening public, but are also determined 'in separation', which renders the power of an individual listener to reciprocate to a broadcast ineffectual unless other unknown listeners reciprocate in the same way, in which case reciprocity is 'gathering of reciprocity in one voice' (Sartre 1990: 272). The plurality of the gathering is therefore a chimera, compounded by the vested influence over the broadcasts by capital and state. Sartre maintains that even if an individual has experience of making an effective critique of, say, government policy by virtue of some group membership elsewhere, that individual *as a listener* is defined by 'receptivity', or 'passive activity', which is felt as impotence.

There was no way out of this, inasmuch as it would not be resolved by the listener becoming a broadcaster, since the same inhuman relations would pertain, while there was no possibility of engaging with each of the millions of listeners serially, one by one. Sartre saw this relation of serial absence as a characteristic of all mass media. For example, if a listener were to publish a critique of a broadcast in a newspaper, they would simply be 'opposing one serial relation with another', reaching the thousands of separate listeners only in so far as they were also separate readers. Moreover, a listener would also become aware that, inasmuch as they were bound to other unknown listeners in an impotent relation, so they too were an Other in the midst of Others. The key, for Sartre, lies in the radio voice which is 'mystifying' in the way it seems to address the listener directly, which would imply reciprocity, but instead the listener, in not being able to reciprocate as in a face-to-face encounter, is reified, not treated as part of a human relation.

This is a particularly eloquent account of the persistent association of the privatized public with passivity. But it can be challenged on various counts – and not just that Sartre himself since the 1940s had used the radio as a platform for his ideas. First, lack of reciprocity is a common feature of public life, not least in the constitution of the reading public. It is the resounding of the public word through broadcast speech that introduces the spectre of a muted public of listeners. Second, the equation of listening with passive reception fails to give credit to the listener to engage in the critical activity of reflection and critique, despite this being assumed for the reader (who, despite this abstraction, may well be the self-same person). Third, it is, perhaps, the 'liveness' of radio which gives rise to the unrealizable expectation of reciprocity in the moment and reciprocity in kind.[13] And finally, the focus on the structural conditions of reception overlooks the specificities of the broadcasts which may have a more or less public character. These are all questions which are explored in more detail in the final section of the book. For now, though, this chapter concludes with an examination of the kind of listening that was most closely associated with the domestic and with passivity, with a view to excavating its public dimensions.

A Distracted Public

Very soon after its introduction into the private sphere, the radio became defined as a secondary medium with fragmentary, ephemeral content listened to while doing other things. This was a new, *distracted* way of listening, possibly quite different from ways of listening that had gone before. To listen is to pay attention to sound and meaning. It assumes intention and a degree of concentration that distinguishes it from 'mere' hearing. And yet here is a new hybrid form of attention that was the subject of much controversy in the early years of broadcasting, compounded by the fact that it was associated primarily with women in the private sphere. There was a similar anxiety about distraction in the cinema, but while the distracted gaze was recuperated by some critics as a new form of perception (*Zerstreuung*), appropriate to the alienation and fragmentation of modernity in place of the contemplative absorption of an earlier age (Kracauer 1926/1995; Benjamin 1936/1992a), the distracted ear was has not attracted such luminous critical defenders, and certainly the dominant discourse about domestic listening through radio's 'golden age' was precisely about learning how to listen in a concentrated and purposeful fashion.

Even those critics and practitioners who lobbied for acoustic montage techniques, that might have elicited the same kind of jolt out of unreflective apprehension as was hoped for in the jump cut, could still lament the passivity and irresolve of the domestic listener. Rudolf Arnheim, a champion of the radiogenic artform, could still write dismissively about 'those who, to distract themselves in the evening, turn the receiver on without reading through the schedule', and 'the passive listener, who recklessly flicks the knob around [. . .] desiring only to be somehow diverted'. Concentration had to be 'fought for by the listener *against* his surroundings, and he rarely succeeds in doing this' (in Vancour 2010: 184–5).

The assumption here that the listener is male is not just a product of the linguistic bias of the age. It also has to do with the pervasive but unspoken alignment of distracted listening with the domestic and therefore feminine sphere. The male listener has to *struggle* against the feminine surroundings to achieve mastery over the acoustic environment. It is not irrelevant that the discourses and practices of 'audiophilia' reveal this kind of concentrated and purposeful listening discussed in previous chapters to be a stereotypically masculine pursuit. This is not because of any innate differences between the sexes, but because of the material and historical conditions that produce particular modes of perception. Taking the example of Weimar Germany, I have argued in more detail elsewhere (Lacey 2000) that women's engagement with the modern media during the first part of the twentieth century must be set against the differentiated and contradictory integration of women into modernity and the particular ways in which even those women most integrated into the modern would have experienced a sharpening of traditional gender roles and responsibilities (Petro 1989: 43–4). The distracted gaze in the public space of the 'picture palaces' was implicitly a male gaze in contrast to the emotional absorption associated with women's film viewing, as suggested by a term like 'the weepies'.

The gender roles in relation to radio seem, however, to be reversed. Archetypally – and in a way that came to be reflected in the construction of broadcasting schedules on both radio and television – radio in the form of discrete programmes like lectures or dramas was listened to attentively by waged workers in their leisure time, whereas it was listened to distractedly as a constant but fragmented flow during the day by women for whom the home was their place of work – as housewives and consumers. Here we see a dramatic contradiction where those women who were ostensibly least integrated into the modern and the public sphere are the exponents of the most modern – and potentially progressive – mode of perception. Although the way broadcasting was deliberately organized to feed into and reflect the rhythms and practices of the domestic sphere can be read as a means by which women in particular were reintegrated into traditional roles, it is possible, following the logic of the distracted gaze, that the distracted ear would recognize the repetitiveness, isolation and monotony of household routines, and understand that it was a condition shared by countless other listeners. The artificiality of the soundscape accompanying the most familiar routines had the potential to represent 'the everyday made manifest: as a consequence of having lost its essential – constitutive – trait of being *unperceived*' (Blanchot 1987, in Moran 2003: 175). Certainly it was understood by people across the political spectrum that radio could reach women in the home in a way that no other medium of communication could, and arguments flew about whether the radio could be deployed to keep women in the home by offering compensatory distractions, or whether it could be used as an unobtrusive way to mobilize women to participate in different ways in the public sphere (Lacey 1996: 57–96).

The radio offered access to a public world reconstituted for domestic consumption via domestic radio sets that were often designed to blend with the fabric and furnishings of the home, further collapsing the sense of distance from the sound event. In this, the radio followed the pattern of the phonograph before it and all audio media that have followed in the trajectory towards miniaturization and concealment, taking up less visual space while becoming more ubiquitous and enhancing the sense of immediacy. To paraphrase Benjamin (1936/1992a: 217) on film, radio offered the distracted listener the illusion of an equipment-free reproduction of reality, wrenching sounds from the 'domain of tradition' and reproducing them in the listener's 'own particular situation'. In so doing, this most denigrated and mundane form of engagement with mediated sound is recast as a mode of perception with radical potential.

In his essay on the Storyteller, Benjamin (1936/1992b: 83–107) argued that the decline of activities like weaving and spinning in the modern age was having a detrimental effect on the culture of community listening. It was this kind of repetitive, haptic activity that was boring enough to allow enough mental relaxation to exercise the 'gift of listening' to stories repeatedly told and retold, and in which the 'dreambird of experience' could be hatched (Benjamin 1936/1992b: 90). Although the relation between storyteller and listener here is an unmediated one, it is instructive to adapt the analysis to broadcasting, the storyteller *par excellence* of the modern age. Radio stands at the heart of a paradox, which makes it the response to the decline of the craft of storytelling, which depends on the boredom it in turn serves to destroy. But more than that, while the attempt by waged workers to escape the boredom of their leisure time by turning on the radio or indeed the phonograph was, in Benjamin's terms, no escape from the spell of the commodity or the repetitive patterns of the workplace (Moran 2003: 170), the housewife tuned in – along with countless others in an invisible community – to listen to stories while still engaged in repetitive, almost proprioceptive domestic labour.

While Benjamin might have been critical of the modern media's dominant informational mode where 'no event any longer comes to us without already being shot through with explanation' (Benjamin 1936/1992b: 89), the genre most closely associated with distracted women's listening, the 'soap opera', was a storytelling device designed to weave into the domestic routine and keep the listeners coming back for more. The narratives of these dramas, listened to while doing other things, became the stuff of conversation, gossip and fantasy, in other words embroidered with home-spun explanations and extensions. Benjamin (1936/1992b: 91) wrote, 'When the rhythm of work has seized [the listener], he listens to the tales in such a way that the gift of retelling them comes to him all by himself'. Here, paradoxically, in relation to the most cynical move of the marketing men and the big corporations to ensnare the listener as consumer into commodified culture, in the most denigrated corner of privatized, distracted listening, is potentially another way of recuperating listening as a potential site of resistance in the face of all the pessimistic critique. There is, even here, a kind of responsiveness in the act of privatized listening as collective endeavour and public practice that is all too often overlooked.

7 The Politics and Practices of Collective Listening

The emergence of the new sound media clearly had profound implications for the ways of listening available to new kinds of publics. However, as the previous chapter argued, the dominant trend through this history was towards the privatization and individualization of the listening public via the technological and textual inscription of an idealized and domesticated listener, albeit that there always remained a public horizon to this experience. The social application of any new technology is complex and convoluted, of course, but too often the contingency and contestedness of the process, particularly in its early phases, is written out of history. So dominant has been the narrative and experience of privatized listening for both recorded and broadcast sound, that it is instructive to look to some of the alternative listening practices that existed alongside or within the dominant 'auditory regime'. This chapter explores some of those exceptions to the dominant historical narrative, by turning attention to instances of civic and collective listening to mediated sound.

Politics on Record

Although the history of the record is dominated by recordings of music and light entertainment, politicians were also among the early adopters of phonograph technology. Of course, many were keen to record their greatest oratorical moments for posterity, but phonography also served more pressing and practical ends. An early example was reported during a Yorkshire election campaign in 1893, where a local politician had 'hit upon an expedient' to address meetings where he was unable to attend in person.[1] Commercial recordings of stump speeches were circulated during the 1896 US presidential election – short simulations of oratory from political rallies presented as if recorded live, together with simulated applause (Bauman and Feaster 2003: 2–3). In Germany too, similar recordings, which aspired to 'liveness' and which were rapidly produced and distributed in the wake of political events so as to intervene in ongoing debates, were also widely circulated. In fact, by 1897 their status in relation to copyright law had to be clarified; their reception by listeners rather than readers ensured they were deemed analogous to a lecture in person, rather than a pamphlet (Gauss 2009: 113).

Recorded voices continued to play a part in electioneering through the twentieth century. In 1906, William Randolph Hearst used recordings to reach rural constituents as part of his campaign to be New York State Governor. His opponents, meanwhile, deployed twenty-five wagon-mounted phonographs to replicate speeches in the Russian and Yiddish vernacular of the East Side (Bauman and Feaster 2003: 6–9). Political culture had long been represented in the homogenizing language of print; here is evidence that recorded speech might be deployed to reach out to diverse publics in more deliberately diverse voices. Two years later, during the 1908 Presidential campaign, Edison's National Phonograph Company produced twenty-two two-minute recordings of candidates William Jennings Bryan and William Howard Taft to be played at home or at rallies – even as reconstituted 'debates' replete with mannequins. Adverts encouraged individual citizen-consumers to buy cylinders, priced at 35 cents each, from both candidates, regardless of how they intended to vote. These recordings were intended for domestic as well as public listening, but the acoustic codes were designed to produce a sense of partaking in politics in conventionally public space. Although they were of limited success at the time, either commercially or as opinion-shifters, these commodified 'sound bites' do represent a first move towards the shorter, pithier soundbites of the modern media age (Rabin 2008), and remind us that it was not only with radio that mediated sound impacted on the form and availability of public political discourse.

Meanwhile in the UK, the Conservative Party in 1907 commissioned a fleet of twenty horse-drawn vans, decorated with cartoons and posters (with slogans like 'British Work for British Hands' and 'Socialism Denies Liberty'), stocked with leaflets and handouts, and equipped with 'a lantern and gramophone', to tour the length and breadth of the country in a promotional campaign. These mobile multimedia propaganda vehicles would pull up outside factory gates in the dinner hour to reach working men, and at public meetings in the evening. Speakers illustrated their talks with slides and entertained the listening public with gramophone records of 'political parodies, set to the tune of well-known songs, and stump speeches by well-known politicians'.[2] This was still the era when popular politics played out in the streets and other public places, but it was a transitional period in which the new media technologies were deployed in these public spaces alongside conventional forms of communication before they came to be used more commonly as means to convey public affairs and political messages directly into the home. Here is an account of a cacophonous moment in the electoral campaign in Croydon in 1909:

> Last night a huge crowd in Katherine-street was entertained with two cinematograph exhibitions, two gramophone concerts, one powerful searchlight, and a dozen hoarsely roared speeches. It was probably just as well that the voices of the speakers drowned one another.[3]

The fact that the phonograph was a recording as well as a playback device meant it was relatively easy to make recordings for specific purposes and locations, be they commercial, social or political. In January 1905, *Talking Machine News* reported an interesting experiment in the US by a debating society that used the phonograph to organize debates over distances of thousands of miles, with one local group recording a proposition, sending it to another and a reply being recorded in turn. It listed the advantages and disadvantages as follows:

> It is fatal to verbosity, for the time at the disposal of the speakers is limited. Bashfulness also need no longer hinder the aspiring orator now that he is enabled to make his speech at home [. . .] The objection is that this is not debating, as the word is commonly understood, though it may, of course, be a passable substitute for it.

This practice occupies a liminal space in media history. The report focuses on how recordings enable debate over distance, albeit interrupted; but print had long since overcome distance and with that same delay between interventions. The phonograph is appropriated, therefore, to 'breathe life' back into the word, but the very vitalism of the voice serves only to emphasize the interruption of time and distance. The report therefore compares the benefits and deficiencies of recorded debate in relation to face-to-face debate rather than in relation to writing, with which it had at least as many affinities. Comparison to telephony is lacking altogether, already firmly associated as it was with private communication and apparently ill-suited to the public genre of the debate. But the experiment also looks forward, without knowing it, to the era of sound broadcasting which would solve the 'problem' of liveness, and even teleconferencing which would solve the 'problem' of interactivity – although the contemporary form with which it shares most in common is, arguably, the podcast. Each incarnation, for all their specificities, is an expression of a desire to connect across distance by the medium of sound and voice and to constitute a listening public.

Collective Radio Listening

Of course the appropriation of broadcast radio for political communication is more familiar and much better documented than phonography. The communicative context of a dispersed and distant public of listeners would have far-reaching implications for the conduct of public and political life and the forms of public discourse (Lerg and Steininger 1975; Scannell 1989; Goodman 2010). But think of the radio audience, certainly in the 'golden age' of broadcasting, and it is the image of the individual or family group listening in domestic space that comes most readily to mind. One aspect of broadcasting history that is much less well rehearsed is the radio listening that took place in public spaces and as part of an explicitly collective endeavour. It is to this aspect of listening to broadcasts collectively in public space that this chapter now turns. Of course, the radio was never only a solitary experience. Radio from the beginning was not only a social phenomenon, but a sociable one, with families and neighbours listening together as a matter of course, or workers in shops, factories and offices working to a background of mediated music. But these familiar privatized or accidental collectivities have come to obscure those historical instances of collective listening that have taken place outside of the familial home in congregations constituted as *publics*. The standard historical narratives by the same token have also tended to obscure the once live debates about the radical possibilities of such listening publics in the media age.

In fact, some of the earliest plans for public radio drew inspiration from public events in the classical sense – the gathering of an audience in a common space to listen to programmes made up of music, lectures and light entertainment via a telephone with a loudspeaker attachment. However, such experiments faltered under the technical limitations of loudspeaker technology, the limited range of reception and also the desire of the electronics industry to reap the profits from the sale of millions of individual wireless sets. Instead, many people's first experience of radio would have been as part of a collective audience partaking in advertising stunts by retailers seeking to sell domestic receivers. In Germany, department stores and upmarket cafés would provide headsets for customers, and special listening cabins were put up in public exhibition spaces such as the Theresienhöhe in Munich or the Lunapark in Berlin (Lenk 1997: 74–6). In London, shops would often stay open late after normal closing time in order to attract commuters to evening broadcasts on their way home from work (although with time broadcasters learned to extend their broadcasting hours into normal trading hours to help promote the sale of sets).[4] In some sense these early listeners were akin to the hams, thrilling more in the wonder of listening than the content, a radio of attractions, to adapt Tom Gunning's (1986) description of early cinema. Later, as the novelty waned, groups would still gather to hear news bulletins, sports reports and 'event' broadcasts, just as television viewers continue to do even in an era of ubiquitous media.

The first such event in the UK was the relay of the General Election results just two days after the British Broadcasting Company first went on air. The following day, 16 November 1922, *The Times* reported the novel phenomenon of 'listening-in parties', when thousands of people were able to 'sit comfortably at home and learn by wireless the news of the polls', and learn, too, of the vast crowds (including notable numbers of women) in London and other cities who had gathered in public places to hear the results as they came in. In Germany, in May 1924, the crowds grew so large to listen to the broadcast election results, amplified in public spaces, that the police were called in to disperse them (Ross 2008: 183). Election results had also been broadcast in the US in 1920, but it was an early experiment in broadcasting live sports that had proved the appeal and commercial viability of such mediated cultural events, namely RCA's broadcast of the world heavyweight championship between Jack Dempsey and Georges Carpentier on 2 July 1921. The Amateur Wireless Association had helped arrange loudspeakers in public halls where listeners could congregate on payment of an admission fee – some 300,000 people were recorded as having participated (Sterne 2003: 195–7).

The BBC, too, with its very different motivations, soon realized that if broadcasting was to be a success, it should 'provide novelties and stunts for the public'.[5] Occasionally, such events were front page news. The *Daily Express* devoted two days' headlines to the must-hear concert with the soprano Luisa Tetrazzini in March 1925, reporting that shops and restaurants had fitted loudspeakers to attract the crowds, that the whole nation, 'from Thurso to the Lizard, from Hull to Connemara, in great liners in the oceans, in shepherds' shieldings, in artisans' cottages, in middle-class villas, in luxurious restaurants' had been 'entranced by a voice . . . millionaires and workmen in a bond of song', concluding that 'no audience was ever so democratic, so widely distributed, so calculated to fire imagination'.[6]

Such media events continued in Britain, as elsewhere, throughout the 1920s and into the late 1930s, and were especially popular for the collective reception of royal occasions, when crowds of several thousand could be reported (Pegg 1983: 173–5). The sense of public occasion was easily translated into narratives of nation-building through a shared acoustic experience that transcended normal social barriers. But perhaps the high point for collective listening in the UK was during the nine days of the General Strike in May 1926, when the political rifts within the nation were at their most acute.

The strike played a momentous part in the history of the BBC as is well known, offering Reith a chance to show what broadcasting could do in an emergency, and setting the scene for the company's subsequent incorporation as a public service by Royal Charter. With the newspaper presses stilled, Reith had immediately negotiated with the government to lift the prevailing restrictions on broadcast news, and the BBC overnight became the only source of national news, ostensibly committed to making 'plain, objective news audible to everybody' in its reporting of the crisis. In fact, its reports tended to reflect the government's position 'in the national interest' and the compromises it made to its impartiality were the subject of controversy then as now. But Reith did steer a path that avoided the very real prospect of the BBC being directly commandeered by the state, which established a reputation for the BBC as an independent and indispensable institution in the life of the nation, and that put the role of broadcasting firmly on the political map (Tracey 2003). These institutional aspects of the story tend to be privileged in the retelling over the effect of all this on the listening public.

Public radio was still in its infancy. By 1926, only two million sets were licensed in a population of 45,000,000 (still a remarkably rapid take-up). But two million sets translates into many more than two million listeners even in normal times. In a time of crisis, with no alternative source of news, many millions more gathered in public and private places to listen to the five daily bulletins, with sets specially installed in clubs and pubs, shops and town halls. Newspapers, when they did manage to publish emergency editions, drew their information from the BBC bulletins (themselves composed from agency wires and government statements), and bulletins were transcribed and displayed in shops and town halls, and of course relayed by word of mouth. The bulletins were interspersed with the regular fare of talks and music, designed to impart a sense of calm and normality to listeners.

People listened to the bulletins for information, but in the heightened political climate, they certainly also listened critically.[7] Though union leaders were denied access to the airwaves, strikers listened in for want of any other source of information – their own papers and publications being stalled by the strike (Pegg 1983: 175–84). However, the unions and the Labour Party did warn their members not to believe anything they heard on the wireless since it was under the control of the government.[8] The heightened presence of the BBC during this short period was extraordinary, and as a consequence of its new status and its exposure to innumerable new listeners, not only did numbers of licences increase by nearly a third, but listening, collectively and privately, became more firmly established as an activity in the public sphere.

While most receivers during this time were located in the home, its status as a *public* organ meant its role and remit was widely understood to range much more broadly than the domestic context. Scannell and Cardiff (1991: 269) describe how the radio in this period was used as a kind of bulletin board for a diverse 'network of local, neighbourhood activities'. The radio would be used routinely to announce all kinds of community events in schools, churches and village halls, as well as theatres and conference venues. They give a flavour of the variety of events and associations, in reproducing an announcement made during the strike, that in both form and content offered reassurance that public life would soon return to normal:

> The Sixteenth Annual May Lecture of the Institute of Metals, two perfor-mances of *The Human Touch* at King George's Hall, the Annual Conference of the National Association of Head Teachers, the Services and Meetings in celebration of the 67th Anniversary of the Universities' Mission to Central Africa, the examinations of the College of Violinists, the sixth Montgomery County Musical Festival, the Ramsey Hunt Hospital Carnival in aid of the Peterborough and District Council of the Spiritualist Union, the Dinner of the National Federation of Iron and Steel Manufacturers, the Dunmow Flitch and the 1250th Anniversary Celebrations of the See of Hereford were all, for the moment, postponed (369–70).

What this extraordinary list also shows is how radio was seen as belonging squarely in the weft and warp of associational life. The odd assortment of organizations descriptively and performatively reflects the variegated daily expression of public life and, by association, also radio's odd assortment of listeners. Radio had a public role to play not only in announcing to the various memberships of these organizations whether their particular event was going ahead, but in presenting the vibrancy of associational life back to its listeners who were constituted as a new and all-encompassing associa-tion. Radio's public aspect in bringing people together in temporary com-munities of interest chimed with listeners' identities outside the home, as much as ever it did with their identities as family members gathered around the domestic hearth. This was true in Germany as well, where early listener groups would be formed in association with churches, women's groups, the unions and veterans' associations. Two examples will underscore this point – the attempts to organize public associations of listeners to mitigate their isolation as privatized members of the public, and the attempts to organize group listening.

Listener associations

Organized pressure groups played an important role in Britain in the formative years of broadcasting (Pegg 1983: 65–91). Some were technical or commercial organizations, like the Radio Society of Great Britain, founded in 1913, whose lobbying contributed to the establishment of the British Broadcasting Company in 1922; or the Radio Association, founded in 1922 to vet wireless traders, educate the public in 'radio science' and to 'protect the interests of listeners' – in short, to do for the radio public what the Automobile Association had done for 'the driving public'. It claimed 3,000 members by 1925 and its Chairman gave evidence before both the Sykes and Crawford Committees.[9] Another, larger organization was the Wireless League, founded in 1925 by Lord Beaverbrook of the *Daily Express* to oppose any extension of the BBC's monopoly when it was up for review the following year.[10] The *Express* likened the licence fee to 'taxation without representation' and argued 'the British listener-in must show the characteristic British sense of public duty, and the British aptitude for civic organization. He must not leave it to the next man to defend his rights. He must join up himself with the Wireless League'.[11] The very next day another banner headline proclaimed 'Enthusiastic Support for the Wireless League: Success Assured in One Day', with telegrams and letters of support having come in from all over the country and from all walks of life. Over the next few days the paper reproduced endorsements from prominent figures, representatives of provincial radio societies, and 'ordinary' listeners-in.[12] Within a fortnight, it claimed to be the largest such organization in the country, and by 1926 had grown to 80,000 (mainly middle-class) members organized into 150 regional branches, having incorporated or crowded out other nascent associations.[13]

The BBC was initially wary and refused the League 'microphone publicity' because of its association with 'newspaper interests' that had been critical (and covetous) of its monopoly.[14] But by July 1925 the League had become independent of the *Express* and, under the Chairmanship of Sir Arthur Stanley, began to enjoy friendlier relations with the BBC, to the extent of being given monthly airtime for broadcast talks. This rapprochement led to a more radical breakaway group, the New Wireless League, spurring the BBC in turn to work *with* the Wireless League and give up its own plans for a national listeners' organization (Briggs 1995: 227). Instead, on becoming a public corporation in 1927, the BBC invited representatives of the principal listeners' organizations to a new Wireless Organization Advisory Committee, though it seems not to have been very active, and did not survive beyond 1930. In 1934 the first BBC Central Advisory Committee was formed, which included 'eminent men and women, broadly representative of educated opinion among listeners' who were enjoined to 'interpret the policy and practice of the Corporation to the various sections of the community with which they may be associated'. However, the Ullswater Committee in 1936 recommended wider representation of listeners' rather than experts' views and before long the Corporation began engaging in listener research.[15]

Group listening and democracy

Another way the BBC sought to deliver on its Charter obligations was in promoting adult education, and for many years it tried to generate interest by promoting collective listening in public spaces. The 'Group Listening Scheme' was driven by daily programmes at peak listening times designed to inspire discussion on themes such as *This Changing World*.[16] The hope was that listening in groups would stimulate 'the capacity to listen to other people's ideas even when they are unpalatable, and to follow up by discussion and calm analysis'.[17] Active discussion, it was thought, would be a useful defence against accusations that broadcasting was 'mechanizing' people's thoughts and habits. Experiments to compare the virtues of individual over group listening, headphones over loudspeakers, and different forms of presentation were conducted in various locations, including the YMCA, universities and the Women's Institute.[18] A test with 15-year-old schoolboys found that headphones increased concentration in 'duller boys' but that 'the loudspeaker made the listening group much more conscious of each other' and so encouraged 'a greater sense of corporate listening'.[19]

A Central Council for Broadcast Adult Education was set up in 1928 to supervise programmes to be listened to by 'discussion groups', be that a small group of friends listening 'by the fireside' in one of their homes, to groups of 40 or so meeting in a public library, or groups organized by existing associations like the YMCA, the Co-operative Society, the British Legion, trade unions or groups of unemployed miners. Groups might also be less 'voluntary', being organized in 'prisons, workhouses and reformatories, or again in recreation-rooms and rest-rooms connected with their place of work'.[20] The Council was more concerned to inspire collective listening and discussion (including by loan and repair of receivers in 'distressed areas') than to impose rules about how groups should be organized. Often groups came together around a specific programme or series; sometimes discussions were guided by a group leader. The broadcasts might include suggestions for reading, or would set questions for the listeners to debate, or would invite listeners to conduct experiments at home along with the speaker, courtesy of equipment they could send off for in advance (e.g. *First Steps in Biology*, broadcast in February 1929).

Up to 20,000 people listened to the five weekly collective listening broadcasts in the late 1920s. Though this represented a small proportion of the total audience, the BBC remained committed to programming for groups because these listeners conformed, in principle at least, to the *ideal* listener who was serious, selective and attentive. As Filson Young (1933: 109) put it, employing a rather unfortunate ovine image, 'the listener is invariably willing. He is listening because he wants to listen, because he wants to be educated; because he is one of the hungry sheep looking up to be fed.' Evidence that plenty of listeners were not willing, however, came in newspaper reports about public resistance to the programmes, with listeners complaining of dull, patronizing and didactic programming where they would prefer more dance music and light diversion.[21]

The Group Listening broadcasts were supplemented by illustrated pamphlets, called 'Aids to Study' (2d post-free fom any BBC station), and talks might be reproduced in the *Radio Times*, but a more permanent record of programmes that would 'otherwise be lost in the ether' was deemed desirable in a 1928 report entitled 'New Ventures in Broadcasting'.[22] The result was the launch of *The Listener* in January 1929 which, declared the first issue, was 'an enterprise in the service of broadcasting, undertaken in discharge of an important part of the Corporation's responsibilities towards *the* listener, the citizen'.[23] Apart from clearly signalling the listener as citizen and the citizen as listener, the title reflected Reith's determination to discourage the term 'listener-in', a signal perhaps that together with the invitation to listen in attentively, the idea was about listening *out* to different ideas and different voices.[24] The ambitions were lofty, to say the least. Group listening represented 'a concerted effort to overcome prejudice which should, in a short while, turn the tradition of free speech and free controversy into a reality practised by every man. When that day comes we shall have a surer foundation for world peace than any institutional or governmental guarantee.'[25]

Though now largely forgotten, Group Listening was the place where the seeds of audience research were first sown in the UK. The BBC was famously averse to pandering to public taste, and eschewed any systematic gathering of audience data until 1936. Broadcasting to specific institutional groups, however, gave rise to correspondence with those groups about who was listening, when, how and with what response. The following extracts from letters written in 1929 will give some flavour. A group leader from a Sheffield library listening group wrote about a 'spirit of friendliness and comradeship' that grew in the group, and how he had 'personally witnessed the remarkable development of a working boy who at the first meeting in February expressed himself somewhat haltingly but with a great deal of shrewd reasoning power, and who at the debate on April 16th was able to clothe his ideas in admirable English.' This kind of paternalist elitist attitude was echoed in the report of another group leader from a Suburban Men's Institute who wrote, 'Even these humble students – mainly men from the engineering shops, the docks, gas-works, saw-mills and street-barrows – had got something in greater or less degree from a wireless talk, and most of them were willing and in some cases eager to talk about it. The effort to concentrate had apparently not been too much for them.' But self-constituted groups also reported back positively; for example, one listener, who walked every Tuesday evening for six weeks for an hour and a quarter 'over hill and dale' to join a community group to listen to a scientific series, reported that it gave members, 'from youngest [9] to oldest [81] – a peep into an unsuspected wonderland'.

Each week *The Listener* included a section entitled 'Links with Listeners' that reported on listener groups around the country and questionnaires were sent to libraries and retailers to log loans and sales of the various publications referred to in the programmes.[26] In addition, an investigative tour of listening groups across the country was undertaken in 1931 to generate more qualitative data. For example, at the Cinderford Miners' Welfare Institute, unemployed miners and others listened to morning and evening talks and 'even the billiards stop when our talks come on'. A 'definitely middle class' group in Bristol that included one general, one colonel and a naval captain listened to 'Commerce the Peacemaker' with 'real interest'. An audience in Dumfries at the Ewart Library met 'in a rather chilly chamber lined with dusty and half-empty museum cases, and we sat in rows facing the loud-speaker'. The audience, 'though mainly of the artisan type', had done 'an amazing amount of reading'. The meeting was a rather solemn affair, but the BBC researcher, Mr Milliken, gathered that 'this is often to be expected in Scotland'. A headmistress in an isolated Scottish village 'seemed depressed' that her group had fallen from 50 to 30, but Mr Milliken thought that 'to look at the place one would not think there were more than 50 people in it'. A group of six men and four women met at the Stourbridge Presbyterian Chapel to listen to 'Whither Mankind?'.

The talk 'promoted a really first-rate discussion in which Conservative, Moderate and Left-Wing points of view were freely expressed'. Researchers also went to groups in private homes by invitation, although had to be careful not to give the impression of an 'inspection'.[27] Limited though these efforts were, they do represent an early attempt at some kind of qualitative audience research, almost ethnographic in approach. In the transitional period between complete rejection of research 'at the listening end' and the development of increasingly sophisticated ways of measuring, describing, analysing and accommodating the listening practices and tastes of its audience, it is not insignificant that the BBC began its forays into audience research by examining these listening groups that looked most like conventional theatrical audiences and were constituted somewhere between the privatized reading public and the conventional congregations of the public meeting.

Formalized group listening was also initiated in the US by proponents of adult education, often via radio stations owned by educational establishments. There had been talk of 'listeners' rights' there since the term was first coined by Herbert Hoover in 1924, when, as Secretary for Commerce, he had declared that radio was 'a public medium, and its use must be for the public benefit' (in Toro 2000: 14). Throughout the 1930s there was a prominent tradition of 'radio forums' that brought debate and discussion of local, national and international affairs onto the air, with a view to stimulating the tolerant exercise and exchange of opinion and decision making among their listening publics (Goodman 2011: 193–218). Increasingly, these were accompanied by organized listening groups to encourage dynamic engagement with the broadcasts and so inculcate an active civic disposition. As many as 15,000 listening groups were estimated by the late 1930s, involving up to half a million people (Hill and Williams 1941: 38). One celebrated example was a series of programmes for parent-teacher listening groups in Iowa, which in 1935 generated 144 groups with over 2,000 members. A similar New Jersey-based series had up to 300 groups. Many local organizations arranged group listening at one time or another – churches, women's organizations, libraries, luncheon clubs, while other listening groups emerged organically – like the book clubs that grew up around literary programmes. In some remote communities, collective listening was the norm, or was actively encouraged. For example, the Agriculture Department at the University of Kentucky in 1933 installed fifteen battery-operated sets in community halls and stores in the remotest settlements, in order to pass on the latest agricultural knowledge and to integrate rural listeners into the modern life of the nation (Waller 1946: 334–5). The best-known, and perhaps most influential, example of nationwide listener groups, however, were those associated with *America's Town Meeting of the Air*, broadcast from 1935 by NBC (Loviglio 2005: 42–6; Goodman 2011: 199–212). Well over 100 groups registered with the programme for a fee, for which they received further information and support for their events. The information sheet for one such group in Colombus, Ohio, in 1940 gives some flavour of such groups' ambitions:

> We do not expect our discussions to settle questions or to provide all the answers. For some, the discussions will merely sharpen areas of conflict. But for all who listen, opinion will become more informed, and thinking will be stimulated, and freedom against the sway of mass emotion will be strengthened (in Goodman 2011: 215).

Meanwhile, despite the BBC's efforts to encourage group listening, by 1934 it was clear the tide was against them, and specialized broadcasts were cut back to three a week (Siepmann 1934). The first three series of early evening half-hour programmes were *Poverty in Plenty* on the economics and politics of the Depression, *The Child, the Parent and the Teacher* about contemporary education, and *Freedom and Authority in the Modern World*, examining a problem that had 'become newly acute in these days of dictatorships and the fading of the general faith in universal suffrage, liberal institutions, and responsible government'.[28] The programmes sometimes experimented with presentational styles. *Men Talking* was an example in October 1938 of 'impromptu discussions' on topics 'of everyday interest'. The novelty lay in the studio guests (men and women) starting to talk, unscripted and unrehearsed, before the microphone was 'made alive' and carrying on after the broadcast was over. In this way, it was hoped, 'listeners will genuinely overhear a spontaneous conversation and have all the pleasures of eavesdropping with no harm to the conscience'. It was supposed those listeners who had followed the previous season's *Clear Thinking* series would be particularly well placed to critique such unrehearsed discussions, and to contribute their own arguments. A report on groups listening to *Men Talking* includes, to take just one example, the North Sunderland Evening Class in which sixteen members were enrolled, aged 24 to 71, including three housewives, a lady shop assistant, two clergymen, a bootmaker, gardener, labourer, lorry-driver, man of leisure, two master builders, a baker, and a schoolmaster as leader. All reportedly joined in the discussion.[29]

In 1936 a review of Talks Policy found an undue amount of effort and attention was expended on group listening. It argued the division between group and individual listeners was 'fallacious', and laid the Corporation 'open to attack for devoting too much attention to a minority'.[30] The Advisory Committee put up a spirited defence, arguing group listeners were a minority only because it had not been properly cultivated 'at the listening end' and because of the persistent reduction in suitable talks. It insisted,

> the encouragement of critical listening and discussion by even a small section of listeners is one of the most valuable contributions by the BBC to contemporary life, and the abandonment of this part of its policy seems to mean a surrender to the popular clamour for 'giving the public what it wants'.[31]

The Area Councils raised similar objections, but the Director of Talks found many of the interventions so emotional and misguided as to 'lower the value to be placed upon their opinion in this matter'.[32] Eventually, the Adult Education Department within the BBC was merged with the Talks Department. A Central Committee for Group Listening, with representatives from the regions, was established with a limited remit in 1937 and continued for the next ten years, when it, too, was folded.[33]

Despite the growing acceptance that these programmes should also be of interest to 'serious' listeners in their private homes, support for group listening continued. Almost 1,500 groups were reported in 1937, half as many again as the year before. Numbers continued to grow the following year as the atmosphere of crisis deepened, boosted by around 100 junior groups organized around the 'Under Twenty Club' series. At least 179 local educational authorities were involved in running groups, or supporting various conferences and weekend schools for group listening. The *Manchester Guardian* carried a lengthy report on group listening in the summer of 1939. It supported groups in their encouragement of 'clear thinking', arguing that the groups offered 'some counterbalance to the legion of cheap visual appeals of to-day'. It recognized group listening as 'an exacting task' equal to 'the application of mind to print' which, while never likely to become a mass movement, held out the 'promise of establishing a thinking nucleus among the masses'.[34] Here is a suggestion that, if listening aspired to the critical reasoning associated with the reading public, it was a skill best learned in collective practice.

The outbreak of war saw a concerted effort to organize groups for the forces around informational series like *Our Allies* or *Battle-fronts*, or the weekly *Radio Reconaissance*. Both Ed Murrow and Alistair Cooke broadcast programmes direct from the US for the group listening scheme. There were also reports in 1940 of group listening in wardens' posts, first aid centres, refugee hostels and air-raid shelters. However, conditions for both broadcasters and listeners meant that numbers of programmes and listening groups inevitably declined. A report at the end of the war, commissioned to consider whether or not to continue the scheme, noted the very small numbers involved, varying between 8,500 and 16,000 per session (three sessions annually). The high point had come in 1932–3 with 1,748 groups, with the highest number for a single series 1,200. The average number of students registered for adult education classes was 60,000 over the same period. In 1947 the Director-General, Sir William Haley, reported that 'Looking back, we could not escape the conclusion that group listening had never lived up to the hopes which its originators had framed. Figures are not everything in life, but figures over seventeen years have, I think, some significance.'[35] The decision was made to stop talks designed specifically for group listening and any responsibility for the organization of groups, although the BBC would retain its commitment to adult education.

The Parliamentary Report of the 1949 Broadcasting Committee, noting that the Group Listening Scheme had been abandoned after two decades for lack of popular support, commented (in a section entitled 'The Listening Public') that the BBC's Charter requirement to provide 'information, education and entertainment' was increasingly understood in reverse order by its public. The Workers' Educational Association reported that they had 'watched the BBC listening group movement disappear "unwept, unhonoured and unsung".' The Report concluded that the overall objectives were worth pursuing despite the setbacks, and that the BBC should liaise with other institutions interested in adult education to work together under the framework of the recent 1944 Education Act. It is worth quoting Paragraph 285 of the Report in full, since it sums up the establishment view of the listening public mid-way through the twentieth century:

> Broadcasting as an influence on men's minds has great possibilities, either of good or evil. The good is that if broadcasting can find a serious audience it is an unrivalled means of bringing vital issues to wider understanding. The evil is that broadcasting is capable of increasing perhaps the most serious of all dangers which threaten democracy and free institutions today – the danger of passivity – of acceptance by masses of orders given to them and of things said to them. Broadcasting has in itself a tendency to encourage passivity, for listening as such, if one does no more, is a passive occupation. Television may be found to have this danger of passivity in even stronger form. The Group Listening Scheme, as a frontal attack on passivity, had more to be said for it than is allowed for by the Workers' Educational Association. It was abandoned because the cost seemed excessive in relation to the number of those who listened in groups. Now that the Third Programme has come for serious listeners, regardless of numbers, a fresh attempt is justified to make some of them into active listeners again, whether in groups for

discussion or in the more natural way of listening at home. In more hopeful days the BBC made attempts, not only to stimulate listener activity to discussion through the Group Listening Scheme, but to stimulate reactions and activity by audiences in other ways. Determination to attempt this and to encourage audience participation, so far from being surrendered, should now be strengthened.

This conclusion demonstrates some of the ambiguities surrounding the act of listening to mediated sound. Listening is recognized as an activity with civic importance, and yet needs to be nurtured and encouraged if it is not to decline into passivity. One way to nurture active listening was to bring it, literally, out into the public, to bring listeners together in the same physical location. Critical listening could be encouraged – and monitored – only in public space, and only in connection with public discussion. To this extent, the hopes for a critical listening practice were bound up with the faith in embodied, face-to-face encounters that is prevalent in so much political discourse.[36] Listening to the radio in the home is thought the more 'natural' way to receive programmes, but the home is only reluctantly acknowledged as a place for political activity. The whole discussion is framed with a certain urgency born of the experience of the recent war and the role that propaganda had been purported to play in underpinning the Nazi regime, where ordinary people had apparently simply accepted what they were told and had followed orders unquestioningly.

The passage also resonates with the hierarchical ordering of listeners as 'serious' and 'casual' that had been a feature of BBC policy since the 1920s, as well as demonstrating that the concern for audience participation and interactivity was on the agenda long before the advent of computer-mediated communication. What is also striking is the interest with which the question of active, critical listening is attended to in the public domain of government and public service broadcaster. From the point of view of the establishment, public service broadcasting, with its mix of entertainment and education, could offer a sense of national and social cohesion and train the newly extended electorate in the principles and practices of democratic citizenship. Educational broadcasting and the general guidance in the art of critical listening were couched in terms of both self-improvement and civic duty. Michael Bailey (2007: 106) has argued that this emphasis on self-improvement was also inculcating a regime of self-regulation, and that public service broadcasting should be seen as a cultural apparatus deployed to make the populace more 'governable'. David Goodman (2011: 71) has made a similar argument in relation to American radio in its 'golden age'. Listeners to commercial radio in the US were also widely addressed as 'citizens who listened to the contrasting opinions of others and formed their own individual opinion'. Whether listening in groups or as individuals, American listeners were actively encouraged to be 'civically aware, cosmopolitan, yet locally active'. Goodman (2011: 97) concludes that the 'active audience – inasmuch as it was being critical, opinionated, outspoken [. . .] was complying with the individualizing demands of the system'.

Group listening was therefore a double-edged sword, being a disciplinary as well as an educational technology, encouraging listeners to 'translate the values of a higher and distant authority into their own terms', to ensure that 'the listening public both in its entirety and as individuals cared more about its civil responsibilities', and to produce 'a politically obedient citizenry'. However, there is a paradox insofar as the aim of critical listening as inculcated by the Group Listening Scheme was to provide citizens with the requisite skills to question rather than to accept what they listened to, to be critical rather than simply be 'politically obedient'. The political classes might well have wanted to recreate the listening public in its own idealized image of a cultivated and engaged political body, but that idealized image contained within it a self-transformative potential. The Group Listening Scheme might have been a top-down experiment in a public form of listening, but it nevertheless was going against the grain of the dominant mode of individualized home-based listening that, as discussed in the previous chapter, was a more explicit way of *domesticating* the public. Listening in groups always brought with it at least the potential for something unexpected, unpredictable. As the BBC critic Filson Young (1933: 25, 30–1) put it:

> there are things in broadcasting which you would pass over or ignore if you were listening to them alone, but which would not pass muster if subjected to the test of being listened to in company. The tell-tale glance, the meeting of eyes in disparaging or approving agreement, may be most effective [. . .] the effect is more fertilizing, so to speak, when listened to in company [. . .] Listening in company requires more than tolerance – it requires broadness of understanding.

Similar conclusions about the promise of collective listening for the inculcation of a democratic culture were found in a cross-national comparison of listening groups between the US and the UK, commissioned by the Federal Radio Education Authority and published in 1941. The author of the American section, Frank Ernest Hill, argued the benefits of group listening were felt by educators, broadcasters and listeners alike, and that group listening went a long way to making people learn to be more tolerant of opposing points of view. The author of the British section, F.E. Williams, while more circumspect about the educational value of group listening, agreed there was a more diffuse social value and that the development of 'critical listening' in the public would strengthen democracy:

> The savour of democratic life does not depend on large numbers of bookish people, but on a vast number of citizens ready to face arguments and facts not necessarily agreeable to them, and in making up their minds not on the basis of wide reading but on material as presented to them (Hill and Williams 1941: 257).

Of course, the struggle for democracy was no idle question during this period, and it is pertinent now to turn to the German case to examine a particularly politicized and polarized take on collective listening.

Collective Listening and Propaganda

Hörgemeinde or 'listening communities' had been a feature of the broadcasting landscape throughout the Weimar Republic, becoming increasingly formalized as the 1920s wore on (Lacey 2007). Like the BBC, the national broadcaster, the Deutsche Welle, as well as regional stations in Cologne, Leipzig and Berlin, began to make programmes specifically targeted at congregations of listeners for the purposes of adult education or public information, with series, for example, on contemporary political ideologies or the problem of unemployment. By the end of 1931, there were 749 reported groups, mostly in rural areas and mostly led by teachers, priests or other local community leaders. There were also some 166 groups associated with existing organizations, 66 with bookshops and 26 in adult education colleges (Merkel, 1996: 239). Rising unemployment swelled the numbers, with around 500 unemployed groups reported in 1932 (Neels 1932: 58).

Beyond these educational and associational listening groups, however, the most significant instances of collective listening in Weimar Germany were organized by the workers' radio clubs which had mushroomed after 1924, when licences to build sets had become prohibitively expensive in the government's bid to control and centralize the airwaves. The clubs taught workers how to build low-cost transmitters and receivers, wrote scathing reviews of 'bourgeois' broadcasting, campaigned for a workers' station, and occasionally jammed or hijacked transmitters.[37] But with no legitimate access to the airwaves, one of their main objectives was to encourage a critical ear in their members by organizing collective listening. Groups as large as 500 would gather in public halls to listen to the radio and to generate a critical public discussion of the output, not just in the hall, but by sending reports of the proceedings to the party press and to the radio authorities.[38] In 1932, amid increasingly extremist politics, nationalist radio reforms presaged the Nazi takeover a few months later (Lacey 1996: 47–53). The workers' radio clubs organized a series of demonstrations, attracting tens of thousands in Leipzig, Essen and Düsseldorf. Although they never achieved their aim of a workers' station, it is clear that these listener organizations made a considerable impact through the latter years of the Republic, and that collective listening was a regular experience for large sections of the working class (Marx 1932).

But there was another section of the disaffected audience that was also excluded from the airwaves through the Weimar period, and that self-consciously learned from the organizational strategies of the workers' radio clubs – the right-wing nationalists and the National Socialists. Though the Nazis had burst onto the political scene at the same time as the first broadcast in the autumn of 1923, their voices were banned from the airwaves and the organization concentrated on other forms of political action and propaganda.[39] However, by the end of 1930, the regional Party organizations had begun appointing radio lieutenants to organize what they called 'the struggle for the radio', under the auspices of the anti-Marxist *Reichsverband der Rundfunkhörer*, the 'National Union of German Radio Listeners', which claimed to be above party politics, but was effectively taken over by the National Socialists in 1932.[40] The move was intended to build a power base among the listeners equal to that of the Marxist organizations and to form an active battle troop (*Kampfverband*) for the cause of national socialism and against the 'Jew-infested' radio with its false gods of objectivity and neutrality.[41] The leader, Eugen Hadamovsky, called on all 'nationally-minded' Germans to work towards broadcasting's destiny as the monolithic voice of the national will.[42] A promotional flyer for the union's illustrated magazine, *Der Deutsche Sender*, addressed to 'German Radio Listeners' gives a flavour of the language deployed in these campaigns:

> Break the red broadcasting terror! [. . .] The red radio raises the highest fees in the whole world and with your money has turned the microphone into the strongest propaganda tool of cultural bolshevism, negrofication and corruption of the *Volk*. [. . .] *German be the radio!*[43]

The Party organized a new listening service in every region where radio lieutenants would listen to and report weekly on the 'Marxist cultural propaganda' broadcast by a given list of stations, both local and foreign. The documents indicate there were at least twenty-four local groups in Hamburg alone.[44] At this stage, then, the Party did have a notion of an active listening public and one that could be stimulated by the practice of collective, critical listening. However, once the Nazis came to power, while the radio activists were romanticized and aggrandized in the re-telling of the 'time of struggle', all such notions of a critical public sphere were abandoned. The listeners' groups were lauded in hindsight as a 'revolutionary movement', but now the revolution was considered complete and the task became keeping listeners in line, as Hadamovsky, made clear:

> We went into the radio as Hitler's soldiers under the orders of Dr Goebbels. [Our task is now . . .] to make every fellow German a radio listener and so bring each and every one into direct contact with the political and spiritual leadership of the nation.[45]

All the listener groups of the Weimar period were disbanded or *gleichgeschaltet*, including those nationalist ones which had once been their allies, and the lieutenants were to report any attempts to regroup.[46] Collective listening was still on the agenda, but was now to be achieved by the installation of loudspeakers in factories and public places, where people were expected to down tools and listen attentively – and uncritically – whenever the Führer spoke to the nation. Central to radio's propagandistic value was its ability to speak directly to the people, and at the heart of the propagandistic strategy to win over the listening public to the national socialist cause was a faith in the ability of the Führer's voice to move those who heard it, 'whether in the home, in collective listening situations or through radio stations in the street' (Puetzfeld 1939).

Hitler's charisma as a public speaker had been hugely influential in his ascent to power. It had never been heard on the radio, but the speeches he made during the 1932 Reichstag elections were recorded, with around 50,000 copies distributed nationwide (Gauss 2009: 210). It became a priority in the new regime to have his voice heard by as many people as possible. The guidelines for the broadcast of a speech on 3 March 1933 in the Hamburg region give some indication of the attempt to saturate public and private spaces with the sound of 'his master's voice': in addition to being broadcast simultaneously on all available transmitters, loudspeakers were to be installed in all the main public halls, larger restaurants and gardens; telephone connections in special listening rooms were to be provided for the press; a local recording would be made for distribution on disc after the event; and radios were to be placed in open windows so the speech could be heard by passers-by.[47] The new regime referred to this kind of broadcast as a *Gemeinschaftssendung* or 'community programme', and considered these radio events as the 'most fundamental and radiogenic' programming form.[48] In the first year, such broadcasts included the 'Tag von Potsdam', May Day and the Nuremberg Party rally. A press release defended the lack of listening choice on such days in the following terms:

> on such days all listeners became participants – in the truest and finest sense of the word – in the life of the nation; no-one needed to feel disadvantaged, nobody needed to take other listeners into consideration, because each and everybody was being 'spoken to'. The whole German listenership had a united relationship to the radio and to their fellow listeners; the whole of Germany became like one great big room in which innumerable people of the same mind were gathered together.[49]

These were clearly attempts to translate public rallies and assemblies as directly as possible to the radio. Radio in these early days of the regime was imagined less as an intimate domestic companion, and more as a public platform, with the entire country transformed into a sounding chamber for the bombast and demagoguery of the new regime. Party rallies would be relayed, military music blared out, and the schedules filled with overt and insistent propaganda by Party functionaries. The official line was that the propaganda alone would not work, since the listeners too had a *responsibility* to surrender their own desires to the general will. Though radio had become the mirror of the government, this would be far from dull since the state was so 'lively' it could easily 'fill the radio with life'.[50] However, it seemed that the listeners were not impressed with this official line and soon began to turn off their radios, or tuned in to foreign stations, in what was later described as a 'listeners' strike' (Hagemann 1938: 46). In response, the audience was accused of not knowing *how* to listen, of unfairly expecting it to be a personal gramophone, or mistaking it for an 'Ich-Erlebnis' instead of a 'Wir-Erlebnis' (a 'me-experience', not a 'we-experience').[51] Not for nothing was the official radio set called the *Volksempfänger* – the people's receiver. But the truth was that it was not so easy to force or chide the audience into listening, and before long Goebbels realized that a more effective propaganda strategy would be, in effect, to listen more to the listeners, and provide them with more of the light entertainment they craved to sugar the propaganda pill. In a radio address in July 1936, Hadamowsky, by now the head of German radio, encapsulated this new ideological position:

We are not speaking to individuals, but members of the *Volksgemeinschaft*. Who could find the right tone for all the millions of different individuals? But that, thank the Lòrd, is not our task. Which is much simpler and clearer: to speak – and act and sing and make music *for* the millions of members of our listening community, our *Volksgemeinschaft*, and foreign *Volksgemeinschaften*. And we want to find the right tone, especially as far as our nation is concerned. Because we are part of this nation too; we belong to this community. The more often we listen to the heartbeat of this community, the better we will know how to hit the right note for our people, and so better serve German art and German culture.[52]

Within months of coming to power, the Party's propaganda division began an audit of broadcasting in preparation for its centralizing policy of *Rundfunkeinheit*, or radio unity. The ultimate objective was the 'political mobilisation of the entire German radio audience'. The *Funkwarte*, the regional radio lieutenants, were to report back on the various technical, political and cultural radio organizations, providing details of their remit, membership (including political affiliations) and the extent of their 'public presence'.[53] They also reported on the available cable facilities in public squares and assembly halls that could be used to relay radio broadcasts. The most important venues, such as the Olympic stadium in Berlin, and exhibition halls in major cities, were directed to have permanent systems installed.[54] Special radio sets called *Deutsche Arbeitsfrontempfänger 1011* (German labour front receivers) were produced for use in factories. The number 1011 was a reference to a speech Hitler had broadcast from a Siemens factory on 10 November 1933 that had been massively promoted to the extent that every factory siren in the country was sounded before the broadcast and all production came to a standstill while he spoke.[55]

In 1935, two years after coming to power, the regime embarked on a plan to install a nationwide system of public loudspeakers that would be *jederzeit einsatzbereit* (ready at any time) to broadcast messages from the Führer and other propaganda.[56] Loudspeakers had been used for public events for several years, but had always been temporary installations. At first, the plans faltered because of financial and technological hurdles. The Propaganda Ministry's solution was to bring loudspeaker technology together with the already ubiquitous *Reklamesäule*, the columns traditionally used for advertising and public announcements, so that costs could be partly offset by advertising revenue. The Ministry for Post was charged with providing the necessary infrastructure of high frequency radio cables, while a limited company dedicated to the project – the Reichs-Lautsprechersäulen-Treuhand-GmbH – was set up under the direction of the Propaganda Ministry in 1937. Although a private company, any profits above 4% would be requisitioned for 'mutual purposes' by the Ministry.[57] The first loudspeaker column was presented at the Berlin Radio Exhibition in 1937,[58] and a prototype network of 100 columns was unveiled by Goebbels in Breslau on 23 June 1938.

The official consensus was that the system had successfully met the requirements of providing centralized announcements at any time, which in turn offered the possibility of 'capturing instantaneously and acoustically the whole population'.[59] It was important that this 'ever-ready' system could be installed in air-raid shelters, Party locales, factories and offices, as well as open public spaces, thus providing blanket coverage at a moment's notice. There is also a reference in the official report to evidence of how effective the system was at influencing public behaviour at big public events, such as the national gymnastic and sports festival held in Breslau that year.

New impetus was given to the project with the onset of war.[60] Some 6,600 columns were planned, half of which were to double as advertising columns; the others would be so-called 'Lautsprecher-Pilze' – loudspeaker mushrooms – that would not carry advertising. Albert Speer would be involved in their design. A division of labour was intended between the domestic and foreign news broadcast on radio and 'calming and enlightening instruction about the current situation' provided over the loudspeaker columns. The 'suggestive voice' of the speaker would give guidance to the population in the streets and public squares during air raids, and could continue to provide information in the shelters.[61] The benefits of the system for a totalitarian regime would, however, in principle extend to peace-time, and control of the system would remain squarely with the Party.

Despite widespread support for the plans, the full nationwide system of loudspeakers did not materialize. Nevertheless, the ideologues continued to maintain that even when listened to at home, radio was a *community* medium through and through. More than just an aggregate of atomized listeners, the radio produced *members* of a listening community, and trained them to think and feel as members of the larger *Volksgemeinschaft*. In the end, they accepted it did not matter *where* listeners tuned in, in public or in private, if they listened in their *souls*, providing those souls were of the right political and *racial* character.[62]

Although the various experiments in collective listening in public space sketched in this chapter were ultimately foiled by the pull of privatization, it has demonstrated that during a period riven by economic crisis and political fragmentation, when the definition of the new sound media was not quite settled, there were alternative configurations of the audience available, and the dominant model of the domesticated and disempowered listener was actively and widely contested, right across the political spectrum. Certainly, in the definitional years of both phonography and radio, there is a residual sense that public life takes place *in* public, and that the consequences of listening collectively can produce a new dynamic. What is particularly striking is the variety of ways in which audiences were regarded as active listening publics, not just as passive recipients of political and propagandistic messages. Of course, the histories play out differently in the various national contexts, and the German case reminds us that alternative public spheres are not necessarily nor straightforwardly sites for progressive cultural politics. Yet the lengths the Nazi regime went to in order to control not only the content but also the context of listening in both public and private is some indication that even the most dictatorial state struggles to fully domesticate the listening public.

Although the story of mediated listening across the long twentieth century has been dominated by people listening to both recorded and broadcast sound in private spaces or in privatized forms, there have always been, and continue to be, exceptions to the rule. In the digital age, the facility to share sounds online is characterized by two apparently contradictory trends – listening opportunities that are increasingly personalized but that are also networked in innovative ways. Listeners are able to represent their listening to their social networks and track others' online listening in real or archived time. On the one hand, this means that listening is a practice that is increasingly surveilled and increasingly open to measurement and commodification. On the other hand, it is also a sign of a persistent desire to create and partake in forms of collective listening to mediated music, sound and speech, albeit in virtual space. Perhaps resistance to the prevailing trends of personalization and privatization accounts for the growing trend for 'curated listening' events in public spaces, or even 'listening cinemas' where radio plays and other sonic works are listened to by an audience in the darkened comfort of a moviehouse or planetarium.[63] Listening together in a concentrated fashion in public space without visual stimulation remains so unusual an experience, despite more than a century of media sound, that it still appeals to experimental artists as a way to produce alternative experiences, unpredictable encounters and new ways of engaging in public culture. In an unconscious echo of earlier debates, the discipline of listening in public has been described as 'liberating' for demanding the kind of concentrated attention that is rare in an age of constant overlapping and overwhelming digital distraction, and for promising a listening experience that is 'intimate yet public, collective but anti-social' (Fisher 2009: n.p.).

While not forgetting that collective listening is common practice in our audiovisual culture, coming together *to listen* alone is likely to remain the exception rather than the rule. However, the variety and persistence of examples discussed in this chapter, together with the passion and great expectations with which the proponents of group listening have promoted the practice, suggests at the very least that we should reinsert the notion of a public or collective reception between the dominant terms of individual and mass reception when thinking about the politics and experience of listening in the media age.

Listening in the Public Sphere

8   The Public Sphere as Auditorium

'Listening' is a term that looms large in the language of everyday contemporary politics. Politicians, particularly when on the back foot, pledge to 'listen' to the people, and initiate 'listening projects' and 'big conversations'.[1] In an attempt to re-engage a disaffected electorate, the political classes are keen not to appear to be talking *at* the voters, but listening *to* them. This apparent embrace of a less hierarchical model of communication is a product of the slow but insistent expansion of more personalized forms of political discourse and expression over the long twentieth century (Coleman 2005: 275). Such initiatives are not the subject of this chapter as such, but are a clue to the role that listening has always played in public life, both as an embodied activity and as a metaphor for an interactive politics, despite its neglect in theorizations of the public sphere. In this chapter, theories of the public sphere will be revisited to draw attention to the political action of listening in and on the mediated public. The auditorium is offered as a convenient metaphor for the public sphere, a space in which the political is literally sounded out.

Public life was once lived out entirely in acoustic space. Civic participation in the public debates of ancient city republics was largely confined to the space within which citizens could be within earshot of other public speakers – the *auditorium*. Without the means for further amplification or dissemination, the physical constraints of audibility within a given space were a contributing factor to the political constraints on inclusivity (alongside cultural restrictions to do with gender and social status). In his 'natural history' of the information age, Paul Levinson (1997: 78) acknowledged the acoustic framing of the ancient democracies by coining the term 'acoustocracy'. The acoustic limits of public space were gradually overcome by the adoption of *representative* politics – representation being achieved through delegation on the one hand and symbolic mediation on the other. In his influential treatise on representative government, J.S. Mill (1867: 17) recognized that to surmount the acoustic obstacle to establishing a democratic polity beyond a local civic community, 'required the press, and even the newspaper press, the real equivalent, though not in all respects an adequate one, of the Pnyx and the Forum'. Mill did not elaborate on the inadequacies of the press in this passage – perhaps it was simply a comment on the shortcomings of contemporary journalism; but perhaps he was expressing a nostalgia for the small civic state that allowed for direct democracy with all its face-to-face participation, live debate and power of the spoken word, a nostalgia in other words for a polity in which participation was a matter of speaking and listening.

Mill, like democratic theorists before and since, certainly placed great faith in political discussion at every level, with Parliament as the institutional incarnation of a national 'conversation'. The press would stimulate, engage in and report on that conversation, not stand in for it, but in breaking down the spatial – and temporal – barriers of the auditorium it would involve a shift from a listening to a reading public. The press (together with other communications technologies like the roads and the railways) enabled the communication of ideas to travel more easily across time and space, and gave communities an expanded repertoire of recording the events of public life and extending their reach. In the process, the public was constituted as a collectivity in the moment of representation, in the moment when it was represented back to itself.

In the post-acoustocratic world, there *is* no public before or outside of representation. No longer do citizens appear before each other in shared acoustic space. It is precisely the *mediation* of the public sphere which makes possible the imagining of a collective subjectivity and which serves as a common frame of reference. The move from the ear to the eye in public affairs was, then, literally a *dislocation* – a dislocation from embodied physical space to the disembodied, abstracted and imagined community. The fact that this space, this public, is *imagined* does not make it any less *real*. But nor did the dominance of print and the politics of representation mean that the auditorium was entirely abandoned. This is not only because of the way writing stores sound, but because politics and public affairs remained in significant part a matter of spoken debate and discussion, albeit referenced to, suffused with, contextualized and recorded by the written text. The invention and application of technologies to record and reproduce sound and image gradually helped to loosen, or at least reconfigure, the hegemony of the printed word and heralded a series of transformations in the organization of sensory experience that have been explored in preceding chapters. Walter Ong famously called this the move to an era of secondary orality, although the formulation occludes the parallel development of secondary aurality. In fact, Ong (1982: 136) did recognize the listening relationship and, furthermore, stressed its *publicness*:

> This new orality has striking resemblances to the old in its participatory mystique, its fostering of a communal sense, its concentration on the present moment, and even its use of formulas. [. . .] Like primary orality, secondary orality has generated a strong group sense, for listening to spoken words

forms hearers into a group, a true audience, just as reading written or printed texts turns individuals in on themselves. But secondary orality generates a sense for groups immeasurably larger than those of primary oral culture – McLuhan's global village. Moreover, before writing, oral folk were group-minded because no feasible alternative had presented itself. In our age of secondary orality, we are groupminded self-consciously and programmatically. [. . .] We are turned outward because we have turned inward.

Here, although it is not stated explicitly, is a recognition of the political *action* of listening in and on the mediated public, and an indication of just how profound a change to politics, and to political subjectivity, would be enabled by the *re-sounding* of the public sphere.[2] In the shift from a reading to a listening public there is, in other words, a shift in emphasis from the individual to the plural, from the subjective to the intersubjective, from the local to the cosmopolitan. However, Ong follows his paean to the collective potential of listening in the age of secondary orality with a passage that laments the demise of stirring oratory and agonistic politics. For Ong, the transformation in the listening audience under the new technologized regime – distanced, absent and shaped by the discipline of the alphabeti-cized word – tamed and contained political speech, where any display of spontaneity is mere artifice.

If there was a lack of spontaneity, it was produced by the requirement for participants to reflect on the activity and context of listening at a dis-tance which produced new forms of speech. Practitioners of the new sonic media were faced with the challenge of translating the conventions of print media into auditory form. The absence of visual clues, the impossibility of interlocution with the speaker, and the heterogeneity and dispersal of the listening public meant that simply reading aloud from printed material designed for other purposes was soon found to be thoroughly unsatisfactory as a listening experience. The director of the first German news service, the Drahtloser Dienst, for example, warned that writing for listeners as if they were readers would be like 'trying to take a photograph with a violin'.[3] Lengthy guidelines were provided for contributors, reminding them to compose sentences, 'calculated for the ear', that were not 'paperly', but checked for 'listenability'.[4] The performance for the listener should disavow the scriptedness of the speech and aspire to the sound of spontaneity. As the *BBC Handbook* of 1929 (129–31) put it, 'We must all be unassumingly natural at the wireless tribunal.'

The very fact these apparently self-evident guidelines had to be set out in this way is just one indication of the radical shift in the practice of public journalism required by the reintroduction of sound into public discourse.

And it was more than just a superficial stylistic change. Over time, directives like these, worked out and refined by people struggling to define and place the new media, represented a far-reaching move in public speakers attuning to the conditions of reception. Moreover, the anonymity of radio listeners – in principle, anybody and everybody out there could be listening in – meant nothing could be taken for granted, and a mode of address had to be found which was accessible and meaningful to a *general* public, not like the striated and specialist reading publics that had become established in the silent world of print. In other words, here in the formative years of radio as a public medium is a key moment in which the institution and recognition of the *listening* public has profound consequences for the communicative practice of the public sphere.

Radio as a technological form seemed to pay scant regard to physical, political or social boundaries. Of course, the technology had been developed by vested commercial, military and political interests and, of course, access to both production and reception was hardly universal, but it was nevertheless marked by a distributive, or at times even a *redistributive*, ethic that equated citizenship with listenership, underscored by the medium of a common, spoken language that seemed to require no special skills in literacy. These attributes were cause for both celebration and alarm in different quarters – celebrated either as a truly modern democratic forum – a public good – or feared as a dangerous propagandistic tool. The different interpretations hung, ultimately, on whether listening could be countenanced as a political activity.

Take, for example, Horkheimer and Adorno's (1988: 129) contrasting of the telephone as a democratic medium with radio as an authoritarian one, which was based on radio's lack of the machinery of rejoinder. The telephone – by mid-century firmly established as a medium between two private individuals – is considered more democratic than radio – with its involvement of whole populations – because the mark of democratic participation is 'to speak' and not 'to listen'. Even those who celebrated the democratic potential of radio would do so in terms of it providing information to enable *subsequent* political participation, participation being measured by the act of speaking up. Listening itself is rarely considered participatory or as a political activity in its own right. This bifurcation of the public sphere into its 'informing role' and its 'conversational role' is something that can be traced back in debates about the press, where the 'passivity' of reading also struggled at times to be recognized as a political activity. But the reintroduction of listening into the public equation, associated as it was with *passive* reception, gave new succour to transmission models of media communication with their pessimistic assessments of a pliable and powerless audience.

Listening and Political Action

Yet for all its association with passivity, and despite its neglect in political theorizing, listening can, at some fundamental level, be construed as a pre-condition for political action. Though Hannah Arendt rarely discussed the subject of listening directly, her work offers valuable ways of thinking about the role of listening in political action. In *The Human Condition*, she contrasts the *vita activa* – the realm of human labour, work and (political) *action* – with the *vita contemplativa*, the realm of thought and contemplation, separate and free from material needs and desires. In the tradition of Aristotle, Augustine and Aquinas, Arendt agrees that the *vita contemplativa* requires peace and quiet, although she resists the classical privileging of the contemplative life *over* the active life, arguing that the concern that underlies the *vita activa* 'is not the same as and is neither superior nor inferior to the central concern of the *vita contemplativa*' (1958: 17). In the classical and Christian traditions, absolute quiet was required for the contemplation of Truth and the eternal, including the subordination and exclusion of all bodily movement, sensations and cravings of the flesh. Contemplation required isolation from the *noise* of the world, both literally and metaphorically. Philosophers and writers might still recognize this kind of withdrawal. In his recent philosophical treatise on listening, for example, Jean-Luc Nancy (2007: 1) suggests that the philosopher is someone 'who cannot listen, or who, more precisely, neutralizes listening within himself, so that he can philosophize'.

But if the contemplative life requires closing one's ears to the noise of the world, then it follows that the active life is one in which activity is defined by being open to listen to and engage with the world. Listening is at the heart of what it means to be *in* the world, to be active, to be political. Thinking in this way about listening as a political action in and of itself is strangely counterintuitive. Listening tends to be taken for granted, a natural mode of reception that is more passive than active, but listening is, I would argue, a critical category that ought to be right at the heart of any consideration of public life.

The distinction between the *vita contemplativa* and the *vita activa* in all their various incarnations always tends to rest on the distinction between 'quiet and unquiet' – the most decisive distinction for Aristotle, according to Arendt (1958: 15). In *The Inhuman Condition*, Keith Tester describes how this image of quiet and unquiet operates at two levels, the experiential and the situational. The *experience* of quietude includes the culturally conditioned choice to develop a contemplative (rational) subjectivity. The *situation* of quietude includes the environmental conditions that enable the contemplative life. Tester (1995: 84) argues that on both counts the simple distinction between quiet and unquiet is no longer tenable in the face of 'assaults which are directed towards the experience and the situation of quiet by the simultaneously literal and metaphorical un-quiet of contemporary social and cultural relationships'. In a world that has become *literally* noisier, it becomes both more difficult and less desirable to find the conditions of quiet for contemplative life. At some level, it is precisely the noisiness of the world that provides the incentive for the retreat into oneself, into the quiet life.

At the turn of the twentieth century, Simmel had identified the defensive strategies required by modern city dwellers for whom visual relations had displaced verbal exchange with neighbours, acquaintances and strangers. But, as discussed in chapter 4, even the retreat into the private or interior realm is more often achieved by a retreat into other forms of technologically conditioned sound as we drown out the noise – and the silence – with our music and media. Tester (1995: 101) argues that unquiet has become so much second nature that quiet seems 'too empty and too demanding' to provide an escape route. At a metaphorical level, the desire for 'the quiet life' as expressed in the prevailing 'culture of contentment', to use J.K. Galbraith's formulation, represents a retreat from political engagement, but one that is also always aware of the possible intrusion of 'unquiet' in the form of global economic, technological and environmental processes beyond the control of the individual consumer. For Tester, then,

> un-quiet becomes the source, place and avenue of engagement. [. . .] A sense of unquiet becomes the basis of an ability to do something other than quietly accept the benefits one gains from the culture of contentment. A sense of un-quiet might be able to transcend situational quiet and the emotional withdrawal from the world which noise precipitates (Tester 1995: 105–6).

Susan Bickford (1996) has also turned to Arendt in her groundbreaking interrogation of the political practice of listening. For Bickford, Arendt's version of agonistic, pluralist politics allows a way of theorizing political listening in conditions of acute 'unquiet' – that is to say, in conditions of conflict and inequality. In the rare instances where political theorists have registered listening as part of the political process, it has tended to be in terms of an empathetic listening, a listening out for things in common, for the things that unite. Bickford credits Benjamin Barber with being the first theorist to take listening seriously as a political practice, but finds his focus on listening as a 'mutualistic art that by its very practice enhances equality' presupposes a degree of consensus that is by definition not extant in situations of conflict and difference (in Bickford 1996: 13). For the same reason, Bickford finds Habermas' understanding of communicative action wanting, inasmuch as it requires all participants to be oriented to 'achieving, sustaining and renewing consensus' (Bickford 1996: 17). *Political listening* is proposed as a corrective to the conformative limitations of consensus-based politics:

> Such listening does not require the purification of motives or abstracting from our identity, nor does it involve empathy for one another or a strong sense of community. It is a constitutive element in the process of figuring out, in the face of conflict, what to do. Listening – as part of a conception of adversarial communication – is a crucial political activity that enables us to give democratic shape to our being together in the world (Bickford 1996: 18–19).

Listening, then, constitutes a kind of *attention* to others (and otherness) and, importantly, *being attended to* that is the prerequisite both of citizenship (as distinct from community) and of communicative action. Politics itself is made possible only by this listening attention to one another. A political argument is made in order to persuade those listening to it. The speaker must therefore attend to those listening, just as the listeners attend to those speaking. Without such attention to the listener, democratic communication withers away.

We normally think about agency in the public sphere as speaking up, or as finding a voice; in other words, to be listened to, rather than to listen. And it goes 'without saying' that one of the central tenets of modern democratic theory is the freedom of speech; and yet what really goes unsaid is that speech requires a listener. What is actually at stake here is the freedom of *shared* speech or, to put it another way, the freedom to be heard. But this formulation still puts the speaker centre stage; it is still formulated as the politics of *voice*. The presence of a listening public is simply assumed, and no special freedoms or protections are afforded to the act of listening. But inasmuch as there is a mutual responsibility (or *response-ability*) in any communicative exchange between speaker and listener, the question arises whether there is not also another freedom implicit in the proper functioning of democracy, the freedom of *listening*. There is an ethical dimension to this question which will be pursued in the following chapter. For now, it is enough to recognize that the privileging of speech over listening in political theory can be challenged on logical, philosophical and ethical grounds.

To start simply – without a listener, speech is nothing but noise in the ether. More to the point, without a listener there would be no reason, no *calling*, to speak. And if the speaker is not also at turns a listener, only a perverted version of communication remains. Bakhtin (1986: 68) argued that in fact the distinction between speaker and listener is only sustainable in the abstract as a 'scientific fiction', and only if the critical perspective is skewed to the speaker's point of view. If listening is properly understood as an active, responsive attitude rather than a passive, receptive one, then it would follow that, 'any understanding is imbued with response and necessarily elicits it in one form or another: the listener becomes the speaker'. Bakhtin is not just referring to the notion of turn-taking here, but is suggesting a much more radical rejection of the dichotomy speaker/listener. Speaking and listening are rather interchangeable elements in the communicative process, a process in which the silence of the listener also speaks (because it always already speaks) and is heard, and in which the speaker is also always already a respondent because 'he is not, after all, the first speaker, the one who disturbs the eternal silence of the universe' (Bakhtin 1986: 69). The listener's response may not be verbally articulated, and may not follow immediately, but this does not diminish the fact that 'all real and integral understanding is actively responsive, and constitutes nothing other than the initial preparatory stage of a response (in whatever form it may be actualized).' Listening, as Alice Rayner (1993: 20) has put it, 'is not simply auditory; it is a framing of the speech'.

This more expansive understanding of the responsiveness of listening is a hugely important insight in relation to mediated listening that is so often dismissed as passive because of the absence of immediate response in kind. Listening seems passive only from a perspective that demands a rather straitjacketed version of reciprocity, where a listener has the opportunity to become a speaker whose voice will carry equally far and resonate in just the same space, and without any delay or distortion. But this is a perspective that presupposes an ideal speech situation, to borrow a phrase, in which participants to a dialogue have equal status and power, and are already in agreement about the rules of engagement and turn-taking.

In fact, it is apposite to think of speech as *resonating* with the listener. Resonance is a property of acoustic space that is a form of causality, but not the linear causality associated with visual culture. Resonance is therefore about responsiveness, but it need not be responsiveness in kind, nor need it be immediate. A speech can resonate with a listener without the listener responding in speech. Moreover, resonance can also generate a great deal of acoustic energy from a small sound event so, to continue the analogy, the speech act is effective to the extent that it resonates with those listening who may well, in the age of mediated listening, number in their millions. Listening also shapes the speech that is listened to since a speaker is 'actively oriented precisely toward such an actively responsive understanding' and 'does not expect passive understanding that, so to speak, only duplicates his own in someone else's mind. Rather, he expects response, agreement, sympathy, objection, execution, and so forth' (Bakhtin 1986: 69). It is notable here that listening stands in for all understanding (Bakhtin suggests the same relations broadly pertain between written and read speech). It is the listening relation that provides the template for human communication and understanding *tout court*. Listening is, after all, 'how we get into language in the first place' (Scannell 1996: 165).[5]

Although the figure of the listener is a shadowy one in political theory, it is necessarily implicit in the idea of freedom of speech, inasmuch as the listener is the Other of the speaker. In *On Liberty*, J.S. Mill (1859: 39) recognized opinions expressed in public discourse were only reliable inasmuch as they were the product of listening to counter-arguments:

> any person whose judgment is really deserving of confidence [. . .] has kept his mind *open* to criticism on his opinions and conduct. Because it has been his practice to *listen* to all that could be said against him (my italics).

In his critical discussion of Mill's 'stoic notion of the listening citizen', J.D. Peters (2005: 130–2) describes the difficult and disciplined civic duty of listening to – and listening out for – opinions that contradict, challenge, test one's own opinion, the better to hone opinions into reasons and arguments, although this exposes an unresolved contradiction in Mill's schema which finds that citizens 'are supposed to listen with ice and speak with fire' – in other words, to listen dispassionately but to speak with conviction. But there is another way of conceiving listening in political terms that is not only reactive in these binary terms. In terms reminiscent of Bakhtin's, Amit Pinchevski (2001: 79) puts it as follows:

> freedom of speech, to paraphrase Levinas, is a difficult freedom; a freedom realized only in relation to what resides outside the active speaker who is always already situated within a context of alterity which is calling, imploring a response. Responsibility comes before freedom: it presides even if one does not recognize its authority or if one does not know how to respond. The

practice of the freedom of speech – along with its politics, rights and regulations – emerges out of this responsibility, or rather from the split, or the
différance, of responsibility and free speech.

The right to free speech, then, is intimately bound up with the responsibility to listen, a responsibility that is *shared* between the speaker and the
listener. Indeed, politics itself could be described at its most basic level as
the dynamic *between* the act of speech and the act of listening (Bickford
1996: 4). The speech act alone is static; only the presence of an active listener introduces the dynamic, introduces the element of intersubjectivity.
For Arendt, this 'in-between', this sense of relatedness and difference, is
both the precondition and the motivation for communication and for
politics. Communication is only possible because of the similarities we share
in the human condition, and only necessary because of the inevitable differences and space between us. But what happens when the speaker and
the listener are not face-to-face but at a distance, not live but recorded, not
two private individuals but any number of participants, anytime, anywhere?
In other words, how are we to think through the freedom of listening in
the modern age of mediated communication?

For Arendt, it is precisely the world of things we share in common – the
public world – that relates and separates us. She famously used the metaphor of a table that we sit at to come together in discussion, to speak and
to listen, but that the public world itself is a thing in the world that sits
between us (Arendt 1958: 52). In the next sentence, though, she laments
the way in which mass society has 'lost its power to gather [people] together,
to relate and to separate them [. . .] people gathered around a table might
suddenly, through some magic trick, see the table vanish from their midst,
so that two persons sitting opposite each other were no longer separated
but also would be entirely unrelated to each other by anything tangible'. It
is hard not to read into this account a dismissal of the modern media of
mass communication as a means to real *communion*. In this pessimistic
reading of mass society, Arendt had much in common with other critics
of her time; but as Silverstone (2006: 36, 84) has most persuasively argued,
it is simply not realistic to dismiss the media or the way in which the
mediated world has become, or has at least the potential to become, in
effect the 'table' at which we sit. In the modern, globalized world, the
media provide a 'space of appearance', a public world that we share in
common, relating and separating us and where the 'proper distance' required
of a moral view of communication has to be nurtured and maintained –
not only by those who speak in the mediapolis, but also by those who
listen.

Of course these questions are at one level just another spin on the familiar and fundamental questions of any study of media communication, which raises the question of why, if it is really so central to the question of communication, has listening been so long neglected in political and communication theory? There seem to be three main reasons: the problem of property, the problem of dialogue, and the problem of consensus-building.

Listening and the problem of property

The modern public sphere emerged out of the historical confluence of the rise of print culture, capitalism, nationalism and the Enlightenment. The public that formed in the crucible of these forces was constituted, significantly, as a *reading* public, a situation that seemed to privilege the eye over the ear. But the neglect of listening as a political act also has to do with the freedom of speech being caught up in the idea of the liberty of the individual, where individual expression is treated like a *property*, to be defended and protected insofar as and as long as the rights of others are not violated in the process. The speech act as 'self-expression' was conceived as a product to be circulated and exchanged in the free marketplace of ideas. The act of listening could not be conceptualized in this way, could not *belong* to an individual subject. The act of listening is more difficult to observe, to measure, to record, to reproduce. Whereas the visual subject of Cartesian perspectivalism is fixed in space, inhabiting and *in possession of* a singular point of view, a subjectivity extended to the reading subject, the listening subject inhabits 'a more fluid, mobile and voluminous conception of space' (Connor 1997: 207) that evades appropriation.[6] The defence of the freedom of speech as a property right could not, then, be extended to embrace the freedom of listening or the freedom of *communication* more broadly. The freedom of speech is concerned with the communicative context only insofar as that individual right to self-expression is guaranteed. The freedom of listening, by contrast, inheres in the space *between* individuals, and is concerned precisely with guaranteeing the context within which freedom of expression can operate as communication.

The way this individual right was extended to the press and other media has been critiqued by Onora O'Neill. The freedom of expression, unconstrained as it is by requirements to truth, accuracy, civility or transparency, is a foundational but 'innocuous' freedom at an individual level; but its translation to an institutional level has been problematic, 'because it marginalizes communication, and because it dismisses any requirement to attempt effective, accurate or ethically acceptable communication' (2009: 169–70). The shift from a reading to a listening public involves a shift in thinking about a public as a collective of sovereign individuals to a public constituted intersubjectively. It is a shift that then does require institutional speech to attempt to communicate effectively, accurately or ethically. This is echoed in the shift from a substantive to a discursive concept of rationality in Habermas' work that represented 'a move away from the epistemology of the subject towards a view of the irreducibility of intersubjectivity' (Dahlgren 1995: 100).

Listening and the problem of dialogue

The next problem to acknowledge in the elision of listening from the field of political and communication theory is that a dialogic model of communication has been sutured onto print and mediated culture and into dominant political (democratic) theory. The fit is not always an easy one, and not only for reasons of scale. The dialogue (or conversation) is returned to again and again in political and communication theory of all colours on the basis of its status as a universal and primary form of human communication. It is even there in arguments for the restoration of listening in political communication (Penman and Turnbull 2012). It is a form of communication that is predicated on a face-to-face interaction and is assumed to connote all sorts of positive qualities: sincerity, spontaneity, reciprocity, egalitarianism, complexity, warmth, reason. It is held up as a *personable* form of communication in contrast to mediated communication. But this is already an idealized version of what a dialogue can be. Face-to-face encounters can equally be one-sided, insincere, awkward, artificial, stereotypical, cold or just at crossed purposes. In other words, even dialogue in embodied and unmediated practice does not necessarily live up to the dialogic ideal. As Zygmunt Bauman (2000: 10) puts it, 'ambivalence resides at the heart of the "primary scene" of the face-to-face'. The distinction is further blurred by the pervasive 'conversationalism' (Schudson 1978, 1997) of a whole spectrum of media and other public forms, from the intimate address of broadcasting to representations of social participation, to the increasing use of vernacular and intimate language in everything from advertising copy to political speeches (thanks to the realization that audiences are paradoxically maximized by a personalized address).

At the same time, face-to-face talk has arguably been re-ordered by the communicative characteristics of 'modern speech machines' with their 'uncertainties of address, delays of response, and dubious delivery' (Peters

2006: 121). In other words, the less than ideal experience of living in a mediated world itself stimulates a nostalgic fantasy of a golden age of unmediated and effortless interaction, and a longing for 'presence'. This in turn is a sublimation of a longing for things like trust, authenticity, reliability, reciprocity, equality and accountability – things that have widely been seen as under threat in modern conditions of mediation – or rather, nostalgically re-imagined in the media age. As Peters (1999: 141) puts it, only in an age of phantasmatic representation could there be any currency in the phrase 'appearing in person'. This same nostalgia for presence and 'the real' shaped the discourses of sound fidelity as was described in an earlier chapter, and this trust in the mediated to appear real and unmediated is key to the power and the possibility of the mediated public sphere. It also can be seen as having shaped the development of audience research, with interviewers being sent out to meet and converse with the otherwise unknowable public 'in the flesh'.[7] And the trace of this faith in the presence of the audience through forms of dialogic interaction remains in the hyperbole surrounding interactive broadcast genres and social networking sites.

The face-to-face ideal underpins theories of community as much as theories of communication. Iris Marion Young (1986/1995: 246) listed a series of objections to this nostalgia for dialogic communication in an influential essay critiquing the idea of community, so often evoked as a remedy for the ills of modern society:

> It presumes an illusory ideal of unmediated social relations, and wrongly identifies mediation with alienation. It denies difference in the sense of time and space distancing. It implies a model of the good society as consisting of decentralized small units which is both unrealistic and politically undesirable. And finally, it avoids the political question of the relation among the decentralized communities.

For all its shortcomings, though, the dialogic ideal has remained a powerful trope in political philosophy and media studies. Normative democratic theory is full of references to the forum, the coffee house, the town hall meeting, and so on, with all their dialogic connotations of assembly, participation and interaction that are simply out of kilter with the scale and organization of modern states. And these references persist despite the widespread recognition that the modern bourgeois public sphere was, from the beginning, 'international in scope and constituted as a textual artefact' (Peters 1997: 9), and despite the fact that a public must *by definition* be a relation among strangers. As Warner (2002: 58) explains, a public unites people by their participation in the discourse that constitutes them as a public, not by any pre-given or positive sense of collective identity (like nations, religions or unions, etc.). A public is constituted precisely in its *impersonal and indefinite* address – in other words, a mode of address diametrically opposed to that of the face-to-face encounter.

A dialogue implies, by convention if not strictly by definition,[8] two interlocutors. The term tends to conjure an image of two speakers rather than a speaker and a listener or two speaker-listeners. The image of two listeners would be ridiculous in a way that the image of two speakers could never be. And yet *public* speech only exceptionally takes the form of a dialogue between two interlocutors. The speaker, even in the public auditoria of ancient city states, would speak to *many* listeners – all of whom had, crucially, the *potential* to speak back, but who in practice must have been more often and more continuously in the position of listener, listening not only to the present speaker, but also listening to the other silent listeners, in the sense of bearing a responsibility to the potentiality of those listeners to break their silence by speaking. In this Bakhtinian sense, even the speaker does not give up the responsibility to listen in the act of speaking. These listeners *actively* constitute the public, they are not mere bystanders. They are not members of a public by virtue of their mere presence or by virtue of their 'identity'. They are members of a public by virtue of the act of listening, by the active decision to participate in the discursive address. A public is contingent on there being people willing to actively take up that address, to listen. The agency of a public, which is an imaginary association with no institutional form or formal power, rests on this active will to be addressed, this active mode of attention (Warner 2002: 61).

A dialogic model of public speaking is hardly adequate, then, even in apparently ideal conditions of co-presence (where participants are not only physically together in the same auditorium, but share a common culture and values and, in terms of a debate, share in a situation of common purpose and practice). Indeed, holding dialogue up as the measure of public speech inevitably leads to the denigration of those participants in the process who listen more than speak, or those who never speak. From a dialogic perspective, a speech that is not reciprocated *in speech* can only be deemed a monologue. And if that monologue is addressed to a multitude of silent listeners, it is but a short step then to deem it propaganda.

Acknowledging the active, responsive attitude of the listener offers a different approach that does not restrict reciprocal public speech to the dialogic form, and therefore is better able to accommodate forms of communication, mediated or otherwise, between two *or more* participants.[9]

This is important when we consider the obvious but easily forgotten fact that it is possible for more than one listener, indeed a whole multitude of listeners, to listen to a single speaker, whereas more than one (uncoordinated) voice speaking at the same time becomes hard to decipher, becomes babble. The dialogic model, however, in seeking a balance between the 'two sides', tends to suppose that the multitude of listeners would listen as one, and that the one has been stripped of its voice and its potential to reciprocate. Here is the root of the distrust in 'mass' communication as dissemination, indeed as representation – and it rests in the failure to recognize the activity and responsiveness of the listener, and on an instrumentalized understanding of reciprocity.

In an influential article critiquing conversational ideals in democratic theory, Michael Schudson (1997) also took issue with the widespread idea – expressed most forcibly by John Dewey – that the *spontaneity* of conversation produces a more authentic form of political communication (Evans 2001). On the contrary, Schudson reminds us, democratic communication is contrived, rule-governed and essentially *civil* – after all, conversations are not exclusive to democratic societies, and nor can democracy be said therefore to derive from conversation. Conversationalism is idealized as an exchange between equals, but public conversations cannot and should not assume equality of status or cultural capital between participants. This is another useful reminder of the possibility that a focus on listening alongside speaking allows for a space for openness to other views and time for reflection and measured judgement rather than the unreflective, immediate response valorized in 'authentic' interpersonal dialogue.

In this regard, it is fitting to consider the way in which Arendt (1986: 106–7) invokes the figure of 'the mask' in political communication (Bickford 1996: 101–2; Moruzzi 2000). Although the mask is often conceived of as a visual metaphor (as in theories of the masquerade), the Latin word for mask, '*persona*', reveals it to be a device that lets 'sound through' – *per sona*. Originally used by actors on the Greek stage to disguise their own features while allowing their voices to resound in the auditorium, Arendt suggests the mask is a suitable metaphor for the way individual attributes and distinctions are masked by political and legal devices that give an individual a political or public 'persona' that legitimates their participation in public affairs as equals. The mask does not deprive individuals of their distinctiveness, but directs attention to that which connects and equalizes them, while acknowledging that the distinctive individual perspective will 'sound through'. This performative idea of 'persona' seems to be a more mutable, contingent and creative term than the term 'identity' as commonly deployed. Indeed, Arendt was keenly aware of the limitations and dangers of the conservative essentialism that underpins much identity politics, and saw the public mask as a tool of free political agency, a device that recognizes the proper artifice of the public realm. The mask is deployed precisely to direct attention away from 'what' we are, to 'who' we are, as revealed through performative speech and action. The idea of 'persona' occupies a space somewhere between the twin extremes of 'identity' and 'otherness' that are the common currency of mediated representations.

It might be countered that the concept of the active responsive listener has also been derived from a dialogic model of communication, albeit a model that does not *a priori* privilege the speaker over the listener. But the use of the singular here is misleading. Even with just one additional participant to the 'dialogue', we are likely to find two listeners to one speaker at any one moment, if there is not to be communication breakdown.[10] The listener can be, indeed arguably most often is, part of a collectivity. The experience of listening is, both potentially and very often in practice, an experience of plurality. The experience of speaking, in the moment of speaking, is, in contrast, an experience of singularity. This is especially evident if we consider how the media pluralize the audience not only in terms of multiplying the potential number of listeners, but also in terms of dispersing them across space and time. The listening public of any particular instance of recorded expression can in principle be almost infinitely expanded across continents and across the generations. It can even be expanded to include the 'speaker', listening back to a recording of their own speech. Moreover, a 'public' is rarely constituted in relation to a single text (although a single text can address a public). Rather a public is constituted in the *reflexive circulation* of discourse, a 'concatenation of texts through time' (Warner 2002: 62).

Listening and the problem of consensus

Such a radical dispersion could be seen as being detrimental from the point of view of conventional notions of a 'public' that rest on ideas of consensus and consensus-building. However, if we follow Arendt, and recognize that plurality, rather than consensus, is not only a pre-condition for politics, but its *achievement*, then this radical dispersion of the audience is cast in a more positive light. Consensus, after all, can too easily slide into conformity, or be (ab)used to universalize particular interests. Harmony, in the end, is only achieved by the exclusion of discordant tones.

This reference to harmony suggests it is worth pausing for a moment to consider the prevalence of musical metaphors in political discourse

– evidence perhaps of the sublimation of the idea of listening in political theory. Nancy S. Love (2002, 2006) has traced the use of musical metaphors in democratic political theory, and has argued that the three dominant perspectives – aggregative, deliberative and agonistic democracy – use musical, vocal and sonic metaphors in significantly different ways.[11] Aggregative politics, the system most prevalent in contemporary Western states, are concerned with soliciting and representing the aggregate view of the populace (defined in terms of their competing self-interests rather than reasoned justifications) via a system of competitive elections and the institutionalization of power. Visual metaphors dominate in the descriptions of such systems, with talk of 'perspectives', 'viewpoints', 'symmetry' and 'mirroring'. The 'voice' of the people is understood primarily in terms of the vote. The 'voice' of the people in 'deliberative' models is understood in terms of 'speech' and 'argument', albeit often a narrowly defined version of rational argument that belies its origins in Enlightenment thought and the age of print. Proponents of agonistic democracy, meanwhile, tend to embrace a much less restrictive interpretation of 'voice', specifically including all forms of embodied or paralinguistic vocal communication, not least applications of the voice that register particularity, emotion and passion. Iris Young (1997: 65; 2000), for example, writes of 'communicative democracy' where all forms of communicative interaction are valorized, where people try to 'reach understanding'. Habermas, too, in his elaborations on deliberative democracy, recognized the role these aspects of vocality play in the 'sounding board' of civil society, but argued these sounds produce only a cacophony until translated into a literate, public 'text' (1996: 344, 367). In contrast, theorists of agonistic democracy regard these aspects not as something to be contained or translated, but as constituent and necessary expressions of political communication. At this end of the theoretical spectrum, musical metaphors become more prevalent. The musical form of the counterpoint, for example, has been particularly influential in feminist and post-colonialist critiques. Musically, counterpoint refers to a kind of melodic interaction that involves two or more distinct musical lines, themes or 'voices' that are independent in contour and rhythm, but interdependent in harmony. Counterpoint offers 'a way to listen to many voices, as themes and variations on themes, and to correct for not listening to particular themes' (Gilligan et al. 1990, in Love 2002: 68).

Roger Silverstone (2006: 85–90) also took up the notion of the contrapuntal from Edward Said in his study of the 'mediapolis'; it is a notion that recognizes there is a dialectical tension between different 'voices' – dominant and subordinate, present and absent, constant and shifting. In the contrapuntal, the individual elements are meaningful only in their relation to each other, and that relation is constantly shifting. A dominant voice or theme might subside or disappear altogether, although still shaping the whole by its absence. The interplay of different voices might work to create consonance or dissonance, as interpreted in the act of listening. But the act of listening is also constantly in flux. Edmund Husserl reflected on how listening to music requires the listener to manage overlapping perceptions – of the sound in the present (as each sound exists only in the present), of the retained impression of the preceding sounds and of the leaning towards the sound to come. What this suggests, as Jean-Luc Nancy (2007: 18) summarizes, is that listening takes place in a present that 'is not instantaneous, but differential in itself' with melody becoming, therefore, 'the matrix of a thought of unity *of and in* diversity [. . .] as much as of a diversity or divergence *of and in* unity'. Extended to the apprehension of other mediated sound, this would mean that the act of listening is not straightforwardly determined by any particular media text in the moment of its apprehension, but is part of an active contextualizing and framing on the part of the listener.

The figure of the listener is crucial in the translation of the contrapuntal from the musical to the sociological and political realm, where the focus is not on a single unified artistic composition, but the agonistic polyphony, or even cacophony, of the political and cultural scene. Listening, then, becomes an active way of engaging analytically and politically with the plurality of the world. Iain Chambers (1996: 51), for example, has proposed listening as a model for understanding the post-colonial world that both resisted the hegemonic visual models of the past and allowed new voices and new perspectives to emerge:

> In the dispersal of a single History, whose omniscient word legislates the world, I begin to hear composite voices crossing and disturbing the path and patterns of the once seemingly ineluctable onrush of 'progress'. In the movement from concentrated sight to dispersed sound, from the 'neutral' gaze to the interference of hearing, from the discriminating eye to the incidental ear, I abandon a fixed (ad)vantage for a mobile and exposed politics of listening – for a 'truth' that is always becoming.

This reference to a 'truth' that is always becoming is an important aspect of the listening, pluralist perspective that is both its condition and its achievement. The 'truth' of living in the world must be a polyphonic truth, a truth that is capable of accommodating a plurality of potentially discordant voices. This politics of recognition (Taylor 1992; Fraser and Honneth

2003) is in many ways a politics of voice, but it is also a politics of listening, a politics of 're-cognition' – listening out for and listening in to voices in order to hear what they are saying, in the sense of understanding, but also in the sense of 're-thinking' one's own position in relation to what is heard.

It is worth repeating that this condition of listening as plurality is a feature of the non-mediated public sphere, not just something that comes into play in the era of mediated sound. Lewis Hyde (2008), for example, has written about the lecture hall of the Philadelphia Academy, that Benjamin Franklin had had constructed in 1739, as a space that would welcome the preachers of any and all religions and be open to all the people of the city, pledging that 'even if the Mufti of Constantinople were to send a Missionary to preach Mahometanism to us, he would find a Pulpit at his Service'. The hall represented an open, uncensored space in which all and any could be heard – a democratic experiment in agonistic pluralism and the 'freedom of listening'.

Plurality as a democratic virtue is normally conceived of in terms of a plurality of voices guaranteed by the freedom of speech. But plurality also has to be guaranteed by the freedom of listening. This is more than just a question of simply being heard. Hearing is not yet listening. It is in listening that an active, responsive attitude inheres. Plurality is guaranteed by the freedom of listening because an individual experiences, or *inhabits* plurality in the act of listening more than in the act of speaking. It is only in listening, indeed, that we can apprehend and acknowledge the plurality of voices. If the public sphere is an auditorium where the freedom of speech is exercised, then it is the members of the listening audience who become the 'auditors' of public exchanges and performances.[12] The listeners, in other words, hold the responsibility not to close their ears to expressions of opinions with which they might not agree, and, by extension, to ensure that the whole spectrum of opinion gets to be heard. Media plurality is not, in fact, guaranteed by the freedom of speech, or at least not by freedom of speech alone, for those who speak might all speak with the same voice, either through choice, coercion or the conditions of the marketplace. It is in the freedom of listening that limitations on plurality are registered, whether that be the dominance of certain voices or the absence, marginalization and censorship of others. Even silence may register in the politics of listening as a marker of agency, a political strategy *not* to engage in a particular incarnation of the public sphere.

It is worth recalling the discussion about collective listening in public spaces from the previous chapter in this regard, where one of the great benefits of coming together to listen was the hope of nurturing an openness to different voices. Frank Ernest Hill, one of the leading advocates of group listening, summed up their importance in terms that echo the hopes of the Philadelphia Academy:

> They serve society as a whole. They promote leadership, they make for a better informed electorate, they encourage the habit of discussion upon which a democracy must rest, and they break down the prejudice and increase tolerance. Moreover, they already do these things on a greater scale, in proportion to the effort expended, than any non-radio agencies can hope to do them; and they hold the possibility of exerting much more power than they have already manifested (in Waller 1946: 345).

Similarly, radio reformers in America during the 1930s had advocated the listener's *right* to hear a diversity of voices on the air (Toro 2000: 14; Fones-Wolf 2006). These various examples all circle around the idea of offering a hearing without prejudice, a listening of toleration and openness. This sort of listening involves a certain risk and vulnerability, but it is not a question of listeners simply giving themselves over passively and self-sacrificially to the speaker.[13] Just as a speaker draws on a shared cultural tradition of language and thought in producing an utterance (much of which will have been encountered as a listener, of course), so does the listener bring with them their own horizon of understanding, a horizon that is itself always shifting according to context and circumstance. Gadamer's hermeneutics of reading can be adapted to the listening situation – listening as interpretation is the collision of the world of the speaker and the world of the listener. As the listener enters the world of the speaker, that world is transformed by the act of listening. The collision makes for 'lived experience' (Abulad 2007: 18). The listening subject is also transformed in and through practices of listening; in Foucauldian terms, listening is a 'technology of the self', a 'moment of silence that makes possible the constitution of the self' (Beard 2009: 11; Levin 1989: 119). Moreover, the perception of difference in perspective between the listener and that which is listened to opens up in principle and in practice an awareness of plurality.

Falling silent in order to listen is not, then, an act of passivity, nor an act of submission, but is an active part of the communication process. Listening to another is not simply to put oneself in the place of the speaker, or to abandon one's sense of self, as is often proposed (Levin 1989: 224–5; Corradi Fiumara 1990: 73). Moreover, listening to another is not necessarily to silence one's inner voice in order to hear the external world, but to modify and switch the focus from one to the other. Speaker and listener are mutually interdependent, but it is the *openness* of the listening position – on either side – which produces the space in and across which communication can take place. This openness represents:

> a willingness to construct certain relations of attention, relations in which neither of us has meaning without the other. This kind of listening and speaking together engages both agency and situatedness: I cannot hear you except against the ground of who I am, and you are speaking, not in the abstract, but to me – to who you think your listeners are (Bickford 1996: 147).

The situatedness of the embodied listener is important. Since listeners cannot entirely abandon listening from their own perspective, and must recognize that the perspective of the other is doubly filtered (through the speaker's perspective and their own as listener), the act of listening opens up a space for intersubjectivity. There is a certain courage required in this political listening, the courage to be open to the opinions of others, neither refusing to listen, nor simply identifying uncritically and selflessly with the position of the speaker.[14] It takes courage because it entails the possibility of one's sense of self being challenged or changed in the process of the encounter. It requires an attitude, as Bickford (1996: 168) puts it, 'somewhere between sheer defiance and sheer docility'. Listening in this way forms the bedrock of a democratic practice.

The Freedom of Listening

Freedom of listening, then, is a normative ideal that encompasses both a responsibility and a right to listen. It is to be understood, therefore, as distinct from the freedom *to* listen. The freedom of listening is a 'first order' right based on the principle of liberty that is distinct from the freedom *to* listen, a 'second order' right based on the principle of equality. The freedom to listen, understood in terms of a right of access to and partipation in public debate, is of course integral to any practical definition of democracy, inasmuch as the channels of public communication ought to be accessible to all members of the public. Accessibility is measured in terms of economic, social and cultural capital. It is a matter of having access to the media of communication through either private or collective ownership, having the requisite skills in media literacy (or media *audition*, perhaps), and also having an invitation or inclination to participate – the sense of having a legitimate part to play in the communicative exchange. The freedom *to* listen, then, is as much a material condition of the freedom of listening as it is a constituent part of the normative ideal. However, when the freedom to listen is understood only as a right and not also as a responsibility, it is a poorer guarantor of plurality, for listeners might decide to exercise their right to listen only to those speakers whose opinions resonate with their own. This constitutes a refusal to listen, itself a powerful exercise of power and censorship.

If the freedom of listening is a normative ideal that, while rarely acknowledged in these terms, underpins the freedom of speech and is identifiable in unmediated forums of democratic communication, it is arguable that it became an increasingly urgent freedom in the era of mass and mediated communication, when access to the dominant public forums of debate (as 'speakers') became increasingly restricted, both by the technologically transformed *scale* and specialization of the forum, and by the vagaries of the marketplace which tends to concentrate ownership and favour conformity. The potential of listening as a political and profoundly democratic activity opens up new ways of understanding and assessing non-dialogic, non-interactive forms of mediation – still the dominant media mode. If the public sphere is to be understood as a space in which a plurality of voices can be heard, then those voices must be able to express themselves in a plurality of ways, not just in the image of a dialogue. There must, clearly, be a place for performance, for lectures, for presentations.[15] The freedom of expression is not confined to a dialogic mode, but it does presuppose an audience, and, implicitly, an audience with active choices and with active responsibilities.

Even the contemporary proliferation of outlets, the rise of 'user-generated content' and new modes of interactivity have not diminished the relevance of the freedom of listening. It is there, for example, in contemporary debates about the digital divide and net neutrality and the fragmentation of the public into self-selecting identity and interest groups (Dahlberg 2007; Welton 2002: 201). It is also a possible response to the 'fantasy of abundance' in political networked communication in capitalist democracies that Jodi Dean has critiqued. Her argument is that the proliferation of voices circulate as 'contributions' rather than as 'messages' and that there 'is a significant disconnect between politics circulating as content and official politics' (Dean 2005: 53).[16] Public discourse, she argues, has taken on the characteristics of economic rather than communicative exchange. In other words, participation in the public sphere has been reduced to performance without an audience, a display and experience of activity that disavows a lack of real political agency, and certainly a performance that need not be listened to by those in power. The implication is that without a public that is listening, the communicative act of speaking up in the auditorium of the public sphere is turned in on itself and ironically – and dangerously – rendered 'passive'. The ethical responsibilities that this implies for the listening public are the subject of the final chapter.

9   Media and the Ethics of Listening

There has been something of an 'ethical turn' in media studies in recent years. New questions have been posed by changes in the media ecology – the increasing global reach of more forms of mediated communication and the growing number of people enaged in the *production* of media content. Usually media ethics asks how to guide and evaluate these new conditions of production – questions about representation, distribution and address. For many critics, to *act* in the media ecology is to engage in media production. But the practices of reception – reading, viewing and listening – cannot easily be separated out from the content that is produced. They have to be thought of *in relation* – and not just after the fact, but as a constitutive part of the making and meaning of that content. They have to be considered as part of the dialectic at the heart of any communication process, between response and responsibility. Moreover, they cannot only be thought of as the activities of isolated individuals, but also, and arguably more urgently, as collective activities that render them, by definition, *public* – with all the ethical responsibilities that implies.

This focus on the ethics of production to the neglect of the ethics of reception has a very long history (Christians 2000). But this blindspot in contemporary media studies is all the more remarkable given how prominent a topic it was in the early days of radio. It is well known, for example, that broadcasting in Britain under the direction of John Reith was as much as anything else a *moral* crusade. This missionary zeal rested on a faith in a shared and unquestioned moral understanding, and a determination that the technical miracle that was radio deserved to be used for the greater good. To have used it 'merely' for entertainment and distraction would have been 'a prostitution of its powers' and an underestimation of the potential of the listeners who made up its public (Reith 1949: 108). The decision to organize broadcasting as a service to the public was therefore taken on ethical as well as political grounds (Scannell 2004: 100). The ethic here is a *distributive* (or even re-distributive) one that characterized much wider discussions about public service and the welfare state (Scannell 1989; Currid 2006: 41). It is an ethic that puts *accessibility* at the centre, recognizing that participation (in health care, education and so on, as well as democratic culture) is dependent on having the *means* to participate. In practice, of course, there were and are shortcomings with a model that assumes a moral certitude about the right to decide which are the right goods for the good of the public, but the real virtue of the distributive ethic lies in its self-transformative potential. As long as a service is provided in the name of the public, then any individual or group who feels excluded from – or 'not spoken to' – by that service has a legitimate reason to demand reform, to demand a form of address that resonates with them as citizen listeners. Though broadly speaking broadcasting developed as a *consumer good* in the US, sold to targeted markets rather than *public goods* available to all citizens, this is something of a caricature, for American radio was also to a greater or lesser degree shaped by a 'civic ambition', albeit ultimately a divisive one (Goodman 2011: xviii; Fortner 2005). The commercial model too rested on a faith in a moral economy that would serve the public interest by distributing goods according to demand (the listeners 'calling' the radio programmers to 'speak').

The distributive model of communication, exemplified by broadcasting with its indiscriminate address, is characterized by its disinterestedness and generosity (Peters 1999: 52; Scannell 2000, 2004; Schrage 2005). It may be less 'efficient' than forms of communication that target particular constituencies, but it is arguably fairer, and better suited to give rise to the unexpected. Moreover, it is a form of non-reciprocal communication that, for Peters, echoes the indiscriminate, ubiquitous and unconditional love of God. The Biblical parable of the sower (the 'parable of parables') provides the central metaphor: The sower sowed (or *broadcast*) his seeds indiscriminately, some falling on stony ground, but some on fertile earth where the crop thrived 'and brought forth fruit'.[1] A sculpture of the sower was created for the foyer of BBC Broadcasting House, opened in 1932, the Latin legend for which includes the prayer that 'the people, inclining their ear to whatsoever things are beautiful and honest and of good report, may tread the path of wisdom and uprightness' (in Avery 2006: 79). This phrase, 'inclining their ear', captures the intentionality, complicity and activity of the listener in the enterprise of broadcasting. The interpretative burden is laid at the ears of the listener. The listener, accepting the invitation to listen, is obliged actively to seek out the meaning. The act of listening literally *makes* sense.

Discriminating Listening

It is not perhaps surprising, then, that much time and energy went in to trying to persuade the listener to 'incline their ear' not only in the right direction (towards beautiful, honest and reputable things), but also in the right way (selectively, attentively and with appropriate discrimination).

Listeners should not be lazy or gluttonous or dissolute, but engaged, selective and resolute. There were constant reminders to listeners that they were not likely to find everything to their liking, and that they should construct their own 'programme' from the schedules provided, since those schedules were designed, in principle, to provide something for everyone, not everything for any one person.[2] Broadcasters railed against 'tap listening' and people who listened with only half an ear. Such listening was disrepectful, a squandering of the valuable cultural resource offered by the custodians of the airwaves. The BBC critic Filson Young went so far as to call such listeners 'wicked' (in Briggs 1981: 54). Although this advice was often couched in terms that suggested the listener would gain personally from proper listening – developing a better appreciation, feeling less dissatisfied, being more in control – there was also an implicit recognition of the ethical obligation on the part of the listener to *make sense* of the broadcast fare as a member of the public. Each member of the audience had an ethical duty to listen actively and to take individual responsibility for their part in a functioning listening public rather than a mass audience, as a 1931 editorial in the *Radio Times* made clear:

> It is something to bear in mind when we feel adversely critical towards programmes: were they not designed, we might pause and ask ourselves, as part of a scheme aimed to please each of us at some time or another, aimed, in fact, to allow us as listeners to retain our separate entities as thinking men and women? A people's strength lies ultimately in its individuality. Individuality is the expression of spirit, and spirit lives in each of us separately – not as a crowd. Nothing must be allowed to swamp that individuality (in Scannell and Cardiff 1991: 372).

The dread prospect of standardization and loss of individuality in the age of mass communication was to be staved off by the practice of active listening. However little this image of the actively engaged listener corresponded to the way in which most people came to use radio primarily as a convenient background companion, and however idealistically or patronizingly the 'art of listening' was propagated, these examples remain nevertheless a practical example of the ethics of listening feeding through into public discourse and the arrangements of media communication.

There were plenty of 'listening reformers' during the early years of radio in the US as well. Often educators concerned with the deleterious effects on levels of attention associated with the new media, these reformers were concerned listening should be 'not just a private or solipsistic activity but something that eventually led outwards to engagement with people in the world' (Goodman 2010: 36). Active, concentrated and discriminating radio listening was taught as a civic skill that would, as one educator put it, 'be our greatest bulwark against threats to democracy' (Goodman 2010: 38). There was a great deal of urgency to these debates during the 1930s when the propagandistic potential of broadcasting was all too evident at home and abroad. Meanwhile, in Germany the new regime, too, for different reasons, and with the threat of sanctions, was imploring its listeners to pay due attention (Lacey 1996: 103–4; Lenk 1997).

Although these early debates about the art of radio listening are very much of their time and tangled up in a variety of religious and ideological discourses, they provide an interesting example of a public concern with the ethics of listening in relation to mediated communication. They are significant, furthermore, because they invite us to think beyond conventional *dialogic* models (and ideals) of communication which in the modern age – not least *because* of broadcasting – no longer offer an adequate basis on which to build a media ethics, broadly conceived. Beyond the conceptual problems with privileging dialogical forms of communication in public settings outlined in the previous chapter, broadcasting introduces the possibility of listening to distant others, of collective listening, of constituting communicative spaces that could transgress physical, political (national) and social boundaries. And it popularizes a mode of communication that is not dependent on a notion of reciprocity. On the other hand, attending to the *activity* of listening also complicates any characterization of broadcasting simply as *dissemination.*

The idea of the 'active audience' has long been common currency in media and cultural studies. Audience activity has been variously read as selectivity, or utilitarianism, intentionality, involvement, or resistance to influence. The active audience is posed against the passive audience, understood to be gullible, faceless, conformist, vulnerable. The 'invention' of the active audience can thus be seen as an attempt to retrieve and revive the classic liberal model of the free and rational individual in the face of mass society critiques that held the audience to be passive and vulnerable. At one level, then, historiographically, the search for evidence of the autonomous activity of the audience can be read as a kind of moral crusade, one that is ideologically predicated on the sovereignty of the individual (Biocca 1988: 55). Allusions to audience activity can be variously descriptive, evaluative, judgemental, normative or prescriptive. But, however they are deployed in detail, the notion of activity, in all its variety, is uniformly valorized over passivity. Terms like 'public', 'rational', 'disinterested', 'autonomous', 'masculine' and 'logocentric' appear on the 'active' side of the balance sheet. On the 'passive' side appear 'private', 'emotional', 'biassed', 'exploitable',

'feminine' and 'sensuous'. These simple binary oppositions are more ideological than real, as feminist scholarship in particular has taught us, but
they are divisions – onto which speaking and listening are also mapped –
that are surprisingly persistent. This book, too, could be said to be caught
up in that same bind, trying (in written form) to haul listening onto the
good, active side of the divide, albeit mindful of the fractal nature of these
distinctions; that is to say, mindful of how the distinctions between active
and passive play out in multiple, complex and often mutually contradictory
ways.

It is noticeable how these debates about the activity of the audience have
receded in recent years with the rise of new forms of 'interactivity', sidelined
either by a fascination with the new platforms for the audience to 'speak
up' or in celebratory accounts of the collapse of any distinction between
producer and consumer (leading to neologisms like 'prosumer' and 'pro-
duser'). The activity of listening, as a mode of active reception anterior and
separate to measurable *expressed* response, is once again elided as audience
activity is thought of in terms of 'speaking up', whether that be via posts
to websites, red buttons pressed, phone votes made or comments tweeted.
In whatever mode activity is understood, however, if the audience is
acknowledged to be active, then it begs the question of whether there are
ethical responsibilities attached to that activity. Roger Silverstone (2002:
772–5) posed the question in terms of the complicity and collusion of the
audience with media power, arguing that to insist on the intellectual and
political agency of the audience was necessarily to raise questions about the
responsibilities of the audience to resist and challenge media power: 'If we
are to be acknowledged as willing participants in mediated culture then
there has to be some meaning in the notion of *willing*.' The responsibilities
of the audience play out at different levels in different contexts, but fundamentally, the audience is implicated in the media game and has responsibilities for the simple reason that, without an audience, there is no 'game'.
'Game' is the term that Silverstone prefers to 'system' or 'industry' and so
on, since it offers a way to acknowledge the 'knowingness' of both producers
and audiences in the conventions and deficiencies of mediated exchange.
Thinking about the media game also moves away from a discourse of universal 'truth' towards a more contingent and contextualized discourse of
conventions and rules that are produced and broadly understood by the
various players in the game, both producers and consumers. Inasmuch as
ethical questions are about the establishment of 'trust', the emphasis can
then shift from a concern with 'lying' to a concern with 'cheating' according
to the prevailing rules and conventions of the game (Silverstone 2002:
773). There is also the question of trusting that all of the players will turn

up to play, that there will be an audience of listeners, listening out and listening in.

The question of trust is central to contemporary debates about communication ethics in the political sphere. Surveys regularly indicate that 'the public' has lost trust in both politicians and journalists. The surveys are taken because of the role that trust plays in a representative political system, trust both in those delegated as political representatives, and in those charged with representing the public world back to us. Modern 'disembedded' relationships, such as those produced via mediatization, require a particular form of trust, according to Anthony Giddens (1991: 19), that involves a leap of faith in the absent other. Meanwhile, Onora O'Neill (2004) has argued that 'trust grows out of listening, not telling'. She points out that the ways in which governments try to tackle falling levels of trust tend to be couched in terms of 'transparency' and 'disclosure' which, while honourable in intent, tend to reproduce the one-directional mode of communication that perhaps undermined the levels of trust in the first place. She argues that such policies are defined by an informational logic (they are simply about 'handling information') that pays scant regard to communication as a two-way process. Listening is a way of being respectful of the electorate, listening to them in all their diversity, and being open to hear the variety of their responses. But if listening *to* citizens is vital to the production of trust in political exchanges, then listening *as* citizens is no less important.

The Ethics of Being Addressed

To consider the ethics of listening in public is to offer a way to balance the ethics of how the media should construct and target their address, with a concern for the ethics of *being addressed*. Silverstone made a significant contribution here in his last book, *Media and Morality*. He begins with Ulrich Beck's notion of the cosmopolitan born into two worlds, the cosmos (nature) and the polis (city/state), or rather the state of being rooted 'in *one* cosmos but in *different* cities, territories, ethnicities, hierarchies, nations, religions – all at the same time' (in Silverstone 2006: 14). The human condition in late modernity is thus, empirically, one of *plurality*. Silverstone argues that since the individual embodies this plurality, this 'doubling of identity and identification', the individual is also ethically obliged 'to recognize not just the stranger as other, but the other in oneself'. The world is full of people who are not 'like us', but we are nevertheless alike in the shared experience of that difference. Significantly, Silverstone takes as a given that our dependence on the media for our connection to the world is 'no longer at issue'. The ethical response to cosmopolitanism in media terms is, then, 'an obligation to listen' (2006: 14). This obligation is one that is laid at the door of media producers and corporations but also, significantly, to 'us' as 'readers, audiences, citizens'.

In fact, in the current 'ethical turn' in media studies, there has been a remarkable interest in the idea of 'listening' as emblematic of a mode of intersubjective and empathetic participation in the public sphere (Downing 2003: 632–3; Silverstone 2006; Couldry 2006). Not insignificantly, these questions about the agency and responsibility of 'listening' are coming to the fore just at the moment when it is possible to talk about 'the end of broadcasting' and when familiar distinctions between production and reception are blurring. As the centralized forms of media production are diminishing, the question of media ethics has to turn again to questions of the audience. In a communications environment where 'speaking up' is valued regardless of who is listening or the nature of the listening response, in an age, that is, of 'cyberbabble' (Loy 2007), the responsibility for meaning-making lies even more heavily with the listening public. Certainly the fetish of participation as 'finding a voice' without taking account of how those voices resonate with listeners is part of a wider critique of contemporary communicative practices (Schudson 2003; Žižek 2006; Couldry 2010; Tacchi 2011).

Silverstone explores the 'obligation to listen' in terms of 'hospitality'. Hospitality, following Derrida's reading of Kant (2002), is taken to be a primary moment of morality and the human condition – namely the requirement 'to welcome the other into one's space with or without any expectation of reciprocity'; it is 'the mark of the interface we have with the stranger' (Silverstone 2006: 139). Ironically, this lack of reciprocity, raised here to a moral ideal, is precisely what in many critiques condemns mediated communication as pathological. Silverstone proposes taking unconditional hospitality as the normative ethical ideal for the 'mediapolis'. He recognizes that the processes of mediation will always involve restrictions and constraints even when the voices of others are welcomed into a particular media space – editorial decisions, professional and presentational codes and the unavoidable manifestations of symbolic power will always and necessarily render media hospitality conditional and imperfect. And yet the normative ideal is, he argues, a necessary fiction to give a 'sense of the limits of what we are doing editorially and politically [. . .] and to conceive of how to transcend those limits'. Ultimately, it reminds us of the requirement to 'respect those who speak in public space' and 'to grant, without qualification, a right of audience to those who would otherwise be beyond the pale' (Silverstone 2006: 142).

This right of audience is understood as a right *to be heard*, a corollary to the right to free expression. But Silverstone also constructs the notion of the *universal audience* to accommodate the presumption that the right of audience is matched by a right to be a member of an audience, a right *to listen*. The political implications of a right to listen as part of a broader freedom of listening were explored in the previous chapter. But the freedom of listening also brings obligations, including moral obligations. For Silverstone this translates into the pressing question of media 'literacy' on an analytical as well as a political level.

The extension of democracy in the nineteenth and early twentieth centuries was matched, broadly, by a political will to extend literacy to all sections of the population. But as the weight of political representation has shifted from print to audiovisual media, the equivalent political will has been lacking to extend literacy programmes to audiovisual media that seemed not to require specialist skills to be deciphered. The discipline of media studies is still often met with derision in the political sphere. Current discussions of information literacy tend to focus on technical rather than critical dimensions, while media literacy in the age of digital participatory culture tends to focus on productive rather than receptive skills – how to post, blog, sample, edit, podcast or mash-up and so on. Silverstone suggests that Ong's era of 'secondary orality' requires the propagation of a 'secondary literacy' (Silverstone 2006: 178–9) that would extend beyond simple technical competency to include critical self-reflexivity, responsibility and ethical judgement. But while the broad point is well made, it is surprising that he retains the notion of 'literacy' in this context (except that it might be a pragmatic shorthand), when 'secondary listening' might seem to be more apposite, both in relation to the spokenness of 'secondary orality' and in relation to his own arguments about there being an 'obligation to listen'. It is also surprising, given his acknowledgement of the centrality of 'listening' to the questions of media and morality, that he habitually elides the act of listening in his discussions of media reception, writing, for example, of the responsibilities of 'spectators and readers' (Silverstone 2006: 46) and letting 'the screen' stand in for the place of mediation (Silverstone 2006: 54–5). Such slippages are a reminder of just how deeply entrenched is our visualized understanding of the audience, and how counter-intuitive it remains for listening to stand in for the range of media competencies required in a multimedia environment. But the easy elision of listening as an appropriate term for the critical responsibilities of the audience is disappointing inasmuch as there are specific qualities in the listening relation that might have something new to offer in debates about media ethics and that might better reflect the tenor of mediated representation in its instantaneity, its embodiedness and its sensory appeal.

Listening as a Responsibility in the Public Sphere

While it is possible to be trained in the arts of public speaking and, in various ways, media literacy, it is rare to find the equivalent opportunities to hone the arts of public listening (in contrast to the legion of books about listening in interpersonal situations). As Romand Coles (2004: 687) has put it, we have 'marginalized the arts of listening'. Coles, in the context of social movement theory, argues that if learning to find a political voice is dependent on learning how to listen, then learning how to listen is dependent on listening to different voices in different locations and contexts: 'to move beyond the limits of one's familiar spaces, faces and primary associations' (Coles 2004: 688). For Coles, this is only realizable through 'literal bodily world traveling', a travelling between spaces of familiarity and strangeness, between home and elsewhere. In the context of city- or community-based politics, he imagines this as an imperative to engage in a variety of face-to-face encounters, and describes walking 'receptively' through unfamiliar neighbourhoods, listening to others' stories and other ways of telling stories. The combination of listening and 'world travelling' results in a lived *experience* of plurality, not merely an *imaginative* act of representative thinking. Coles argues that the radical openness of listening is precisely what is needed in contemporary antagonistic societies, to get 'into the skin' of others' lives. Tanja Dreher (2009: 451) describes this 'listening across difference' as 'a subtle shift, from seeking better understanding of "an other" to listening for better understanding of relationships and complicities, issues and the workings of privilege'. Listening and travelling, then, are thought together in terms of a democratic practice that 'at once *embody* principles like equality, justice, freedom and democratic engagement, and at the same time enable us to re-articulate the meaning of these in different contexts with different people' (Coles 2004: 692). Part of the significance of this approach is precisely that it understands listening not only as a means to an end – the valorization of more voices – but to a certain extent as an end in itself, as the development of a democratic sensibility.

But these are democratic practices that have been discerned in the grass-roots politics of community action and that rely, in Coles' formulation, on the visceral, embodied encounter and engagement with different voices in particular contexts and locations. Such 'lived' encounters are no doubt important and necessary, but they are inevitably limited in scope and reach for most people. Time, geography, resources and inclination all impose their limits on the capacity for the kind of radical democratic listening described in locally-based social movements. Once again, we hear the virtues of embodied presence being sung in the name of a radical inclusivity, while the very reliance on *presence* necessarily excludes absent others. The question of how listening and travelling can operate through representation, through *mediation*, must then come onto the agenda. Listening and travelling, after all, are both ideas covered by the term 'communication' and are both encompassed by the term 'mobile privatization' that Williams (1974) coined to describe and analyse the communicative responses to the paradoxes of modernity that produced 'a society that is both isolating and connecting, atomizing and cosmopolitan, or inward-dwelling but outward-looking' (Groening 2010: 1335).

Listening and travelling can and, via the media, do happen at a distance. A classic statement of how listeners encounter otherness via the media was offered by Cantril and Allport's (1935: 259) influential early study of the psychology of radio:

> A turn of the wrist immeasurably expands his personal world. The poor man escapes his poverty; the country dweller finds refuge from local gossip; the villager acquires cosmopolitan interests; the invalid forgets his loneliness and his pain; the city dweller enlarges his personal world through contact with strange lands and peoples.

In fact, the gap between 'imaginative visiting' and 'engaged listening' may be productively narrowed by recognizing that listening, particularly in relation to storytelling and other forms of mediated encounter, involves the imagination in travelling across boundaries physical, personal, social and temporal. The usefulness of importing these terms of listening and travelling into a media ethics is that it poses ethical responsibilities for the audience as well as for media producers. It poses an ethical responsibility for the media not only to travel and to tell different stories, but to listen to the variety of ways in which those stories are told. In other words, alongside the welcoming ethic of hospitality, we should add an ethic of travelling or visitation. Hospitality, after all, means welcoming others into your home, your space.[3] By the same token, there is also an ethical responsibility for the audience to travel adventurously among those stories, listening out for voices that are unfamiliar or uneasy on the ear. This sort of travel 'away from the self' is, for Levinas, the basis for an ethics beyond the secure and stable subject of Enlightenment thought. It is possible to travel and yet return to 'the same', with one's sense of self unchanged or even reinforced. But an ethical move away from this 'totality' toward an 'exterior' is made possible by journeys 'away from the self, in which one is dissociated from the familiar, the comfortable and the recognizable' (Benson and O'Neill 2007: 33), and which therefore involves an element of risk.

Listening as *Erfahrung*

These two terms, listening and travelling, come together in the German verb *erfahren*, which means 'to experience' but can also mean to hear or to learn about something, and which is built on the root verb *fahren*, to travel. In discussing Benjamin's use of the term *Erfahrung*, Miriam Hansen (1993: 187) points out that it conveys:

> a sense of mobility, of journeying, wandering or cruising, implying both a temporal dimension, that is, duration, habit, repetition, and return, and a degree of risk to the experiencing subject (which is also present, though submerged, in the Latin root *periri* that links 'experience' with 'peril' and 'perish').

The German language also offers another verb for experience: *erleben*. The distinction between them is crucial: *Erlebnis* as the realm of immediate, fragmentary sensory experience and *Erfahrung* as the gradual accretion of tradition and collective memory. *Erfahrung* is the product of connections and correspondences between sensations, information and events unconsciously made against an integrated background derived from a continuity of tradition and collective existence. The superficial and fleeting experiences of *Erlebnis*, on the other hand, register in an individual's conscious memory (*Erinnerung*), making little impact on unconscious or collective remembrance (*Gedächtnis*). That 'meaning' was evaporating under modern conditions was widely testified to in different guises – as alienation, anomie, disenchantment, apathy, ennui. For Benjamin, the shock effects of modern life represented an assault on *Erfahrung* by *Erlebnis*, but *Erfahrung* itself might have so changed under modern conditions, that the alienating, distracting forms of popular culture might be precisely the way in which the alienation and distraction of the shocks and stimuli of modern life could be made 'communicable' and therefore available for criticism (Crary 2000: 48–54; Highmore 2002: 66–9).

There is, then, a social horizon of experience that can include the collective experience of the disintegration of experience in modernity produced and reflected back by the new media of communication (Hansen 2011). The new forms of mediated sound discussed in this book represented a distinctive recombination of individual sense perception and social reality, and thus helped to redraw the social horizon of experience, to remediate the relationship between the public world and the private experience of everyday life. That social horizon of experience is no longer confined to face-to-face encounters, but the lack of presence is not necessarily something to be mourned, although it might be compensated for in a variety of textual and receptive practices. The experience of mediation is by now a thoroughly common experience, fully integrated into the everyday, available for appropriation as part of the mundane, as part of being in the world. Paddy Scannell (1996: 149) has written persuasively, for example, about the 'dailiness' and reliably never-ending flow of broadcasting being perhaps its most significant and astonishing accomplishment. It is a dailiness of availability, combined with an *everydayness* of address marked by familiarity and intimacy that has opened up the world to a newly constituted *general* public, to enable the publicness of the world to appear, in principle, to all, to *bring together* aspects of the world that were discrete in a common space before a common, if diverse and distant, public. The so-called 'legacy' media have by now extended across generations, providing in some cases precisely a sense of anchorage in an otherwise changing world. The new media environment, meanwhile, is one of ambient and pervasive media that afford multiple points of connection between public and personal life, a network that arguably reconstitutes the idea of a general public in terms of an infinite number of lateral connections rather than a single 'sphere' constituted within a national frame. At any rate, the experience of mediation has, over the course of the long twentieth century, become increasingly difficult to think about as somehow separate from 'authentic' experience.

In other words, if the twin practices of listening and travelling are accepted as being fundamental to the development of a democratic sensibility, then they must be thought through in proportion to the kinds of involvement in political communicative practice that most citizens engage in and that can be squared with the networked and global scale of contemporary politics. Listening, and listening *out* in particular, would seem an appropriate term for describing the *experience* of this information network. Reading or spectating suggest a focus on a singular object, whereas the auditory sense is more aware of sounds coming from different directions, more tolerant, in other words, of plurality. The rapid exchanges of text and image aspire to the qualities of talk, but also take on the flavour of background noise, making listening the apposite metaphor for the mode of reception amid these mediated social networks.

And yet, one of the paradoxes of our current experience of information abundance is that there are mechanisms at play, institutional, psychological and algorithmic, to direct our 'travelling' to familiar, homely sites. Where public service radio, for example, was once programmed in a self-conscious attempt to broaden its listeners' horizons by mixed programming so that a listener might encounter something unheard of, radio broadcasting (and the record industry with which so much radio is closely connected) has been characterized by increasing specialization and formatting, to the point now where personal music players and online radio can be tailored to fit the most precise personal tastes. Listening in to more of the same is arguably an expression of a desire to have the world reflect back and echo the listening subject, either as some sort of narcissistic extension and self-confirmation, or an expression of anxiety about difference or the unknown. Andrew Crisell (2002: 121), even before the emergence of web radio platforms like Last FM or Pandora, judged 'choice' between streamlined, targeted stations to be 'an often timid, conservative faculty'. Similarly, Susan Douglas (1999: 348) described the tendency in format radio to cultivate and pander to 'a safe, gated-in listening'. In fact, this pessimism about the docility of the people and the external barriers to the courage required to escape the comfort zone of conformity and deference was already part of Kant's famous answer to the question 'What is Enlightenment?' (Donald 2003: 48), and part of Horkheimer and Adorno's (1988: 42–3) critique of the *Dialectic of Enlightenment* with 'the regression of the masses' being 'their inability to hear the unheard of with their own ears'. So it would be wrong to present these shifts towards increasing personalization and specialization simply as a narrative of decline. Clearly the 'democratic elitism' of the Reithian BBC, however well-intentioned, was wrought with class prejudice and the inequities of monopoly; and clearly, despite the increasing sophistication of techniques by search engines and advertising to attract users to similar sites to those just visited, the web is still a place of wide horizons for the adventurous traveller. So, while there are clearly ethical questions for producers and the institutions of the media here, the 'obligation to listen' rests at least as much with members of the listening public.

Amid the abundance of information, there is a new scarcity of 'time' and 'attention'. Or, to put it another way, amid the 'noise' of unlimited distraction, new listening skills are required. Technical applications and new listening practices are developed in response to the difficulties of navigating the exponential rise in the sounds and voices it is *possible* to listen to. A recent study (Leong et al. 2008) has explored the pleasures and attractions of 'abdicating choice' of what to listen to. Focusing on the relatively random listening enabled by the 'shuffle' function on music devices, they report how listeners find 'richer and more intense listening experiences' because of the process of *defamiliarization* achieved through decontextualization, unexpected juxtapositions and provocative coincidences. Most striking is the listeners' reported thrill at moments of serendipity – meaningful chance encounters with the unknown and the unanticipated. The context here is still all about individual pleasure and consumption, and the automation of the shuffle mode gives the impression of abdicating choice within a context of pre-set control. This could be another example of safe and convenient listening – but perhaps the thrill of relinquishing some of the 'normal' determinations of 'listening in' could translate eventually – or be part of such a translation – into a desire for more adventurous forms of 'listening out'. This is not quite as fanciful as it seems, if we are to take seriously the idea that aesthetic and affective practices in the realm of consumption connect to practices of civic culture and that, in terms of mediated practice and experience at least, the dividing line between consumption and citizenship is neither absolute nor stable (Couldry et al. 2007b). Moreover, in a media world where listening is so directed, so purposeful, so monitored, *just* listening, listening as a state of playfulness without purpose, can itself be a site of resistance or escape (Levin 1989: 233).

Listening Out as Civic Obligation

Listening out is, I am suggesting, a description of the public disposition, the necessary corollary of the indiscriminacy of the public address. But there is also an argument to be made for a more prescriptive understanding of 'listening out', an ethical obligation to listen out for otherness, for opinions that challenge and clash with one's own, for voices that take one out of one's comfort zone. Lisbeth Lipari (2009: 45) has argued that ethics itself arises out of this difficult commitment to engage with difference, this 'listening otherwise' as she calls it. Listening otherwise involves 'a transcendence from self-in-separation to self-in-relation' (Lipari 2009: 53).

This ethical obligation to listen out for otherness might hold in private as much as in public life, but its public dimension intersects with a civic obligation in democratic societies to be well informed in order to form grounded opinions, deliberate well and participate purposefully in public and political life. There is a long history of political theorists understanding the responsibility of the citizen as 'reader' not only to keep well informed, but to develop a sense of shared norms and values: from de Tocqueville writing in 1835 to Habermas' *The Theory of Communicative Action* (1984) and beyond (Schroll 1999: 321). John Rawls (1993/2005: 217), for example, is quite explicit on this point: 'the ideal of citizenship imposes a moral, not a legal, duty – the duty of civility' that includes 'a willingness to listen to others and a fairmindedness in deciding when accommodations to their views should reasonably be made'. It is not for nothing that we speak of giving someone a fair 'hearing'. Note the idea of 'giving' that is connected here with listening, or in the phrases 'to *grant* someone an audience' or 'to *lend* an ear'. Listening, once again, is revealed as an act, an act of choice, an act in relation to others, and an act that *produces* speech in the sense of inviting the other to speak. Moreover, the notion of *fairness* invoked here draws attention to the ethics of care involved in the act of responsible listening, an ethic towards the intentions of the speaker that mitigates against the untrammelled capacity of the active listener to take *any* meaning from the indeterminate polysemy of what is listened to. This duty of fair-minded listening is ethical insofar as the listener is required not only to keep informed but to widen their perspective and commit to the betterment of others as well as self (Schroll 1999: 328).

However, there is a problem if these ideas of 'civility' or 'fair-mindedness' are collapsed into an expectation of consensus-building that would seek to ignore or erase conflict or irreconcilable difference. Writing from a sociological perspective, Les Back (2007: 23) describes the 'art' of active listening as difficult and disruptive, an art that 'challenges the listener's preconceptions and position while at the same time it engages critically with the content of what is being said and heard', whether by one's allies or one's enemies. This need to listen, to *attend to* others, is also implicit in Chantal Mouffe's presentation of agonistic pluralism (2000: 80–107). Like Arendt, she starts from the position that a democratic model that seeks consensus is ultimately self-defeating on various grounds: that if consensus were achieved, then the pluralism which deliberative models seek to protect would be destroyed; that the possibility presented of a rational consensus ignores the relations of power in society; and that those relations of power in society must mean there is an ever-present possibility of antagonism in society. The political challenge for Mouffe then becomes how to transform antagonism into agonism, to make social antagonism compatible with a democratic politics. The problem then is how to turn a 'friend-enemy' relation into an adversarial one in which the adversary's right to express a contrary opinion is not negated, but respected, *listened* to. The openness of political listening, then, is about keeping channels of communication open, accepting ongoing difference and conflicting interests. It is, therefore, a difficult, challenging and risk-laden responsibility. It is not a therapeutic kind of listening, simply 'hearing each other's pain', but is bound up with the process of reaching political judgement through granting a hearing. Following Arendt (1958: 179), listening without political judgement is simply a communicative act; it is not an intrinsic political good unless directed towards the virtues of political judgement and action.

To lay responsibility for adventurous and courageous listening with the public is to engage in what Radcliffe (2005: 28) in her discussion of 'rhetorical listening' has described as 'strategic idealism'. This implies 'a conscious identification among people that is based on a desire for an intersubjective receptivity, not mastery, and on a simultaneous recognition of similarities and differences, not merely one or the other'. This is not about listening simply to decode, absorb or reflect the speaker's intention, but, as Radcliffe puts it, it is a listening to others 'with intent, not for intent'. Again, this is a description of openness, of listening out, rather than – or as a prerequisite to – listening in. There is a public dimension to this ethical obligation inasmuch as a public, the *Öffentlichkeit*, is 'a group of people collectively and freely arriving at judgments of goodness and badness about cultural, political and social matters' (Pinkard in Donald 2003: 46), judgements which are only possible *in community with others*, in other words, judgements arrived at by *cosmopolitan* listeners.

This obligation to listen is the flipside of what Charles Husband (1996) set out as a 'right to be understood', which goes further than Silverstone's 'right of audience'. While the right to be understood might seem a still more idealist formulation than the obligation to listen adventurously, it is perhaps a way of accounting for where that obligation originates, or rather, how it fits in to a circuit of mutual obligations. Arguing that communicative rights have been structured around civil and economic rights of the individual, he proposes a 'third generation' right based on the solidarity of the community and 'a duty to seek comprehension of the other' – other rights of this order would include environmental rights, for example. It is worth citing Husband (1996: n.p.) at some length to recognize the connections with the arguments made thus far:

> The right to communicate in this third generation mode carries with it onerous duties. The right to be understood requires that all accept the burden of trying to understand. Without the inclusion of the subordinate claim of the right to be understood the right to communicate becomes too easily a unidirectional and egocentric democracy of Babel.

The obligation to listen in these terms, to listen out, to listen otherwise, to listen adventurously, then can be understood in general terms as a *response* to the right to be understood. The advantage of such a formulation is that it recognizes difference, intersubjectivity and, for Husband (2009), presupposes that action of some sort is consequent on the understanding aimed at in listening. Understanding without action, he argues, is little more than narcissism, hubris or 'moral voyeurism'. The formulation also draws on a conceptualization of the moral self as prior to the social self. Zygmunt Bauman (2000: 13–14) argues that 'being-for-the-Other rather than for-itself' is precisely the act of self-constitution, and precedes any socially-administered context. He points out that because such moral responsibility is described as 'unselfish', it appears to be about surrendering self-interest; but in fact, he argues, 'the surrender, if any, occurs on the road leading from the moral to the social self, from being-for to being "merely" with. It took centuries of power-assisted legal drill and philosophical indoctrination to make the opposite seem evidently true.' So to listen out in this way is not to surrender self-interest, although it might seem to go against the grain of our current social, political and cultural conditioning. In particular, the construction of the listening public as a commodified audience, made up of self-interested individual 'consumers' controlling privatized soundscapes and listening in to sounds targeted at particular demographics or communities of the like-minded, is the media context within which 'listening out' has come to seem 'contrary to nature'.

In her work on multicultural media, Tanja Dreher (2009: 447) argues her interest in listening is 'situated and strategic, aiming to develop thinking on media change beyond increasingly predictable critiques of representation and a politics of speaking up.' There is, of course, important and difficult work to be done in linking up the ethics of reception with the ethics of production. However, changes at the level of media policy, institution or text do not *necessarily* produce 'better' listening, and 'listening out' as a political or ethical action cannot be captured simply by attending to the productions and producers of the media. To think about the ethics of listening is, in this sense, to *decentre* the media, to understand that cultures of communication exceed the set of activities, productive and receptive, that cluster around particular instances of mediated expression, around particular media texts at particular moments. Listening out is the practice of being open to the multiplicity of texts and voices and thinking of texts in the context of and in relation to difference and how they resonate across time and in different spaces. But at the same time, it is the practice and experience of living in a media age that produces and heightens the requirement, the context, the responsibilities and the possibilities of listening out.

Listening, then, metaphorically and in practice, goes to the very heart of questions to do with the politics and experience of living and communicating in the media age. The experience of listening among media audiences has shaped and re-shaped media technologies, aesthetics and communicative practices. The re-sounding of the public sphere and the alignment of a listening public alongside a reading public has brought with it new dimensions of embodiedness, affect, intersubjectivity and plurality. The politics of listening is an important corrective to conceptualizations of public participation that are restricted to notions of speech, dialogue and text. And the actions of listening in and on the public sphere raise important questions about subjectivity, passivity, cosmopolitanism, democracy and ethics. There is more to media history and more to public participation than listening alone, but theories and practices of media communication and public life miss too much if they don't give the politics and experience of listening a fair hearing.

Notes

Chapter 1: Listening In and Listening Out

1 There are, of course, exceptions, perhaps the best known – and controversial – in the field of media and cultural studies being Adorno's (1938/1991, 1941, 2009) pessimistic analyses of the 'regression of listening' produced by the recording and radio industries. For an interesting discussion of listening, music and mediation, see Born (2010) alongside other articles in a special issue on listening of the *Journal of the Royal Musical Association*.

2 Heidegger (1953/1996: 153) wrote, 'Listening to . . . is the essential being-open of Da-Sein as being-with the other.' Similarly, Hans Georg Gadamer (1979: 324) maintained that 'anyone who listens is fundamentally open. Without this kind of openness there is no genuine human relationship'. David Levin (1989: 203–4) maintains that the rationality rooted in listening 'is essentially communicative, and inherently geared to the achievement of uncoerced intersubjective understanding'.

3 For a succinct overview in relation to the media, see Butsch (2008: 1–14).

4 There are equally interesting but differently suggestive etymological associations in other languages, for example the heteronymic *entendre* in French, that means both to listen and to understand, or the links that the German *hören* (to hear) has with the verbs *zugehören* (to belong to) or *gehorchen* (to obey).

5 These categories are in fact more fluid than this list of binary oppositions would suggest. For more on cross-national radio history, see Lacey (2001).

6 David Toop's *Sinister Resonance* (2010) is a lovely meditation on listening to the haunting sounds and music of silent images and spaces.

Chapter 2: The Modernization of Listening

1 A new anthology of primary documents relating to music, sound and technology in America indicates how historians are beginning to find ways to address this imbalance (Taylor et al. 2012).

2 In this vein, for example, the ethnomusicologist, Veit Erlmann (2010), in his intellectual history of 'modern aurality', rejects the binary oppositions between visual and other epistemologies, and explores how the 'twinned trajectories of reason and resonance clearly disrupt any homogeneous concept of modernity as either ocularcentric or logocentric' and traces how these trajectories run alongside or overlap with 'other lines of demarcation between different conceptual and metaphorical registers of knowledge' (Erlmann 2010: 15–16).

3 This account of 'the alphabet effect' is controversial, not least in its Eurocentricity (Grosswiler 2004: 154–6).

4 The Greek alphabet was notably a unified system for word, number *and* tone, a 'universal alphabet' that somehow prefigures the universal digital language (Kittler 2006: 52).

5 For a rich analysis of Plato's *Phaedrus* in relation to communication more generally, see Peters (1999: 36–51).

6 Emil Berliner's later gramophone (patented in 1887) separated production from consumption, prefiguring Brecht's (1967) famous description of how radio was also 'diverted' from a communicative to a distributive function. For a less schematic account, see Sterne (2003: 204–7) and Morton (2004).

7 The sound of a voice that is stilled. *The Talking Machine & Cinematograph Chronicle*, April 1905, 515.

8 *The Talking Machine News and Journal of Amusements*, February 1923.

9 Memo regarding the statistical survey, 19 January 1931. WAC R44/23/1.

10 Memo from Presentation Director to Controller of Programmes, 21 November 1933. WAC R44/23/1 Audience Research.

11 Introduction to the *BBC Handbook* (1928), 33.

12 WAC R44/252.

13 Can You Listen? *Daily Mirror*, 12 December 1924, 7.

14 The *Daily Mirror* announced such instances on its 'Today's Gossip' page in 1923.

15 Online at the Association for Motion Picture Sound website at http://www.amps.net/newsletters/newformat/Issue36/Issue36_6.htm (accessed 28 October 2008).

16 Anon., Films that speak. British experts on the photophone. *The Times*, 26 September 1921.

17 N.C., The Talking Kinema: Possibilities of the New Invention. *The Guardian*, 4 October 1921.

18 Cf. *The Gramophone Critic and Society News*, 1928.

19 Note the recourse to visual metaphors. Language about film sound is often really about the image of the sound's source (Metz 1980: 29), sound being 'ontologically vague and semantically imprecise' (Dyson 2007: 5).

20 *Wireless Weekly*, June 1923. Cf. Hennessey (2005: 271).

21 *The Daily Mirror*, 9 April 1923.

22 The Latest in Talking Pictures. *The Gramophone, Wireless and Talking Machine*, September 1923, 336.

23 Anon., Films that Speak . . . *The Times*, 26 September 1921, op cit.

24 The Listening of Viewers. BBC Audience Research Dept. News Letter (157), March 1953. WAC R9/18/4; BBC Listener Research Bulletin Supplements 4 (July 1951–4); Trend from Sound to Vision. *Manchester Guardian*, 30 April 1954; 700,000 Fewer Radio Listeners: Influence of Television. *Manchester Guardian*, 15 August 1957.

25 Although there are always exceptions to prove the rule, as in the short-lived experiment in the 1920s with 'telephotography': the broadcast of silent still images to accompany spoken and other events, either on the radio or in public halls. Cf. Broadcast Picture Service. *Manchester Guardian*, 8 August 1928.

26 One such said the programming 'did not give the impression that one wanted or needed to see what was happening'. *Manchester Guardian*, 7 April 1937.

27 Sound from a Television Feature. *Manchester Guardian*, 6 April 1937.

28 In the early 1950s, the BBC would refer to 'the sound public' and 'the television public'. WAC R9/18/4.

29 See *Daily Mirror*, 1 October 1958, 6.

30 Radio's New Deal: BBC Woos the Listener. *Manchester Guardian*; Radio Plans a Come-Back. *Daily Mirror*, 21 August 1957.

31 The metaphor of writing is used for digital coding, though the binary 'language' of code is not bound by linearity or rules of grammar.

Chapter 3: Listening in Good Faith: Recording, Representation and the Real

1 Available to hear at http://www.youtube.com/watch?v=kKBWsy5A2bA (accessed 22 June 2012).

2 http://www.firstsounds.org/ (accessed 22 June 2012).

3 Commentators on early telephony were similarly fascinated by the 'faithful preservation of the individuating tones and accidents of speech and even the non-verbal sounds of the body' (Connor 1997: 205).

4 Cf. full page advert in *The Talking Machine & Cinematograph Chronicle*, September 1905.

5 Cf. *The Times*, 21 November 1910, 8.

6 'Vexatus' in *The Talking Machine News & Cinematograph Chronicle*, June 1905.

7 In a fascinating discussion, Michael Taussig (1993: 208) points out the remarkable fascination of the colonial Westerner with the 'primitive' Other's fascination with the mimetic capabilities of the phonograph once the 'magic' of sound reproduction had been normalized in the West. He suggests that these encounters were staged not only as a disciplinary process of recording and classification, nor only to impress a technological superiority on the natives, but also 'to reinstall the mimetic faculty as mystery in the art of mechanical reproduction, reinvigorating the primitivism implicit in technology's wildest dreams, therewith creating a surfeit of mimetic power.'

8 For further discussion of 'sound fidelity', see Sterne (2003: 213–86) and Gitelman (1999: 269).

9 Based on Alten's *Audio in Media*, in Jones (1993: 242).

10 Most self-confessed 'audiophiles' are white, male, affluent and tend to privilege their 'love of music' over their 'expertise', often keeping older and 'inferior' equipment out of nostalgia, not only for a particular sound quality, but for a lost mastery over their acoustic environment that satisfied their listening desires (Perlman 2004: 785–6).

Chapter 4: Listening Amid the Noise of Modernity

1 Cf. *The Times*, 9 April 1915, 10.
2 Cf. *The Times*, 28 September 1909, 4.
3 *Manchester Guardian*, 3 November 1888, 8.
4 http://www.ecobooks.com/books/whybirdssing.htm (accessed 15 November 2008).
5 When the television service started, intervals were proposed to mitigate against eye strain (Briggs 1981: 199).
6 *Radio Times*, 20 November 1925, 393.
7 For accounts of the aesthetics of noise throughout the long twentieth century, particularly in relation to experimental music, see Ross (2007) and Demers (2010).
8 There is a long history of the power of sound in healing cures, cf. Bynum and Porter (1993) and Gouk (2000).
9 Burrows, meanwhile, was reported to find the continual speaking 'a great strain'. *Daily Mirror*, 16 February 1923, 16.
10 For the company's view of its own history, entitled, 'What Experience Sounds Like', see http://75.muzak.com/# (accessed 9 September 2011).
11 Cf. *The Times*, 17 September 1912, 8. For a discussion of nostalgia and mourning in relation to recording, see Hainge (2005, 2007).

Chapter 5: Listening Live: The Politics and Experience of the Radiogenic

1 Flesch was the first artistic director of Sürag (Frankfurt) and from 1929 to 1933 the director of the Berliner Funkstunde. Here he is paraphrasing Kierkegaard's aphorism, 'At the beginning was boredom': the world was created because the Gods were bored.
2 Benjamin did write for children's radio, but did not engage in acoustic experimentation. For more on Benjamin's 'blindspot' about sound and listening, see Koepnick (2004).
3 There is something of this in Benjamin's (1931/1972, 1992) notion of the 'optical unconscious'.
4 H.N. Brailsford on autumn schedule of plays in the *Radio Times*, 15 August 1930, 326.
5 For more information, and to listen to a reconstruction of the piece, see http://www.mediaculture-online.de/?id=611 (accessed 9 November 2011).
6 Weill collaborated with Brecht and Hindemith on the experimental play *Lindbergh's Flight* in 1929.
7 New routes to the acoustic play. *Westfälischen Neuesten Nachrichten*, January/February 1930. BArch R78/836, 1–42.
8 Available to hear at http://www.last.fm/music/Walter+Ruttman?autostart (accessed 24 October 2008). This 'listening film' attracted international attention, for example, with a review in an early edition of *The Listener* (Herring 1929).

9 *8 Uhr Abendblatt*, 21 March 1930. The actor and director Alfred Braun was one of the most familiar voices on Berlin radio as the main station announcer, with the refrain 'Achtung! Achtung! Hier ist Berlin!' He was also a pioneer of the live radio report, winning widespread acclaim for his coverage of important national events, which he described as his voice 'orchestrating' the reality before him (Braun 1930: 83).

10 *BZ am Mittag*, 21 March 1930.

11 *Vorwärts*, 21 March 1930.

12 The Federal Radio Commission insisted any use of recorded sound be declared on air; live performances were preferred until the late 1930s (Douglas 1999: 227; Hilmes 2008: 154).

13 Tonfilm-Reportage im Radio. BArch R32/345, 37. See also Russo (2010: 77–114).

14 *Magdeburger Generalanzeiger*, 12 August 1930. 'Tageszeitungen und Rundfunk', BArch R78/836, 124.

15 Interestingly enough, Hindemith went on to pioneer *Grammophonmusik*, a new genre of music that might be called 'phonogenic'. The technically innovative music was composed *for* the gramophone, combining musical instruments and voice with recorded and manipulated sound in a complex polyphonic technique that pre-dated multi-track recording and overdubbing by several decades (Katz 2010: 109–11).

16 In the UK, the newspaper lobby successfully prevented the infant BBC from transmitting anything *other* than the sounds of an outside broadcast (sporting, political or cultural events), on the grounds that any kind of commentary rendered it a journalistic report, something that was the proper domain of the press, and not appropriate to a quasi-government monopoly. *Manchester Guardian*, 18 December 1925, 20. See also Chignell (2011: 13–14).

17 Die jüdische Klagemauer. *Pressedienst der deutschen Sender*, 31 August 1933. R78/780, 163–4. Despite this experience, after a short period in exile, Braun later accommodated himself to the regime and was even assistant director to Veit Harlan on the notorious film, *Jüd Süss* (1940).

18 Speech by Dr Goebbels to the directors of radio, 25 March 1933. BArch R78/6, 94–109.

19 Der Führer spricht! *Der Deutsche Sender*, 4(45), 9 November 1933. BArch R78/781, 100.

20 Das funkische Hörwerk. *Pressedienst der deutschen Sender*, 19 December 1933. BArch R78/781, 158–9.

21 Kaffeestunden im Rundfunk?: Wie holen wir den Hörer an den Lautsprecher? – Wie fesseln wir ihn? *Pressedienst der deutschen Sender*, 5 October 1933. BArch R78/781, 47–53.

22 Horst Dressler-Andress, Das wandernde Mikrofon. *Pressedienst der deutschen Sender*, 19 October 1933. BArch R78/78, 151. See also Hermann (1933).

23 Entwurf zu einer Reportage am 30. Januar, 1934. BArch R78/2298.

24 The following guidelines for 'The National Socialist Reportage' come from a six-page document on the topic. 'Nationalsozialistische Reportagen'. 1934? BArch R78/2298.

25 Hadamowsky, E., Individualwirkung oder Gemeinschaftswirkung des Rundfunks? Die Gemeinschaft ist die Grundlage jeder Rundfunkwirkung! Radio speech, 25 July 1936. BArch R78/754.

Chapter 6: The Privatization of the Listening Public

1 Edison intended his phonograph as a transcription device for business and archiving (the term phonography was already in circulation as a term for shorthand), while it was not until 1920 that David Sarnoff reputedly (and disputedly) hit upon the idea of a 'Radio Music Box' in every home (Benjamin 2002).

2 For a detailed exploration of the complexity and implications of these definitional distinctions in the regulatory production of the early broadcast public sphere in the US where private meant both commercial and personal, see Goodman (2012).

3 These textual effects designed to replicate a sense of the face-to-face encounter were famously described as 'para-social interaction' by Horton and Wohl (1956), as if mediated communication were not quite 'authentic'.

4 Anon., The First Ten Years. The Listener, 201, 16 November 1932, 92.

5 An editorial in The Talking Machine News & Cinematograph Chronicle in April 1905 suggested owners of redundant machines sell them to French establishments where there was no such ban, since the penny slots would accept the equivalent French coin.

6 The Talking Machine News & Cinematograph Chronicle, September 1905.

7 Cf. display advert for Spiers and Pond's stores in London, The Times, 22 June 1914, 12.

8 Cf. The Times, 18 January 1918, 10.

9 Cf. Portable Sets at Picnics. Manchester Guardian, 21 June 1927, 12.

10 The Gramophone, Wireless and Talking Machine News, 1923, 261.

11 For a detailed account of the American history, including how these processes were shaped by gendered and ethnic discourses, see Gitelman (2006: 79–82).

12 Cf. The Times, 19 December 1914, 10.

13 It is interesting to note that Sartre's privileging of presence and reciprocity relied on Heidegger's 'preoccupation with the tendency of Dasein to encounter Being in the experience of nearness', a preoccupation which Kittler suggested was first sparked by Heidegger's own encounter with the distancing effects of radio (Mowitt 2011: 14).

Chapter 7: The Politics and Practices of Collective Listening

1 The Straits Times, 27 April 1893, 2.

2 The Unionist Van Campaign. The Times, 12 December 1907, 12; 9 March 1908.

3 Election Intelligence. *The Times*, 29 March 1909, 12. The novelty was slow to wear off: *The Times* (12 May 1928, 14) reported on 'the most modern methods' used in the German elections of 1928, to 'broadcast' recorded speeches during factory siren breaks.

4 Report of Lord Gainsford (Chairman of the BBC) to the Company's Directors, 15 February 1923, WAC CO 7/1.

5 ibid.

6 *Daily Express*, 10 March 1925, 1.

7 Memo from Mr R. Wade to the Director of Publicity, 14 June 1926. WAC CO28.

8 Cf. letter to the BBC about the Strike Bulletin issued by the Oxford Labour Party, WAC CO29.

9 WAC R44/252.

10 'Provisional Wireless Committee'. *Daily Express*, 17 March 1925, 1. The periodic Commissions on broadcasting policy have often inspired lobby groups: The Listeners Association was founded in 1947 to campaign for commercial radio; the (unrelated) Viewers and Listeners' Association, still active today, was responding to the 1962 Pilkington Committee. WAC R41/85/1 and R4/52/4.

11 *Daily Express*, 12 March 1925; 16 March 1925, 1.

12 Photographs of up to 100 staff sorting through sackloads of letters were published. 24 March; 3 April 1925. The League was mentioned in a parliamentary debate as an arbiter on the question of licence fee revenue. The Prime Minister, in the course of his reply, said he would consider broadcasting Parliamentary debates, prompting a joke that MPs would no longer address 'Mr Speaker', but 'Mr Loud Speaker'. *Daily Express*, 26 March 1925. Live broadcasts from Westminster began only in 1978.

13 WAC R44/252.

14 Memo to all stations from the Controller, 23 April 1925. WAC R44/252.

15 WAC R6/36 Advisory Committees.

16 Report on Group Listening to be presented to the General Advisory Council, 15 June 1938, WAC R14/22/1. In fact, a civil servant was seconded to the BBC adult education department as early as 1924 (Bailey 2007: 103).

17 *The Listener*, 23 January 1929, 60.

18 Minutes of the Sub-Committee B of the British Institute of Adult Education and the BBC (Enquiry into the Educational Possibilities of Broadcasting), 23 April 1927. WAC R14/126/2.

19 ibid. 25 April 1927. WAC R14/126/2.

20 How to conduct a wireless discussion-group. *BBC Handbook 1929*, 226.

21 *Daily Mirror*, 17 January 1927. A 'mass protest' among listeners choosing not to listen-in at all, or tuning in to the lighter music broadcast from Paris or New York, was reported.

22 The report was by the Hadow Committee, set up in 1926 between the BBC and the British Institute of Adult Education, under Sir Henry Hadow's chairmanship, *BBC Handbook 1929*, 43.

23 Prejudice and Education. *The Listener*, 16 January 1929, 14.

24 At first, people spoke of 'lookers-in' or 'lookers' in relation to early television, although 'viewer' became the norm during the 1930s (Briggs 1981: 37).

25 *The Listener*, 6 November 1929, 608.

26 Monthly report, 7 November 1929. WAC R14/33/1. Questionnaires sent to listening groups directly were found to put people off. Library loans of books mentioned in broadcasts were presented as proof that radio provided 'democratic education in a very wide and sound sense'. Adult Education. *BBC Handbook 1928*, 139.

27 Report on visits to districts covered by Area Councils or Committees in January and February 1931, 6 March 1931. WAC R14/33/2.

28 *Radio Times*, 28 September 1934, 847.

29 Central Committee for Group Listening: Talks for Discussion Groups, Autumn Term, June 1938, WAC R14/117/1 Adult Education. *Clear Thinking* had been the subject of an experiment in Listener Research, with over 1,000 volunteers responding to a request in the *Radio Times* to submit their views. Of these, only seven had listened in a group. WAC R44/29 Publicity: Audience Research Projects: Clear Thinking, April 1938.

30 Talks Policy, 6 January 1936. WAC R14/33/2.

31 Future of Talks for Discussion Groups: Attitude of Adult Education Advisory Committee, 20 April 1936, 2. WAC R14/33/2, 2.

32 ibid., 3.

33 The BBC did not have any formal responsibility for 'listening-end' work, so this quasi-autonomous organization was set up with BBC support for three years. WAC R14/27/1 Education: Adult Central Committee for Group Listening, Papers and Minutes Feb–Oct 1937.

34 Education for Adults: Group Listening. *Manchester Guardian*, 4 July 1939.

35 Minutes of a joint meeting of the Central Committee for Group Listening and the Programme Sub-Committee, 10 March 1947. WAC R14/117/3, 132.

36 See chapter 8.

37 For example, Communist Party members sabotaged the Cologne regional transmitter and broadcast an election speech. *Berliner Börsenzeitung*, 3 July 1931.

38 Anon. (1931) Richtlinien für Rundfunkhörstunden. *Arbeiterfunk* 45, 549; Funck (1931).

39 By mid-June 1932, an internal Party report claimed, around 50 members had spoken on radio – a successful evasion of the Party's official exclusion. Funkwarte-Tagung am 13. Juni 1932 im 'Schlesischen Hof'. BArch NS26/1178, 36. The Party also distributed regionally produced records of its most popular and effective public speakers, targeted to local listeners and party events. NSDAP Wahlpropagandaleitung Bayern, 15 April 1932. BArch NS22/2. See also Epping-Jäger (2005).

40 Minutes of the Ortsgruppen Funksobleute on 3 December 1931. NS2/1178, 5. See also Koch and Glaser (2007: 101–2). The *Bund Nationaler*

Rundfunkhörer (The League of National Radio Listeners) had a similarly nationalist agenda, but distanced itself from the Nazis. Promotional leaflet, n.d. BArch R431/2001, 260.

41 Die jüdische Klagemauer. *Pressedienst der deutschen Sender*, 31 August, 1933. BArch R78/780, 163–4; Die Eroberung des Rundfunks hat begonnen. *Die Sturmwelle*, 22 June 1931.

42 Hadamovsky, E., Ein Vorkämpfer des nationalen Rundfunks. *Pressedienst der deutschen Sender*, 1933, 2. BArch R78/780.

43 BA Arch NS26.

44 See BArch NS26/1178. Rundfunkorganisation Hamburg; also BArch NS26, 23.

45 Hadamovsky, E., Dienst am Rundfunk ist Dienst am Volk. *Pressedienst der deutschen Sender*, 10 August 1933. BArch R78/780, 124.

46 BArch NS22/1178, 94.

47 'Richtlinien für die Veranstaltung mit dem Führer am 3. März 1933'. BArch NS26/1178, 62.

48 Anon., Der Führer spricht! *Der Deutsche Sender*, 4(45), 9 November 1933.

49 Anon., Hörkultur. *Pressedienst der deutschen Sender*, 33, 19 December 1933. BArch R78/781, 163–4.

50 *Die Sendung*, 10(45), 9 November 1933. *Pressedienst der deutschen Sender*. BArch R78/781, 100.

51 Goerlitz, T.L., Gefällt Ihnen der Rundfunk?; Der Rundfunk als Lebenssteigerung in der Freizeit; Vom missverstandenen Rundfunk: Ein kleines Kapitel Hörphilosophie. *Pressedienst der deutschen Sender*, 7 December 1933. BArch R78/781, 127–31; 139–40.

52 Hadamowsky, E., Individualwirkung oder Gemeinschaftswirkung des Rundfunks? Die Gemeinschaft ist die Grundlage jeder Rundfunkwirkung! Radio speech, 25 July 1936. BArch R78/754.

53 Memo from Horst Dressler-Andress, Reichspropagandaleitung, Munich, 19 May 1933. BArch NS26/1178, 60.

54 Directive from Reichspropagandaleitung, Hauptabteilung V (Rundfunk), Munich, 6 June 1933. BArch NS26/1178, 58. Meanwhile in the US, the Muzak company was broadcasting news clips alongside its 'piped music' during the Depression, as a form of public service (http://75.muzak.com/#/1930s/).

55 See *Handbuch des deutschen Rundfunks* (1938) Heidelberg/Berlin, 16. See also Teichert, H., 'Erfolgreiche Arbeit der Funkwarte: Ausdehnung der Funkwarteorganisation auf die Betriebe' 23 January 1933. BArch R78/780. Factory radio was also considered instrumental in providing distraction and relaxation in rest periods.

56 Unterlagen über den Vortrag beim Führer betreffend Reichs-Lautsprecher-Säulen by the Sachbearbeiter der Abteilung Rundfunk RMVP, 7 March 1939. BArch NS10/46, 215.

57 Telegram to Brigadeführer Bormann, Kanzlei des Führers, from Goebbels, Berlin, 2 May 1939. BArch NS10/46, 212.

58 *World Radio* 629, 1937, BArch R78/1198.

59 Unterlagen . . ., op cit., 215.

60 There was also concern Germany would be left behind, as systems were already installed in cities abroad. Unterlagen . . ., op cit., 218; Telegram, op cit.

61 Unterlagen . . ., op cit., 216.

62 Individualwirkung. . ., op cit.

63 See for example, http://www.soundthreshold.org/season2_introduction.htm; http://invisiblepicturepalace.com; http://www.hoerspiel.com/termine-radio-hoerspiel/hoerkino/ (accessed 18 July 2012).

Chapter 8: The Public Sphere as Auditorium

1 Cf. initiatives of the UK Labour government: 'Listening to Women' (1997), 'The Big Conversation' (2003), 'People's Panels', Citizens' Juries, 'National Conversation' (2007); or the US Democratic Party's 'Listening to America' platform during the 2008 elections; or the 'listening to citizens' element of EU communications strategies since 2005 (Boucher 2009).

2 Note that new sound media entered public life before full citizenship was accorded to all citizens in the US, UK and Germany.

3 Räuscher, J. (1928) Hör-Stil. *Sonderabdruck aus Deutsche Presse* 23. BArch R43I/2000, 196.

4 Bericht des Drahtlosen Diensts, Berlin, 28 April 1927, BA R78/601, 98.

5 Recalling the etymological link between listening and desire in this entry into the communicative world, Levin (1989: 78) writes, 'Very early in life, the child's listening becomes a channel of and for desire, an intentionality of attractions and aversions, entagled in the ego's will to power – its aggressions and defences.'

6 This is also reflected in the gradual denigration of 'hearsay' as admissible evidence in courts of law during this period, as oral traditions were undermined in relation to customary property law, a trend that is arguably in reversal under the influence of new cultural technologies of sound (Hibbitts 1995).

7 Internal memo, 19 January 1931. WAC R44/23/1 Audience Research.

8 The OED definition is 'a conversation carried on between two or more persons', but adds the rider: 'The tendency is to confine it to two persons, perhaps through associating *dia-* with *di-*: cf. *monologue*.'

9 The term 'participant' is preferred from here on in to 'interlocutor', as the latter suggests *speakers* in conversation, rather than *speaker-listeners*.

10 There is, of course, a vital tradition of noisemaking, particularly in protest, which is another form of political communication, although this can be interpreted as a protest against the silencing of marginalization or the inequalities of who gets to speak and be heard. For an example of how this played out in the wake of the French Revolution and the institutionalization of the idea of free speech, see Rosenfeld (2011: 328–34). For a more recent example, take the loud 'pot-banging' protests in Quebec against an unpopular Bill in Spring

2012. See: http://www.globalmontreal.com/6442647845/story.html (accessed 19 June 2012).

11 These are the terms that Love prefers, taken from Young. Note varied terms describe these political forms – liberal, participatory and radical democracy; representative, direct and republican democracy; interest-based, discourse-based and radical democracy among others, but the general schema holds.

12 'Auditing' harks back to checking of accounts by *listening* to figures being read out (Ong 1982: 119). John Uhr (2004: 239) has explored the separation of powers in liberal democratic theory in terms of citizens as 'auditors' holding political representatives to account.

13 Theorists like Corradi Fiurama (1990) and Lipari (2010), and discussions of 'empathetic listening' in therapeutic situations (Walker 1997), talk of listening to others in terms of self-abnegation or self-transcendence.

14 Similar arguments are made in relation to a politics of witnessing, where listening to testimony is both a process of identification and keeping proper distance between the listener and the speaker (Felman and Laub 1992; Chun 1999).

15 Rawls proposed the term 'omnilogue' to capture the variety of communicative practices in public life (in Schroll 1999: 327).

16 In her *Philosophy of Listening*, psychoanalyst Corradi Fiurama (1990: 2) makes a similar point, arguing that 'the mechanism of "saying without listening" has multiplied and spread, to finally constitute itself as a form of domination and control'.

Chapter 9: Media and the Ethics of Listening

1 Matthew 13: 3–8. King James Version.

2 The cartoonists had a field-day imagining incongruous scenarios of people listening to broadcasts not 'destined' for them, like adults listening to *Children's Hour*, working men being 'put through' to the Savoy, or landed gentry learning how to make economical stews (Briggs 1981: 72–3).

3 Cate Thill (2009: 540) has explored this problem in the Australian context, where White Australians might be figured as benevolent hosts with Aboriginal people figured as strangers in their own land.

References

Abel, R. (1988) *French Film Theory and Criticism, 1907–1939: Volume 2, 1929–1939*. Princeton, NJ: Princeton University Press.

Abulad, R. (2007) What is hermeneutics? *Kritike* 1(2), 11–23.

Ackermann, F. (1932) Rundfunk und Schallplatte. *Rufer und Hörer* 12, 534–6.

Adorno, T.W. (1934/1990) The form of the phonograph record. *October* 55, 56–61.

Adorno, T.W. (1941) The radio symphony: an experiment in theory. In: P. Lazarsfeld and F. Stanton (eds.) *Radio Research*. New York: Columbia University Office of Radio Research, 110–39.

Adorno, T.W. (1938/1991) On the fetish character of music and the regression of listening. In: J.M. Bernstein (ed.) *The Culture Industry: Selected Essays on Mass Culture*. London: Routledge, 1–28.

Adorno, T.W. (1991) The schema of mass culture. In: J.M. Bernstein (ed.) *The Culture Industry: Selected Essays on Mass Culture*. London: Routledge, 53–84.

Adorno, T.W. (2009) *Current of Music*. ed. R. Hullot-Kentor. Cambridge: Polity.

Altman, R. (1992) *Sound Theory/Sound Practice*. London: Routledge.

Altman, R. (1995) The sound of sound: a brief history of the reproduction of sound in movie theaters. *Cineaste* 21 (1–2), 68–72.

Altman, R. (2004) *Silent Film Sound*. New York: Columbia University Press.

Anderson, B. (1983/2006) *Imagined Communities: Reflections on the Origins and Spread of Nationalism*. London: Verso.

Angel-Ajani, A. (2006) Expert witness: Notes towards revisiting the politics of listening. In: V. Sanford and A. Angel-Ajani (eds.) *Engaged Observer: Anthropology, Advocacy, and Activism*. Piscataway, NJ: Rutgers University Press, 76–92.

Arendt, H. (1958) *The Human Condition*. Chicago, IL: University of Chicago Press.

Arendt, H. (1986) *On Revolution*. New York: Penguin.

Armstrong, T. (2005) Player piano: poetry and sonic modernity. *Modernism/modernity* 14(1), 1–19.

Arnheim, R. (1933/1979) *Kritiken und Aufsätze zum Film*. Frankfurt a.M.: Fischer.

Attali, J. (1985) *Noise: The Political Economy of Music*. Manchester: Manchester University Press.

Avery, T. (2006) *Radio Modernism: Literature, Ethics, and the BBC, 1922–1938*. Aldershot: Ashgate.

Back, L. (2007) *The Art of Listening*. Oxford: Berg.

Back, L. (2009) Global attentiveness and the sociological ear. *Sociological Research Online* 14(4).

Bailey, M. (2007) Rethinking public service broadcasting: the historical limits to publicness. In: R. Butsch (ed.) *Media and Public Spheres*. New York: Palgrave Macmillan, 96–108.

Bakhtin, M. (1986) *Speech Genres and Other Late Essays*. Austin, TX: University of Texas Press.

Balasz, B. (1931/1970) *Theory of the Film: Character and Growth of a New Art*. New York: Dover.

Barney, D. (2007) Radical citizenship in the republic of technology: a sketch. In: L. Dahlberg and E. Siapera (eds.) *Radical Democracy and The Internet: Interrogating Theory and Practice*. New York: Palgrave, 37–54.

Barnouw, D. (1994) *Critical Realism: History, Photography, and the Work of Siegfried Kracauer*. Baltimore, MD: Johns Hopkins University Press.

Barry, E.D. (2010) High-fidelity sound as spectacle and sublime, 1950–1961. In: D. Suisman and S. Strasser (eds.) *Sound in the Age of Mechanical Reproduction*. Philadelphia, PA: University of Pennsylvania Press, 115–40.

Barthes, R. (1985) Listening. In: *The Responsibility of Forms: Critical Essays on Music, Art, and Representation*. New York: Hill & Wang, 245–60.

Bassett, C. (2011) Twittering machines: antinoise and other tricks of the ear. *differences: A Journal of Feminist Cultural Studies* 22(2–3), 276–99.

Baudry, J-L. (1976) The apparatus. *Camera Obscura* 1 (Fall), 104–26.

Bauman, R. and Feaster, P. (2003) Oratorical footing in a new medium: recordings of presidential campaign speeches, 1896–1912. *Texas Linguistic Forum* 46(3), 1–19.

Bauman, Z. (2000) *Postmodern Ethics*. Oxford: Blackwell.

Beard, D. (2009) A broader understanding of the ethics of listening: philosophy, cultural studies, media studies and the ethical listening subject. *International Journal of Listening* 23(1), 7–20.

Beck, A. (1999) *Radio Theory*, online book, section 2.11.6a: http://speke.ukc.ac.uk/sais/sound-journal/Beck19991Chap2.html (accessed 24 May 2003).

Bellamy, E. (1887/1982) *Looking Backward*. New York: Penguin American Library.

Benjamin, L. (2002) In search of the Sarnoff 'Radio music box' memo: Nally's reply. *Journal of Radio Studies* 9(1), 97–106.

Benjamin, W. (1992) *Illuminations* (trans. H. Zohn). London: Fontana.

Benjamin, W. (1931/1972) A short history of photography. *Screen* 13(1), 5–26.

Benjamin, W. (1932/1972) Zweierlei Volkstümlichkeit: Grundsätzliches zu einem Hörspiel. In: *Gesammelte Schriften* IV.2. Frankfurt a.M.: Suhrkamp, 671–3.

Benjamin, W. (1936/1992a) The work of art in the age of mechanical reproduction. In: *Illuminations* (trans. H. Zohn). London: Fontana, 211–44.

Benjamin, W. (1936/1992b) The Storyteller: reflections on the work of Nikolai Leskov. In: *Illuminations* (trans. H. Zohn). London: Fontana, 83–107.

Benson, P. and O'Neill, K.L. (2007) Facing risk: Levinas, ethnography and ethics. *Anthropology of Consciousness* 18(2), 29–55.

Bergh, A. and DeNora, T. (2009) From wind-up to iPod: techno-cultures of listening. In: N. Cook, E. Clarke, D. Leech-Wilkinson and J. Rink (eds.) *The*

Cambridge Companion to Recorded Music. Cambridge: Cambridge University Press, 102–15.

Bhaba, H. (1992) Postcolonial authority and postmodern guilt. In: L. Grossberg, C. Nelson and P. Treichler (eds.) *Cultural Studies*. New York: Routledge, 56–68.

Bickford, S. (1996) *The Dissonance of Democracy: Listening, Conflict, and Citizenship*. Ithaca, NY: Cornell University Press.

Bijsterveld, K. (2008) *Mechanical Sound: Technology, Culture, and Public Problems of Noise in the Twentieth Century*. Cambridge, MA: MIT Press.

Biocca, F. (1988) Opposing conceptions of the audience: the active and passive hemispheres of mass communication. In: J. Anderson (ed.) *Communication Yearbook 11*. Newbury Park, CA: Sage, 51–80.

Biocca, F. (1990) Media and perceptual shifts: early radio and the clash of musical cultures. *Journal of Popular Culture* 24, 1–15.

Bischoff, F.W. (1926) Die Aesthetik des Rundfunks. *Funk* 2, 72–4.

Blanchot, M. (1987) Everyday speech. *Yale French Studies* 73, 12–20.

Bliss, E. (1991) *Now the News: The Story of Broadcast Journalism*. New York: Columbia University Press.

Boddy, W. (1994) Archaeologies of electronic vision and the gendered spectator. *Screen* 35, 105–22.

Boddy, W. (2004) *New Media and Popular Imagination: Launching Radio, Television, and Digital Media in the United States*. Oxford: Oxford University Press.

Bolter, J.D. and Grusin, R. (1999) *Remediation: Understanding New Media*. Cambridge, MA: MIT Press.

Born, G. (2010) Listening, mediation, event: anthropological and sociological perspectives. *Journal of the Royal Musical Association* 135 (S1), 79–89.

Boucher, S. (2009) If citizens have a voice, who's listening? European Policy Institutions Network Working Paper 24, June.

Bourdieu, P. (1986) *Distinction: A Social Critique of the Judgement of Taste*. New York: Routledge & Kegan Paul.

Bramen, S. (2007) When nightingales break the law: silence and the construction of reality. *Ethics and Information Technology* 9, 281–95.

Braun, A. (1930) *Rundfunk. Ein Handbuch*. Berlin: n.pub.

Brecht, B. (1967) Radiotheorie 1927–1932. In: *Gesammelte Werke* I. Frankfurt a.M.: Suhrkamp, 119–29.

Briggs, A. (1995) *The History of Broadcasting in the UK*. Oxford: Oxford University Press.

Briggs, S. (1981) *Those Radio Times*. London: Weidenfeld & Nicolson.

British Broadcasting Corporation (BBC) (1928) *BBC Handbook 1928*. Savoy Hill, London: BBC.

Brown, I. (1925) Broadcasting and propaganda. *The Wireless Gazette* August, 25.

Buck-Morss, S. (1998) Aesthetics and anaesthetics: Walter Benjamin's artwork essay reconsidered. In: R. Krauss, A. Michelson, Y.-A. Bois, B.H.D. Buchloh, H. Foster, D. Hollier and S. Kolbowski (eds.) *October: The Second Decade, 1986–1996*. Cambridge, MA: MIT Press, 375–413.

Bull, M. (2000) *Sounding Out The City: Personal Stereos and the Management of Everyday Life*. Oxford: Berg.

Bull, M. (2007) *Sound Moves: iPod Culture and Urban Experience*. London: Routledge.

Bull, M. and Back, L. (2003) (eds.) *The Auditory Culture Reader*. Oxford: Berg.

Burghart, R. (2008) *The Conditions of Listening: Essays on Religion, History and Politics in South Asia*. Oxford: Oxford University Press.

Butsch, R. (2008) *The Citizen Audience: Crowds, Publics, and Individuals*. London: Routledge.

Bynum, W.F. and Porter, R. (1993) (eds.) *Medicine and the Five Senses*. Cambridge: Cambridge University Press.

Camlot, J. (2003) Early talking books: spoken recordings and recitation anthologies, 1880–1920. *Book History* 6, 147–73.

Cantril, H. and Allport, G. (1935) *The Psychology of Radio*. New York: Harper & Brothers.

Carey, J.W. (1986) Walter Benjamin, Marshall McLuhan, and the emergence of visual society. *Prospects* 11(1), 29–38.

Carpenter, E. and McLuhan, M. (1960) Acoustic space. In: E. Carpenter and M. McLuhan (eds.) *Explorations in Communication: An Anthology*. Boston, MA: Beacon Press, 65–70.

Casetti, F. (2008) *Eye of the Century: Film, Experience, Modernity*. New York: Columbia University Press.

Cavell, R. (2010) Specters of McLuhan: Derrida, media, and materiality. In: P. Grosswiler (ed.) *Transforming McLuhan: Cultural, Critical and Postmodern Perspectives*. New York: Peter Lang, 135–62.

Caygill, H. (1998) *Walter Benjamin: The Colour of Experience*. London: Routledge.

Chambers, I. (1996) Signs of silence, lines of listening. In: *The Post-Colonial Question: Common Skies, Divided Horizons*. London: Routledge, 47–64.

Chanan, M. (1995) *Repeated Takes: A Short History of Recording and its Effects on Music*. London: Verso.

Chignell, H. (2011) *Public Issue Radio: Talks, News and Current Affairs in the Twentieth Century*. London: Palgrave Macmillan.

Chion, M. (1994) *Audio-Vision: Sound on Screen*. New York: Columbia University Press.

Christians, C.G. (2000) An intellectual history of media ethics. In: B. Pattyn (ed.) *Media Ethics: Opening Social Dialogue*. Leuven: Peeters, 15–58.

Chun, W.H.K. (1999) Unbearable witness: toward a politics of listening. *differences: a Journal of Feminist Cultural Studies* 11(1), 112–49.

Coleman, S. (2005) Blogs and the new politics of listening. *The Political Quarterly* 76(2), 272–80.

Coles, R. (2004) Moving democracy: industrial areas foundation social movements and the political arts of listening, traveling, and tabling. *Political Theory* 325, 678–705.

Connor, S. (1997) The modern auditory I. In: R. Porter (ed.) *Rewriting the Self: Histories from the Renaissance to the Present*. London: Routledge, 203–23.

Connor, S. (2000) *Dumbstruck: A Cultural History of Ventriloquism*. Oxford: Oxford University Press.

Connor, S. (2002) Edison's Teeth: Touching Hearing. Conference paper. *Hearing Culture*, Osaka, Mexico, 24–28 April. Available at: http://www.bbk.ac.uk/eh/skc/edsteeth/ (accessed 2 February 2011).

Connor, S. (2003) Ears have walls: On hearing art. Public talk. Tate Modern, London, 21 February. Available at: http://www.bbk.ac.uk/english/skc/earshavewalls/ (accessed 2 November 2011).

Corbin, A. (1995) *Time, Desire and Horror: Toward a History of the Senses*. Cambridge: Polity.

Corbin, A. (1998) *Village Bells: Sound and Meaning in the 19th Century French Countryside*. New York: Columbia University Press.

Corradi Fiumara, G. (1990) *The Other Side of Language: A Philosophy of Listening*. New York: Routledge.

Cory, M.E. (1992) Soundplay: the polyphonous tradition of German radio art. In: D. Kahn and G. Whitehead (eds.) *Wireless Imagination: Sound, Radio, and the Avant-Garde*. Cambridge, MA: MIT Press, 331–72.

Couldry, N. (2003) *Media Rituals: A Critical Approach*. London: Routledge.

Couldry, N. (2004) Liveness, 'reality,' and the mediated habitus from television to the mobile phone. *The Communication Review* 7(4), 353–61.

Couldry, N. (2006) *Listening Beyond the Echoes: Media, Ethics and Agency in an Uncertain World*. London: Paradigm.

Couldry, N. (2010) *Why Voice Matters: Culture and Politics after Neoliberalism*. London: Sage.

Couldry, N., Livingstone, S. and Markham, T. (2007a) Connection or disconnection? Tracking the mediated public sphere in everyday life. In: R. Butsch (ed.) *Media and Public Spheres*. New York: Palgrave Macmillan, 28–42.

Couldry, N., Livingstone, S. and Markham, T. (2007b) 'Public connection' and the uncertain norms of media consumption. In: K. Soper and F. Trentmann (eds.) *Citizenship and Consumption*. Basingstoke: Palgrave Macmillan, 104–20.

Crary, J. (1989) Spectacle, attention, counter-memory. *October* 50, 96–107.

Crary, J. (1993) *Techniques of the Observer: On Vision and Modernity in the Nineteenth Century*. Cambridge, MA: MIT Press.

Crary, J. (2000) *Suspensions of Perception: Attention, Spectacle, and Modern Culture*. Cambridge, MA: MIT Press.

Crisell, A. (2002) Radio: public service, commercialism and the paradox of choice. In: A. Briggs and P. Cobley (eds.) *The Media: An Introduction*, 2nd edn. Harlow: Pearson Education, 121–34.

Crook, T. (1999) *Radio Drama: Theory and Practice*. London: Routledge.

Crouthamel, J. (2003) War neurosis versus savings neurosis: working-class politics and psychological trauma in Weimar Germany. *Journal of Contemporary History* 37(2), 163–82.

Cullen Rath, R. (2003) *How Early America Sounded*. Ithaca, NY: Cornell University Press.

Currid, B. (2006) *A National Acoustics: Music and Mass Publicity in Weimar and Nazi Germany*. Minneapolis, MN: University of Minnesota Press.

Curtis, J.M. (1978) *Culture as Polyphony: An Essay on the Nature of Paradigms*. Columbia, MO: University of Missouri Press.

Dahl, P. (1983) *Radio: Sozialgeschichte des Rundfunks für Sender und Empfänger*. Reinbek bei Hamburg: Rowohlt.

Dahlberg, L. (2007) Rethinking the fragmentation of the cyberpublic: from consensus to contestation. *New Media and Society* 9(5), 827–47.

Dahlgren, P. (1995) *Television and the Public Sphere*. London: Sage.

Dayan, D. and Katz, E. (1992) *Media Events: The Live Broadcasting of History*. Cambridge, MA: Harvard University Press.

de Certeau, M. (1996) Vocal utopias: Glossolalias. *Representations* 56(Fall), 29–47.

de Kerckhove, D. (1997) *The Skin of Culture: Investigating the New Electronic Reality*. London: Kogan Page.

Dean, J. (2005) Communicative capitalism: circulation and the foreclosure of politics. *Cultural Politics* 1(1), 51–74.

Demers, J. (2010) *Listening Through the Noise: The Aesthetics of Experimental Electronic Music*. Oxford: Oxford University Press.

Derrida, J. (2002) *On Cosmopolitanism and Forgiveness* (trans. M. Dooley and M. Hughes). London: Routledge.

Doane, M.A. (1990) Information, crisis, catastrophe. In: P. Mellencamp (ed.) *Logics of Television: Essays in Cultural Criticism*. Bloomington, IN: Indiana University Press, 222–39.

Döblin, A. (1930) Literatur und Rundfunk. In: *Dichtung und Rundfunk: Reden und Gegenreden*. Berlin: Reichs-Rundfunk-Gesellschaft, 7–11.

Doerksen, C. (2005) *American Babel: Rogue Radio Broadcasters of the Jazz Age*. Philadelphia, PA: University of Pennsylvania Press.

Döhl, R. (1982) Nichtliterarische Bedingungen des Hörspiels. *Wirkendes Wort* 32(3), 154–79; reproduced at http://www.mediaculture-online.de/Hoerspiel.124+M5e6e89ea85c.0.html, 1–36 (accessed 9 September 2012).

Donald, J. (2003) Kant, the press, and the public use of reason. *Javnost: The Public* 10(2), 45–64.

Douglas, S.J. (1999) *Listening In: Radio and the American Imagination*. London: Time.

Downing, J. (2003) Audiences and readers of alternative media: the absent lure of the virtually unknown. *Media, Culture and Society* 25(5), 625–45.

Dreher, T. (2009) Listening across difference: media and multiculturalism beyond the politics of voice. *Continuum* 23(4), 445–58.

Dreyer, E.A. (1934) *Deutsche Kultur im neuen Reich: Wesen, Aufgabe und Ziel der Reichskulturkammer*. Berlin: n.pub.

Drobnik, J. (2004) *Aural Cultures*. Banff: YYZ Books.

Dussel, K. (2004) *Deutsche Rundfunkgeschichte*. Konstanz: UTB für Wissenschaft.

Dyson, F. (2007) *Sounding New Media: Immersion and Embodiment in Arts and Culture*. Berkeley, CA: University of California Press.

Edison, T. (1878) The phonograph and its future. *North American Review* 126 (May–June), 527–36.

Edwards, B. (2004) *Edward R. Murrow and the Birth of Broadcast Journalism*. New York: John Wiley.

Eisenberg, E. (1988) *The Recording Angel: Explorations in Phonography*. London: Picador.

Eley, G. (2002) Politics, culture, and the public sphere. *Positions* 10(1), 219–36.

Elsaesser, T. (2006) Early film history and multi-media: an archaeology of possible futures? In: W.H.K. Chun and T. Keenan (eds.) *New Media, Old Media: A History and Theory Reader*. New York: Routledge, 13–26.

Epping-Jäger, C. (2005) Stimmräume: die phono-zentrische Organisation der Macht im NS. In: D. Gethmann and M. Stauff (eds.) *Politik der Medien*. Zurich: diaphanes, 341–50.

Erlmann, V. (2004) But what of the ethnographic ear? Anthropology, sound and the senses. In: V. Erlmann (ed.) *Hearing Cultures: Essays on Listening, Sound and Modernity*. Oxford: Berg, 1–20.

Erlmann, V. (2010) *Reason and Resonance: A History of Modern Aurality*. Cambridge, MA: Zone Books.

Evans, K. (2001) Dewey and the dialogical process: speaking, listening and today's media. *International Journal of Public Administration* 24(7/8), 771–98.

Evens, A. (2005) *Sound Ideas: Music, Machines, and Experience*. Minneapolis, MN: University of Minnesota Press.

Farmer, R. (2010) Jean Epstein. *Senses of Cinema: Great Directors* 57, 20 December. Available at: http://sensesofcinema.com/2010/great-directors/jean-epstein/ (accessed 3 September 2012).

Feaster, P. (2009) Reconfiguring the history of early cinema through the phonograph, 1877–1908. *Film History* 21(4), 311–25.

Felman, S. and Laub, D. (1992) *Testimony: Crises of Witnessing in Literature, Psychoanalysis, and History*. New York: Routledge.

Fischer, S.R. (2003) *A History of Reading*. New York: Reaktion.

Fisher, C.S. (1992) *America Calling: A Social History of the Telephone to 1940*. Berkeley, CA: University of California Press.

Fisher, M. (2002) *Ezra Pound's Radio Operas: The BBC Experiments 1931–1933*. Cambridge, MA: MIT Press.

Fisher, M. (2009) A love letter to collective listening. *Dummymag* 22 November. Available at: www.dummymag.com (accessed 18 July 2012).

Fones-Wolf, E. (2006) Defending listeners' rights: labour and media reform in postwar America. *Canadian Journal of Communication* 31(3), 499–518.

Forsey, M.G. (2010) Ethnography as participant listening. *Ethnography* 11(4), 558–72.

Fortner, R.S. (2005) *Radio, Morality, and Culture: Britain, Canada, and the United States*. Carbondale, IL: Southern Illinois Press.

Fraser, N. and Honneth, A. (2003) *Redistribution or Recognition? A Political-Philosophical Exchange*. London: Verso.

Führer, K.C. (1996) Auf dem Weg zur 'Massenkultur'? Kino und Rundfunk in der Weimarer Republik. *Historische Zeitschrift* 262, 739–81.

Funck, H.M. (1931) Die Frau und der Rundfunk. *Arbeiterfunk* 9(1).

Gadamer, H.G. (1979) *Truth and Method*. London: Sheed & Ward.

Gal, S. (2002) A semiotics of the public/private distinction. *differences: A Journal of Feminist Cultural Studies* 13(1), 77–95.

Gauss, S. (2009) *Nadel, Rille, Trichter: Kulturgeschichte des Phonographen und des Grammophons*. Cologne: Böhlau Verlag.

Gay, P. (1969) *Weimar Culture: The Insider as Outsider*. London: Secker & Warburg.

Gehrke, M.M. (1930) Das Ende der privaten Sphäre. *Die Weltbühne* 26(2), 61–4.

Gehrke, P.J. (2009) Introduction to listening, ethics, and dialogue: between the ear and the eye: a synaesthetic introduction to listening ethics. *International Journal of Listening* 23(1), 1–6.

Giddens, A. (1990) *The Consequences of Modernity*. Cambridge: Polity.

Giddens, A. (1991) *Modernity and Self-Identity: Self and Society in the Late Modern Age*. Cambridge: Polity.

Gilfillan, D. (2009) *Pieces of Sound: German Experimental Radio*. Minneapolis, MN: University of Minnesota Press.

Gilligan, C., Lyons, N.P. and Hammer, T.J. (eds.) (1990) *Making Connections: The Relational Worlds of Adolescent Girls at Emma Willard School*. Cambridge, MA: Harvard University Press.

Gilloch, G. (1996) *Myth and Metropolis: Walter Benjamin and the City*. Cambridge: Polity.

Gitelman, L. (1999) *Scripts, Grooves, and Writing Machines: Representing Technology in the Edison Era*. Stanford, CA: Stanford University Press.

Gitelman, L. (2006) *Always Already New: Media, History, and the Data of Culture*. Cambridge, MA: MIT Press.

Goffmann, E. (1966) *Behaviour in Public Places: Notes on the Social Organization of Gatherings*. London: Free Press.

Goggin, G. (2011) *Global Mobile Media*. Oxford: Routledge.

Goodman, D. (2010) Distracted listening: on not making sound choices in the 1930s. In: D. Suisman and S. Strasser (eds.) *Sound in the Age of Mechanical Reproduction*. Philadelphia, PA: University of Pennsylvania Press, 15–46.

Goodman, D. (2011) *Radio's Civic Ambition: American Broadcasting and Democracy in the 1930s*. New York: Oxford University Press.

Goodman, D. (2012) Making early American broadcasting's public sphere: radio fortune telling and the demarcation of private and public speech. *Historical Journal of Film, Radio and Television* 32(2), 187–205.

Goodyear, J. (2012) Escaping the urban din: a comparative study of Theodor Lessing's *Antilärmverein* (1908) and Maximilian Negwer's *Ohropax* (1908). In:

F. Feiereisen and A. Merley Hill (eds.) *Germany in the Loud Twentieth Century: An Introduction*. Oxford: Oxford University Press, 19–34.

Gorham, M. (1946) Television is coming back. *BBC Handbook 1946*. London: BBC, 20.

Gouk, P. (2000) (ed.) *Musical Healing in Cultural Contexts*. Guildford: Ashgate.

Groening, S. (2010) From 'a box in the theater of the world' to 'the world as your living room': cellular phones, television and mobile privatization. *New Media and Society* 12(8), 1331–47.

Grosswiler, P. (2004) Dispelling the alphabet effect. *Canadian Journal of Communication* 29(2), 145–58.

Gunning, T. (1986) The cinema of attraction[s]: early film, its spectator and the avant-garde. *Wide Angle* 8(3–4), 63–70.

Gunning, T. (1991) Heard over the phone. *Screen* 32(2), 184–96.

Habermas, J. (1962/1991) *The Structural Transformation of the Public Sphere: An Inquiry into a Category of Bourgeois Society*. Cambridge, MA: MIT Press.

Habermas, J. (1984) *The Theory of Communicative Action*. Boston, MA: Beacon Press.

Habermas, J. (1996) *Between Facts and Norms: Contributions to a Discourse Theory of Law and Democracy*. Cambridge, MA: MIT Press.

Hagemann, W. (1938) *Handbuch des deutschen Rundfunks*. Heidelberg/Berlin: n.pub.

Hainge, G. (2005) No(i)stalgia: on the impossibility of recognising noise in the present. *Culture, Theory and Critique* 46(1), 1–10.

Hainge, G. (2007) Vinyl is dead, long live vinyl: the work of recording and mourning in the age of digital reproduction. *Culture Machine* 9, n.p.

Hansen, M. (1991) *Babel and Babylon: Spectatorship in American Silent Film*. Cambridge, MA: Harvard University Press.

Hansen, M. (1993) Unstable mixtures, dilated spheres: Negt and Kluge's *The Public Sphere and Experience* twenty years later. *Public Culture* 5(2), 179–212.

Hansen, M. (2011) *Cinema and Experience: Siegfried Kracauer, Walter Benjamin, and Theodor Adorno*. Berkeley, CA: University of California Press.

Havelock, E.A. (1986) *The Muse Learns to Write: Reflections on Orality and Literacy from Antiquity to the Present*. New Haven, CT: Yale University Press.

Hay, G. (ed.) (1975) *Literatur und Rundfunk 1923 bis 1933*. Hildesheim: H.A. Gerstenberg.

Heidegger, M. (1953/1996) *Being and Time: A Translation of Sein und Zeit*. Albany, NY: State University of New York Press.

Hendy, D. (2010) Listening in the dark: night-time radio and a 'deep history' of media. *Media History* 16(2), 215–32.

Hennessey, B. (2005) *The Emergence of Broadcasting in Britain*. Lympstone: Southerleigh.

Hermann, T. (1933) Von der Reportage zur Hörmontage. *Rufer und Hörer* 3(9), 427–8.

Herring, R. (1929) An experiment with sound images. *The Listener* July 10, 54.

Herzog, H. (1941) On borrowed experience. *Studies in Philosophy and Social Science* 9(1), 65–95.

Heumann, M.D. (1998) *Ghost in the Machine: Sound and Technology in Twentieth Century Literature.* PhD thesis, University of California, Riverside.

Hibbitts, B. (1995) The metaphor is the message: visuality, aurality and the reconfiguration of American legal discourse. *International Journal for the Semiotics of Law* 8(1), 53–86.

Highmore, B. (2002) *Everyday Life and Cultural Theory: An Introduction.* London: Routledge.

Hill, F.E. and Williams, W.E. (1941) *Radio's Listening Groups: The United States and Great Britain.* New York: University of Columbia Press.

Hilmes, M. (1997) *Radio Voices: American Broadcasting, 1922–1952.* Minneapolis, MN: University of Minnesota Press.

Hilmes, M. (2005) Is there a field called sound culture studies? And does it matter? *American Quarterly* 57(1), 249–59.

Hilmes, M. (2008) Television sound: why the silence? *Music, Sound and the Moving Image* 2(2), 153–61.

Hilmes, M. (2012) *Network Nations: A Transnational History of British and American Broadcasting.* London: Routledge.

Hofstra, M. and Porter, R. (eds.) (2001) *Cultures of Neurasthenia from Beard to the First World War.* Amsterdam and New York: Rodopi.

Hörburger, C. (1977) Zum Problem der literarischen und rundfunkpolitischen Anpassung der Hörspielautoren der 20er Jahre an das Medium Rundfunk. In: H. Kreuzer and V. Canaris (eds.) *Literaturwissenschaft – Medienwissenschaft.* Heidelberg: Quelle & Meyer, 44–60.

Horkheimer, M. and Adorno, T. (1988) *Dialektik der Aufklärung: Philosophische Fragmente.* Frankfurt a.M.: Fischer.

Horton, D. and Wohl, R. (1956) Mass communication and parasocial interaction: observations on intimacy at a distance. *Psychiatry* 19, 215–29.

Howells, R. and Negreiros, J. (2012) *Visual Culture.* Cambridge: Polity.

Husband, C. (1996) The right to be understood: conceiving the multi-ethnic public sphere. *Innovation: The European Journal of Social Sciences* 9(2), n.p.

Husband, C. (2009) Between listening and understanding. *Continuum* 23(4), 441–3.

Hyde, L. (2008) Freedom of listening: an eighteenth century root for net neutrality, *Publius Project*, The Harvard Berkman Center for Internet and Society. Available at: publius.cc/freedom_listening_eighteenth_century_root_net_neutrality (accessed 1 December 2008).

Idhe, D. (2007) *Listening and Voice: Phenomenologies of Sound.* Albany, NY: State University of New York Press.

Jackson, A. (1968) Sound and ritual. *Man* 3(2), 239–99.

Jay, M. (1992) Scopic regimes of modernity. In: S. Lash and J. Friedman (eds.) *Modernity and Identity.* Oxford: Blackwell, 178–95.

Jay, M. (1993) *Downcast Eyes: The Denigration of Vision in Twentieth Century French Thought*. Berkeley, CA: University of California Press.

Johnson, J.H. (1995) *Listening in Paris: A Cultural History*. Berkeley, CA: University of California Press.

Jolowicz, E. (1932) *Der Rundfunk: Eine psychologische Untersuchung*. Berlin: Max Hesses Verlag.

Jones, S. (1993) A sense of space: virtual reality, authenticity, and the aural. *Critical Studies in Mass Communication* 10, 238–52.

Jones, S. (2000) Music and the internet. *Popular Music* 19(2), 217–30.

Jones, S. and Schumacher, T. (1992) Muzak: on functional music and power. *Critical Studies in Mass Communication* 9, 156–63.

Jossé, H. (1984) *Die Entstehung des Tonfilms: Beitrag zu einer faktenorientierten Mediengeschichtsschreibung*. Freiburg/Munich: Karl Alber.

Jütte, R. (2000) *Geschichte der Sinne. Von der Antike bis zum Cyberspace*. Munich: C.H. Beck.

Kahn, D. (1992) Histories of sound once removed. In: D. Kahn and G. Whitehead (eds.) *Wireless Imagination: Sound, Radio, and the Avant-Garde*. Cambridge, MA: MIT Press, 1–29.

Kahn, D. (2001) *Noise Water Meat: A History of Sound in the Arts*. Cambridge, MA: MIT Press.

Kahn, D. (2002) Concerning the line: music, noise and phonography. In: B. Clarke and L.D. Henderson (eds.) *From Energy to Information: Representation in Science and Technology, Art, and Literature*. Stanford, CA: Stanford University Press, 178–94.

Katz, M. (2010) *Capturing Sound: How Technology Has Changed Music*. Berkeley, CA: University of California Press.

Kemritz, M. (1934) 1934. *Rufer und Hörer* 3(10), 433–4.

Kenney, W.H. (2003) *Recorded Music in American Life: The Phonograph and Popular Memory, 1890–1945*. Oxford: Oxford University Press.

Killen, A. (2006) *Berlin Electropolis: Shock, Nerves, and German Modernity*. Berkeley, CA: University of California Press.

Kittler, F. (1995) *Aufschreibesysteme: 1800. 1900*. Munich: Wilhelm Fink Verlag.

Kittler, F. (1999) *Gramophone, Film, Typewriter*. Stanford, CA: Stanford University Press.

Kittler, F. (2006) Number and numeral. *Theory, Culture and Society* 23(7–8), 51–61.

Koch, H. and Glaser, H. (2007) *Ganz Ohr: Eine Kulturgeschichte des Radios in Deutschland*. Cologne: Böhlau Verlag.

Koepnick, L. (2004) Benjamin's silence. In: N.M. Alter and L. Koepnick (eds.) *Sound Matters: Essays on the Acoustics of Modern German Culture*. Oxford: Berghahn.

Kracauer, S. (1924/1995) Boredom. In: *The Mass Ornament: Weimar Essays* (trans. T.Y. Levin). London: Harvard University Press, 331–6.

Kracauer, S. (1926/1995) Cult of distraction. In: *The Mass Ornament: Weimar Essays* (trans. T.Y. Levin). London: Harvard University Press, 323–30.

LaBelle, B. (2010) *Acoustic Territories: Sound Culture and Everyday Life*. New York: Continuum.

Lacey, K. (1996) *Feminine Frequencies: Gender, German Radio and the Public Sphere, 1923–1945*. Ann Arbor, MI: University of Michigan Press.

Lacey, K. (2000) Towards a periodisation of listening: radio and modern life. *International Journal of Cultural Studies* 3(2), 279–88.

Lacey, K. (2001) Radio and political transition: public service, propaganda and promotional culture. In: M. Hilmes and J. Loviglio (eds.) *The Radio Reader: Essays in the Cultural History of US Radio Broadcasting*. New York: Routledge, 21–40.

Lacey, K. (2007) The invention of a listening public: radio and its audiences. In: K.-C. Führer and C. Ross (eds.) *Mass Media, Culture and Society in Twentieth-Century Germany*. London: Palgrave, 61–79.

Lanza, J. (2004) *Elevator Music: A Surreal History of Muzak, Easy-Listening and Other Moodsong*. Ann Arbor, MI: University of Michigan Press.

Lastra, J. (2000) *Sound Technology and the American Cinema: Perception, Representation, Modernity*. New York: Columbia University Press.

Laven, P. (1975) Aus dem Erinnerungsbrevier eines Rundfunkpioniers. In: G. Hay (ed.) *Literatur und Rundfunk, 1923–1933*. Hildesheim: Gerstenberg, 5–33.

Lawrence, A. (1991) *Echo and Narcissus: Women's Voices in Classic Hollywood Cinema*. Berkeley, CA: University of California Press.

Lax, S. (2007) Digital radio and the diminution of the public sphere. In: R. Butsch (ed.) *Media and Public Spheres*. New York: Palgrave Macmillan, 109–21.

LeMahieu, D.L. (1988) *A Culture for Democracy: Mass Communication and the Cultivated Mind in Britain Between the Wars*. Oxford: Oxford University Press.

Lenk, C. (1997) *Die Erscheinung des Rundfunks: Einführung und Nutzung eines Neuen Mediums*. Opladen: Westdeutscher Verlag.

Leong, T., Vetere, F. and Howard, S. (2008) Abdicating choice: the rewards of letting go. *Digital Creativity* 19(4), 233–43.

Lerg, W. and Steininger, R. (1975) *Rundfunk und Politik, 1923–73*. Berlin: Spiess.

Levin, D.M. (1989) *The Listening Self*. London: Routledge.

Levin, D.M. (ed.) (1993) *Modernity and the Hegemony of Vision*. Berkeley, CA: University of California Press.

Levine, L. (1988) *Highbrow Lowbrow: The Emergence of Cultural Hierarchy in America*. Cambridge, MA: Harvard University Press.

Levinson, P. (1997) *The Soft Edge: A Natural History and Future of the Information Revolution*. New York: Routledge.

Liebersohn, Y.Z. (2005) Rhetoric: art and pseudo-art in Plato's Gorgias. *Arethusa* 38(3), 303–29.

Link, S. (2001) The work of reproduction in the mechanical aging of an art: listening to noise. *Computer Music Journal* 25(1), 34–47.

Lipari, L. (2009) Listening otherwise: the voice of ethics. *International Journal of Listening* 23(1), 44–59.

Lipari, L. (2010) Listening, thinking, being. *Communication Theory* 20, 348–62.

Littau, K. (2006) *Theories of Reading: Books, Bodies and Bibliomania*. Cambridge: Polity.

Livingstone, S. (2005) On the relation between audiences and publics: why audience and public? London: LSE Research Online. Available at: http://eprints.lse.ac.uk/archive/00000437 (accessed 2 February 2010).

Love, N.S. (2002) 'Singing for our lives': women's music and democratic politics. *Hypatia* 17(4), 71–96.

Love, N.S. (2006) *Musical Democracy*. Albany, NY: State University of New York Press.

Loviglio, J. (2005) *Radio's Intimate Public: Network Broadcasting and Mass-Mediated Democracy*. Minneapolis, MN: University of Minnesota Press.

Loy, D. (2007) CyberBabel? *Ethics and Information Technology* 9(4), 251–8.

Luhmann, N. (1996) *Die Realität der Massenmedien*. Opladen: Westdeutscher Verlag.

Lupton, E. (2004) *Thinking with Type*. New York: Princeton Architectural Press.

Manovich, L. (2001) *The Language of New Media*. Cambridge, MA: MIT Press.

Marvin, C. (1988) *When Old Technologies Were New*. New York: Oxford University Press.

Marx, A. (1932) Das Wesen des Gemeinschaftsempfanges. *Rufer und Hörer* 2(9), 399–405.

Marx, L. (1964/2000) *The Machine in the Garden: Technology and the Pastoral Ideal in America*. Oxford: Oxford University Press.

McLuhan, M. (2004) Visual and acoustic space. In: D. Warner and C. Cox (eds.) *Audio Culture: Readings in Modern Music*. New York: Continuum, 67–72.

McLuhan, M. and McLuhan, E. (1988) *Law of Media: The New Science*. Ontario: University of Toronto Press.

Merkel, F. (1996) *Rundfunk und Gewerkschaften in der Weimarer Republik und in der frühen Nachkriegszeit*. Potsdam: Verlag für Berlin-Brandenburg.

Merritt, D. and McCombs, M. (2004) *The Two 'Ws' of Journalism: The Why and What of Public Affairs Reporting*. Mahwah, NJ: Lawrence Erlbaum.

Metz, C. (1980) Aural objects. *Yale French Studies* 60, 24–32.

Mill, J.S. (1867) *Considerations on Representative Government*. London: Longmans, Green and Co.

Mill, J.S. (1859) *On Liberty*. London: John W. Parker & Son.

Millard, A. (1995) *America on Record: A History of Recorded Sound*. Cambridge: Cambridge University Press.

Miller, T. (1992) An editorial introduction for radio. *Continuum* 6(1), 5–13.

Mirzeoff, N. (ed.) (2002) *The Visual Culture Reader*. London: Routledge.

Moran, J. (2003) Criticism: Benjamin and boredom. *Critical Quarterly* 45(1–2), 168–81.

Morat, D. (2011) Zur Geschichte des Hörens: Ein Forschungsbericht. *Archiv für Sozialgeschichte* 51, 697–716.

Morruzi, N.C. (2000) *Speaking Through the Mask: Hannah Arendt and the Politics of Social Identity.* Ithaca, NY: Cornell University Press.

Morton, D. (2004) *Sound Recording: The Life Story of a Technology.* Baltimore, MD: Johns Hopkins University Press.

Mouffe, C. (2000) *The Democratic Paradox.* London: Verso.

Mowitt, J. (2011) *Radio: Essays in Bad Reception.* Berkeley, CA: University of California Press.

Nancy, J.-L. (2007) *Listening.* New York: Fordham University Press.

Neels, A. (1932) Gemeinschaftsempfang als Aufgabe und Tatsache. *Rufer und Hörer* 2(2), 55–59.

Negt, O. and Kluge, A. (1993) *Public Sphere and Experience.* Minneapolis, MN: University of Minnesota Press.

Nye, S. (2011) Headphone-Headset-Jetset: DJ culture, mobility and science fictions of listening. *Dancecult: Journal of Electronic Dance Music Culture* 3(1), 64–96.

Nyre, L. (2008) *Sound Media: From Live Journalism to Music Recording.* London: Routledge.

O'Donnell, P. (2009). Journalism, change and listening practices. *Continuum: Journal of Media and Cultural Studies* 23, 503–17.

O'Neill, O. (2004) Earning trust: politics, politicians and the public. Lecture for The Smith Institute, London, 15 September. Available at: http://www.smith-institute.org.uk/transcripts (accessed 5 October 2008).

O'Neill, O. (2009) Ethics for communication? *European Journal of Philosophy* 17(2), 167–80.

Ong, W.J. (1982) *Orality and Literacy: The Technologizing of the Word.* New York: Routledge.

Otis, L. (2002) The metaphoric circuit: organic and technological communication in the nineteenth century. *Journal of the History of Ideas* 63, 105–28.

Palitzsch, O.A. (1927/1994) Gefunkte Literatur. In: A. Kaes, M. Jay and E. Dimendberg (eds.) *The Weimar Republic Sourcebook.* Berkeley, CA: University of California Press.

Pegg, M. (1983) *Broadcasting and Society, 1918–1939.* London: Croom Helm.

Penman, R. and Turnbull, S. (2012) From listening . . . to the dialogic realities of participatory democracy. *Continuum* 26(1), 61–72.

Perlman, M. (2004) Golden ears and meter readers: the contest for epistemic authority in audiophilia. *Social Studies of Science* 34(5), 783–807.

Peters, J.D. (1993) Distrust of representation: Habermas on the public sphere. *Media, Culture and Society* 15, 541–71.

Peters, J.D. (1997) Realism in social representation and the fate of the public. *Javnost: The Public* 4(2), 5–16.

Peters, J.D. (1999) *Speaking into the Air: A History of the Idea of Communication.* Chicago, IL: University of Chicago Press.

Peters, J.D. (2004) Helmholtz, Edison and sound history. In: L. Rabinovitz and A. Geil (eds.) *Memory Bytes: History, Technology, and Digital Culture*. Durham, NC: Duke University Press, 177–98.

Peters, J.D. (2005) *Courting the Abyss: Free Speech and the Liberal Tradition*. Chicago, IL: University of Chicago Press.

Peters, J.D. (2006) Media as conversation, conversation as media. In: J. Curran and D. Morley (eds.) *Media and Cultural Theory*. Oxford: Routledge, 115–26.

Peters, J.D. (2010) Broadcasting and schizophrenia. *Media Culture and Society* 32(1), 123–40.

Petrie, K. and Wesseley, S. (2002) Modern worries, new technology, and medicine. *BMJ* 324(7339), 690–1.

Petro, P. (1989) *Joyless Streets: Women and Melodramatic Representation in Weimar Germany*. Princeton, NJ: Princeton University Press.

Picker, J.M. (2003) *Victorian Soundscapes*. Oxford: Oxford University Press.

Pinch, T. and Bjisterveld, K. (2011) (eds.) *The Oxford Handbook of Sound Studies*. Oxford: Oxford University Press.

Pinchevski, A. (2001) Freedom from speech (or the silent demand). *Diacritics* 31(2), 71–84.

Pinthus, K. (1975) Die literarischen Darbietungen der esten fünf Jahren des Berliner Rundfunks. In: G. Hay (ed.) *Literatur und Rundfunk 1923 bis 1933*. Hildesheim: H.A. Gerstenberg, 41–68.

Plato (1956) *Phaedrus*. Indianapolis, IN: Library of Liberal Arts.

Puetzfeld, C. (1939) Der Rundfunk als politische Waffe. *Völkischer Beobachter* 29 January.

Rabin, D. (2008) The Presidential Debates of '08 – 1908 That is. *All Things Considered*, NPR, Broadcast 1 November. Available at: http://www.npr.org. (accessed 1 January 2011).

Radcliffe, K. (2005) *Rhetorical Listening: Identification, Gender, Whiteness*. Carbondale, IL: Southern Illinois Press.

Rawls, J. (1993/2005) *Political Liberalism*. New York: University of Columbia Press.

Rayner, A. (1993) The audience: subjectivity, community and the ethics of listening. *Journal of Dramatic Theory and Criticism* 7(2), 3–14.

Reith, J. (1924a) *Broadcast over Britain*. London: Hodder & Stoughton.

Reith J. (1924b) In reply to John O'London. *Radio Times* 2(26), 21 March.

Reith, J. (1949) *Into the Wind*. London: Hodder & Stoughton.

Ronell, A (1989) *The Telephone Book: Technology – Schizophrenia – Electric Speech*. Lincoln, NE: University of Nebraska Press.

Rosenfeld, S. (2011) On being heard: a case for paying attention to the historical ear. *American Historical Review* 116(2), 316–34.

Rosenhaft, E. (1996) Lesewut, Kinosucht, Radiotismus: Zur (geschlechter-) politischen Relevanz neuer Massenmedien in den 1920er Jahren. In: A. Luedtke, I. Marssolek and A. von Saldern (eds.) *Amerikanisierung: Traum und Alptraum im Deutschland des 20. Jahrhunderts*. Stuttgart: Franz Steiner, 119–43.

Rothenbuhler, E.W. and Peters, J.D. (1997) Defining phonography: an experiment in theory. *Musical Quarterly* 81(2), 242–64.

Ross, C. (2006) Entertainment, technology and tradition: the rise of recorded music from the Empire to the Third Reich. In: K-C. Führer and C. Ross (eds.) *Mass Media, Culture and Society in Twentieth-Century Germany*. London: Blackwell, 25–43.

Ross, C. (2008) *Media and the Making of Modern Germany: Mass Communications, Society, and Politics from the Empire to the Third Reich*. Oxford: Oxford University Press.

Ross, D. (2007) *The Rest is Noise: Listening to the Twentieth Century*. London: Harper Perennial.

Rubery, M. (2011) *Audiobooks, Literature and Sound Studies*. New York: Routledge.

Rühr, S. (2008) *Tondokumente von der Walze zum Hörbuch: Geschichte-Medienspezifik-Rezeption*. Göttingen: V&R Unipress.

Russo, A. (2010) *Points on the Dial: Golden Age Radio Beyond the Networks*. Durham, NC: Duke University Press.

Saenger, P. (1997) *Space Between Words: The Origins of Silent Reading*. Stanford, CA: Stanford University Press.

Saerchinger, C. (1934) Broadcasting the events of the day. *Radio Times*, 614–15.

Salvaggio, R. (1999) *The Sounds of Feminist Theory*. Albany, NY: State University of New York Press.

Sartre, J.P. (1990) *Critique of Dialectical Reason*. London: Verso.

Scannell, P. (1989) Public service broadcasting and modern public life. *Media, Culture and Society* 11, 134–66.

Scannell, P. (1996) *Radio, Television and Modern Life*. London: Blackwell.

Scannell, P. (2000) For anyone-as-someone structures. *Media, Culture and Society* 22, 5–24.

Scannell, P. (2004) Love and communication: a review essay. *Westminster Papers in Communication and Culture* 1(1), 93–102.

Scannell, P. and Cardiff, D. (1991) *A Social History of British Broadcasting: Volume One 1922–1939*. Oxford: Blackwell.

Scarre, C. and Lawson, G. (eds.) (2006) *Archaeoacoustics*. Oxford: McDonald Institute for Archaeological Research.

Schafer, R.M. (1969) *The New Soundscape*. New York: Berandol and Associated Music Publishers.

Schafer, R.M. (1977/1994) *The Soundscape: Our Sonic Environment and the Tuning of the World*. Rochester, NY: Destiny Books.

Schafer, R.M. (2007) Acoustic space. *Circuit: musiques contemporaines* 17(3), 83–6.

Schirokauer, A. (1929) Kunstpolitik im Rundfunk. *Die literarische Welt* 5(35), 1–2.

Schivelbusch, W. (1982) *Intellektuellendämmerung. Zur Lage der Frankfurter Intelligenz in den zwanziger Jahren*. Frankfurt a.M.: Insel-Verlag.

Schmidt, L.E. (2000) *Hearing Things: Religion, Illusion, and the American Enlightenment*. Cambridge, MA: Harvard University Press.

Schrage, D. (2001) *Psychotechnik und Radiophonie: Subjektkonstruktionen in artifiziellen Wirklichkeiten 1918–1932*. Bonn: VG Bild-Kunst.

Schrage, D. (2005) Anonymus Publikum: Massenkonstruktion und die Politiken des Radios. In: D. Gethmann and M. Stauff (eds.) *Politiken der Medien*. Zurich: diaphanes, 173–94.

Schroll, C. (1999) Theorizing the flip-side of civic journalism: democratic citizenship and ethical readership. *Communication Theory* 9(3), 321–45.

Schudson, M. (1978) The ideal of conversation in the study of mass media. *Communication Research* 5(3), 320–9.

Schudson, M. (1997) Why conversation is not the soul of democracy. *Critical Studies in Mass Communication* 14(4), 297–309.

Schudson, M. (2003) Click here for democracy: a history and critique of an information-based model of citizenship. In: H. Jenkins and D. Thorburn (eds.) *Democracy and New Media*. Cambridge, MA: MIT Press, 49–59.

Schuster, D. (2003) Neurasthenia and a modernizing America. *JAMA* 290(17), 2327–8.

Schwartz, H. (1995) Noise and silence: the soundscape and spirituality. Conference paper. Available at http://www.nonoise.org/library/noisesil/noisesil.htm (accessed 2 November 2011).

Schwartz, H. (2011) *Making Noise: From Babel to the Big Bang and Beyond*. Cambridge, MA: Zone Books.

Sconce, J. (2000) *Haunted Media: Electronic Presence from Telegraphy to Television*. Durham, NC: Duke University Press.

Sennett, R. (1978) *The Fall of Public Man: On the Social Psychology of Capitalism*. New York: Random House.

Sergi, G. (n.d.) The sonic playground: Hollywood cinema and its listeners. Available at: http://www.filmsound.org/articles/sergi/index.htm (accessed 2 July 2008).

Serres, M. (1982) *The Parasite*. Baltimore, MD: Johns Hopkins University Press.

Shimpach, S. (2007) Representing the public of cinema's public sphere. In: R. Butsch (ed.) *Media and Public Spheres*. New York: Palgrave Macmillan, 136–48.

Siepmann, C. (1934) Changes in the talks programme. *Radio Times*, 844.

Sieveking, L. (1934) *The Stuff of Radio*. London: Cassell.

Silverstone, R. (1994) *Television and Everyday Life*. London: Routledge.

Silverstone, R. (2002) Complicity and collusion in the mediation of everyday life. *New Literary History* 33(4), 761–80.

Silverstone, R. (2006) *Media and Morality: On the Rise of the Mediapolis*. Cambridge: Polity.

Silvey, R. (1974) *Who's Listening? The Story of BBC Audience Research*. London: Allen & Unwin.

Simmel, G. (1903/2002) The metropolis and mental life (1903). In: G. Bridge and S. Watson (eds.) *The Blackwell City Reader*. Oxford: Wiley-Blackwell, 11–19.

Skalski, P. and Whitbred, R. (2010) Image versus sound: a comparison of formal feature effects on presence and video game enjoyment. *PsychNology Journal* 8(1), 67–84.

Smith, B.R. (1999) *The Acoustic World of Early-Modern England*. Chicago, IL: University of Chicago Press.

Smith, M.M. (2001) *Listening to Nineteenth-Century America*. Chapel Hill, NC: University of North Carolina Press.

Smith, M.M. (ed.) (2004) *Hearing History: A Reader*. Atlanta, GA: University of Georgia Press.

Spigel, L. (1992) *Make Room for TV: Television and the Family Ideal in Postwar America*. Chicago, IL: University of Chicago Press.

Sterne, A. (1924) 'Radiodiagnosis': when doctors treat by wireless. *Radio Times* 2(21), 15 February, 282.

Sterne, J. (2003) *The Audible Past: Cultural Origins of Sound Reproduction*. Durham, NC: Duke University Press.

Sterne, J. (2007) Media or instruments? Yes. *Offscreen* 11(8–9), 1–18.

Sterne, J. (2012) (ed.) *The Sound Studies Reader*. New York: Routledge.

Stock, B. (1990) *Listening for the Text: On the Uses of the Past*. Philadelphia, PA: University of Pennsylvania Press.

Stoever, J.L. (2007) *The Contours of the Sonic Color-Line: Slavery, Segregation, and the Cultural Politics of Listening*. PhD thesis, University of Southern California.

Tacchi, J. (2011) Open content creation: the issues of voice and the challenges of listening. *New Media and Society* 13(8), 1–17.

Taussig, M. (1993) *Mimesis and Alterity: A Particular History of the Senses*. New York, London: Routledge.

Taylor, C. (1992) *Multiculturalism and 'The Politics of Recognition'*. Princeton, NJ: Princeton University Press.

Taylor, T., Katz, M. and Grajeda, T. (2012) *Music, Sound, and Technology in America: A Documentary History of Early Phonograph, Cinema, and Radio*. Durham, NC: Duke University Press.

Tebutt, J. (2009) The object of listening. *Continuum* 23(4), 549–59.

Tester, K. (1995) *The Inhuman Condition*. London: Taylor & Francis.

Thill, C. (2009) Courageous listening, responsibility for the other and the Northern Territory Intervention. *Continuum*, 23(4), 537–48.

Thompson, E. (1995) Machines, music, and the quest for fidelity: marketing the Edison phonograph in America, 1877–1925. *Musical Quarterly* 79, 131–71.

Thompson, E. (2002) *The Soundscape of Modernity: Architectural Acoustics and the Culture of Listening in America, 1900–1933*. Cambridge, MA: MIT Press.

Thompson, K. (1980) Early sound counterpoint. *Yale French Studies* 60, 115–40.

Thornton, S. (1996) *Club Cultures: Music, Media and Subcultural Capital*. Hanover, NH: Wesleyan University Press.

Toop, D. (2010) *Sinister Resonance: The Mediumship of the Listener*. New York: Continuum.

Toro, A. (2000) *Standing Up for Listeners' Rights: A History of Public Participation at the Federal Communications Commission.* Unpublished doctoral dissertation, Berkeley, CA: University of California Press.

Tosch, D. (1987) *Der Rundfunk als 'Neues Medium' im Spiegel der Münchner Presse 1918–1926.* Munich: Tuduv.

Tracey, M. (2003) *The BBC and the General Strike: May 1926. BBC and the Reporting of the General Strike.* BBC. Wakefield: Microform Academic Publishers.

Uhr, J. (2004) Auditory democracy: separation of powers and the locations of listening. In: B. Fontana, C.J. Nederman and G. Remer (eds.) *Talking Democracy: Historical Perspectives on Rhetoric and Democracy.* University Park, PA: Pennsylvania State University Press, 239–70.

Uricchio, W. and Pearson, R. (1993) *Reframing Culture: The Case of the Vitagraph Quality Films.* Princeton, NJ: Princeton University Press.

Valdar, L. (1923) Inevitable developments of the wireless boom. *Daily Mirror* 23 February, 5.

Vancour, S. (2010) Arnheim on radio: *Materialtheorie* and beyond. In: S. Higgins (ed.) *Arnheim for Film and Media Studies.* New York: Routledge, 177–94.

Vertov, D. (1925/1984) Kinopravda and Radiopravda: by way of a proposal. In: A. Michelson (ed.) *Kino-Eye: The Writings of Dziga Vertov.* Berkeley, CA: University of California Press, 52–6.

Walker, K.L. (1997) Do you ever listen? The theoretical underpinnings of empathetic listening. *International Journal of Listening* 11, 127–37.

Waller, J.C. (1946) *Radio: The Fifth Estate.* Boston, MA: Houghton Mifflin.

Warner, M. (1992) The mass public and the mass subject. In: C. Calhoun (ed.) *Habermas and the Public Sphere.* Cambridge, MA: MIT Press, 377–401.

Warner, M. (2002) Publics and counterpublics. *Public Culture* 14(1), 49–90.

Weber, H. (2008) *Das Versprechen mobiler Freiheit. Zur Kultur- und Technikgeschichte von Kofferradio, Walkman und Handy.* Bielefeld, transcript.

Weill, K. (1925) Möglichkeiten absoluter Radiokunst. *Der Deutsche Rundfunk* 3, 1625–8.

Weintraub, J. and Kumar, K. (1997) *Public and Private in Thought and Practice.* Chicago, IL: University of Chicago Press.

Weiss, A. (1995) *Phantasmic Radio.* Durham, NC: Duke University Press.

Welton, M. (2002) Listening, conflict and citizenship: towards a pedagogy of civil society. *International Journal of Lifelong Education* 21(3), 197–208.

Whitten, W. (1924) The lure and fear of broadcasting. *Radio Times* 2(25), 14 March.

Wiley, S. (1998) Civic journalism in practice: case studies in the art of listening. *Newspaper Research Journal* 19(1), 16–29.

Williams, R. (1974) *Television: Technology and Cultural Form.* London: Routledge.

Winn, M. (2002) *Plug-in Drug: Television, Computers and Family Life.* New York: Penguin.

Wolvin, A. (ed.) (2010) *Listening and Human Communication in the 21st Century.* Chichester: Wiley-Blackwell.

Wolvin, A., Halone, K.K. and Coakley, C.G. (1999) Assessing the 'intellectual discussion' on listening theory and research. *International Journal of Listening* 13, 111–29.

Woolf, D.R. (2004) Hearing Renaissance England. In: M.M. Smith (ed.) *Hearing History: A Reader.* Athens, GA: University of Georgia Press, 112–35.

Wurtzler, S. (2007) *Electric Sounds: Technological Change and the Rise of Corporate Mass Media.* New York: Columbia University Press.

Yamagata, N. (2005) Plato, memory, and performance. *Oral Tradition* 20(1), 111–29.

Young, F. (1933) *Shall I Listen? Studies in the Adventure and Technique of Broadcasting.* London: Constable & Co.

Young, I.M. (1986/1995) The ideal of community and the politics of difference. In: P.A. Weiss (ed.) *Feminism and Community.* Philadelphia, PA: Temple University Press, 233–58.

Young, I.M. (1997) *Intersecting Voices: Dilemmas of Gender, Political Philosophy, and Policy.* Princeton, NJ: Princeton University Press.

Young, I.M. (2000) *Inclusion and Democracy.* Oxford: Oxford University Press.

Zielinski, S. (1999) *Audiovisions: Cinema and Television as Entr'actes in History.* Amsterdam: Amsterdam University Press.

Žižek, S. (2006). *The Parallax View.* Cambridge, MA: MIT Press.

Index